HUSH, LITTLE BABY

HUSH, LITTLE BABY

SHANE DUNPHY ∿

Gill & Macmillan

Gill & Macmillan Ltd
Hume Avenue, Park West, Dublin 12
with associated companies throughout the world
www.gillmacmillan.ie

© Shane Dunphy 2008
978 07171 4387 0

Typography design by Make Communication
Print origination by Carole Lynch
Printed and bound by ColourBooks Ltd, Dublin

This book is typeset in Linotype Minion and
Neue Helvetica.

The paper used in this book comes from the wood pulp
of managed forests. For every tree felled, at least one
tree is planted, thereby renewing natural resources.

A CIP catalogue record for this book is available
from the British Library.

5 4 3 2 1

Hush, little baby, don't say a word,
Daddy's going to buy you a mockingbird.

And if that mockingbird don't sing,
Daddy's going to buy you a diamond ring.

And if that diamond ring turns brass,
Daddy's going to buy you a looking-glass.

And if that looking-glass gets broke,
Daddy's going to buy you a billy goat.

And if that billy goat won't pull,
Daddy's going to buy you a cart and bull.

And if that cart and bull turn over,
Daddy's going to buy you a dog named Rover.

And if that dog named Rover won't bark,
Daddy's going to buy you a horse and cart.

And if that horse and cart fall down,
You'll still be the sweetest little baby in town.

TRADITIONAL LULLABY

CONTENTS

ACKNOWLEDGMENTS

I would like to thank the following people, whose support, friendship and advice made the writing of this book possible:

My wife, Deirdre, and my children, Richard and Marnie. As always, thanks for putting up with me, and for being there.

My agent, Jonathan Williams, whose guidance has been invaluable over the past few years.

All the staff at Gill & Macmillan, for their good humour, enthusiasm and unerring love for what they do.

All the folks at Penguin Ireland, for their confidence in these books, and their faith in what I do.

I wish to particularly thank everyone who has stopped me in the street, or e-mailed, or written, to let me know how much my books have meant, or to share with me a story of triumph over often dire circumstances. It makes it worthwhile to know the work is making a difference.

Every child and each family I have worked with over the years have given me untold gifts. Every time I ponder this strange career of mine, I learn something new.

Finally, to my own parents, Noël and Harry — I wrote *Hush, Little Baby* for you. This book is, as much as anything else, a celebration of our family.

PART ONE

Beginnings

*What put the blood on your right shoulder, Son, come
   tell it unto me.*
*That is the blood of a hare, Mama, you may pardon
   me.*

*The blood of a hare never ran so red, Son, come tell it
   unto me.*
*That is the blood of my youngest brother, you may
   pardon me.*

'WHAT PUT THE BLOOD', TRADITIONAL TRAVELLER
BALLAD, FROM THE SINGING OF JOHN REILLY

Chapter 1 ～

The smell of junk burning on bonfires in the freezing winter's evening was thick, and stuck in my lungs like sawdust. Bricks, blocks of wood and glass bottles, some filled with urine, soared over the high railings with alarming regularity, clattering and smashing off the cracked, frost-whitened concrete and adding to the existing debris.

November: dark clouds, pregnant with rain — or more probably sleet — gathered above the city, an ill omen for the task ahead. From where I stood, a safe distance away among the police cars and marias, I had a clear view of the crowd of angry men and women within the halting site; I could hear their raised voices, and see the accompanying plumes of steam in the darkening air. Some of them were speaking in *Ceannt*, one of the many traveller languages, and I couldn't understand any of the words. I have a smattering of *Shelta*, another nomadic dialect, but the *Sheltan* I could discern was spoken so quickly it was wasted on me. The tone of it all, though, was clear: they were frightened and enraged.

The Travelling People make up a relatively small demographic within Irish society, numbering in the region of 30,000 people. They are generally nomads, preferring to travel from place to place in small familial groups or clans, but since the 1960s Irish governmental policy, combined with the deeply unsympathetic attitude held by the wider settled population, has meant that more than half of their number have moved into houses, mostly in local authority estates. There remain, however, a determined few who spend the year moving around the country, stopping at places that have been traditional halting sites for centuries, and making a living through horse-trading, metal-working and selling scrap — the ancient gypsy trades.

To my left, Ben Tyrrell, my boss, spoke rapidly to Detective Inspector Charles Brophy, going over a map of the halting site, pinpointing the caravan we would be making for, and marking out the homes of possible relatives which could be used as hiding places. The detective and the ten men he had brought with him were dressed in protective clothing — flak jackets and helmets — and carried reinforced plastic shields and metal batons. Ben and I were bundled up in scarves, gloves and overcoats against the elements. We were social-care workers from the Dunleavy Trust, a charitable organisation set up to work with children in extreme cases of abuse, neglect or disturbance, and would not engage in any violence. Our task was to get in and out of the halting site as quickly as possible. The police were there to cover us.

I lit a cigarette and listened to the cries and exhortations of the travellers behind the railing, wishing there was some other way to do this. But I knew there wasn't.

I had been brought into the case at a late stage, only a week previously, and was largely responsible for this stand-off. Under Section 12 of the Child Care Act 1991, the police and social workers can, without resorting to the courts, remove children from their home, by force if necessary, if there is a serious and immediate risk to their well-being. This process of forced removal is usually referred to by the professionals involved as 'doing a Section 12'. I had, after five rather strained visits to the filthiest, tiniest caravan I had ever been in, decided that something needed to be done immediately, and the application of this particular piece of child protection legislation looked to be the best course of action.

The Currans, a transient family, had been living in the halting site for a month. Official, state-approved halting sites were first built in Ireland in the 1980s, in an attempt to quell some of the tensions between the settled and the travelling communities. These sites, unlike their traditional counterparts, many of which are now car parks or farmland, were built on land bought by the state and were properly equipped for traveller families, with points where the caravans could access electricity, water and sewage.

Gerry and Tilly Curran, and their six children, lived in a caravan meant, at a stretch, for two people, and that had no capacity to make use of the available amenities. They eked out a meagre living trading in junk, doing odd jobs and begging. The children, ranging in age from six months to ten years, had never seen the inside of a school, and the public health nurse had been unable to find the family, who were constantly on the move, to carry out any developmental checks. The children were mostly non-verbal, meeting my overtures with vacant, slack-jawed stares. All were desperately undersized for their ages, and the three-year-old, who should have been walking for at least a year and a half, was still crawling and in grey terry-cloth nappies. The family seemed to subsist on a diet of soup and fried bread, and all the children were lice-infested and covered in psoriasis. It remains one of the worst cases of neglect I have ever seen.

Neglect is the most common form of abuse I encounter, if you can really call it 'abuse'. It is more an absence of the things that make up basic care. It is often possible, through working in partnership with the parents involved, to improve the situation greatly. Adults rarely neglect children on purpose. Many are unaware that they are actually *being* neglectful. Despite the horrendous conditions this family were living in, and even though the children were obviously seriously developmentally retarded as a result, I wanted to try to help them. I thought that some regular visits from myself, combined with carefully organised sessions with a family support worker, to assist with things like diet, the management of their finances, and caring for the children, could well set the family on the road to a healthier future. That was until I had visited the cramped mobile home earlier that day.

Gerry Curran, the children's father, had been absent for all my previous visits. This particular morning he was very much in evidence, sprawled across one of the caravan's small couches. He was as filthy as the rest of his family, and reeked of cheap cider and bile. He seemed to be badly hung over, and dozed throughout most of the forty-five minutes I was there. Tilly Curran, the children's mother, had gone out to visit friends in a neighbouring caravan, giving us space to work. The mobile home itself consisted of a single room, each wall lined with cluttered shelves and narrow padded seats that doubled as beds. There was no toilet, no running water and no electricity. Meals were prepared and water, brought from a communal tap outside, was heated on a tiny gas burner. Everything was covered in a fine layer of grease and dirt, and the place stank of sweat, piss and frying.

It was when I was leaving that things went bad. Johnny, the six-year-old, rarely made any sounds at all. He was a skinny, frightened little creature, with a shock of dark hair through which red scabs, where he had broken the skin scratching, could be seen. He had enjoyed the games we'd been playing, and, as I rose to leave, he began to jabber and cry, wanting the fun to continue. This was actually quite a breakthrough for such a silent child, so I decided to play on for another few minutes. As I sat down again, Gerry, who I had thought was asleep, suddenly opened his bloodshot eyes and looked at me.

'You go on now,' he said, his voice guttural and cracked.

'We'll just have one more game,' I said, gently but firmly. 'I won't be in the way more than another five minutes, I promise.'

Johnny, as if to clearly state which side of the argument he was on, went over to his father and said: 'No, Da. Play now.'

It was not spoken in a tone of defiance. There was no challenge there. This was simply a little boy telling his father he wanted to play some more. How was the poor child to know that those four words would unleash a maelstrom that would nearly drown us all?

Gerry Curran, without even pausing for breath, punched Johnny full in the face. I remember the sickening sound of bone crunching as the child's nose shattered, and then his tiny frame crumpling as he fell backwards onto the soiled carpet of the mobile home. The other children went very silent, averting their eyes and moving quietly to stand by the walls, the oldest two picking up the youngest two, neither of whom could walk. I was momentarily stunned, but as the initial shock passed, I sprang up, reaching to grab the man's arm, but he had already leaned over and brought the heel of his fist down on his son's head where he lay on the floor. Again I heard a terrible popping sound, but it was drowned out by my shouting as I caught Gerry and shoved him aside, then bent over to scoop up Johnny's prone figure.

'What … what the fuck are you doing?' I said.

Johnny felt like a rag-doll, a bundle of lifeless limbs. I could smell the rich, metallic scent of blood, which was oozing now from his nose and ears.

'He shouldna' spoke agin me,' Gerry said. 'He won't from now on.'

'You can't hit a child like that,' I said, feeling rage bubbling up in me.

The desire to lash out at him was almost overpowering. With an effort I turned and shoved the door open with my foot. If I had stayed any longer, I would have said and done things I may have regretted. Tilly was standing at the door of a much larger caravan (the travellers refer to them as 'trailers') a few yards away when I emerged into the light. The fact that I was holding the prone body of her son seemed to have little impact on her. She shook her head when I said I wanted her and the children to come with me.

'He's had knocks before. He'll be grand,' she said, looking tired and annoyed.

I couldn't fit all the children in my Austin, and I did not have time to argue with her. I was desperately conscious of the limp child seeping redness into my shirt.

'He's hurt, Tilly,' I said, walking quickly away towards my car. 'I'm taking him to the hospital. I'll be back later for you and the other kids.'

'You can come back,' she called after me as I laid her child in the back seat of my car and tried to get the seatbelts around him. 'We won't be goin' nowhere wit' ya.'

I ignored her. If she wanted to play it that way, then so be it.

———

I have worked with members of the travelling community a great deal, in a number of different roles. I am proud to say that I have friends, quite close friends, in fact, who are travellers. I am fully aware of the shameful history Ireland has regarding its treatment of these indigenous people, and I take no pride in sometimes having to add to the burden society has placed upon them. I knew, as I waited for the doctors to finish making Johnny comfortable, that his injuries and the terrible neglect he and his siblings had grown up with were not the result of his being a traveller. They had been caused by poverty, lack of education, and by generational abuse long predating my dealings with the family. For Gerry and Tilly to believe such brutality was normal spoke of violence in their childhoods. Abuse and neglect cross all boundaries of ethnicity and social stratification.

Johnny had sustained a shattered nose, a broken jaw and a fractured skull. The strain of these injuries on a system already compromised by malnutrition would be severe, the doctor told me. His prognosis was not good. The head trauma in particular could lead to lasting brain damage.

I went to the children's ward, but the boy was still unconscious. He looked small and pathetic in the white hospital bed, his nose packed and reset now, bruises already darkening the area about his eyes, a bandage round his head. I left him, feeling brittle and dry inside, and drove straight to the local police station, ringing Ben Tyrrell en route. It took us a couple of hours to persuade the police that action needed to be taken, but a call to the hospital to confirm Johnny's condition, coupled with several existing complaints on file from concerned travellers the family had encountered on the road, sealed the deal. As a bitterly cold evening settled over the city, I parked my old Austin behind Ben's jeep just outside the halting site and prepared to keep my promise to Tilly Curran.

I had gone in ahead of the police, to see if the children, and prefer-
ably their mother, would come quietly. I had no reason to believe
that Tilly was directly violent towards the children. She had been
supportive of the work I had been doing with them, and I hoped, as
bad as it may sound, that she simply had become acclimatised to the
violence her husband meted out. The police cars and vans had of
course been spotted, and I got some black looks as I walked up the
narrow pathway between the lines of trailers in their berths. Most
were well maintained and clean, decorated with potted flowers,
some painted in traditional gypsy colours of bright red, yellow and
green. Traveller dogs, a peculiar cross-breed of greyhound and Irish
wolfhound, ran here and there, and several berths had piebald
ponies tethered outside, munching on the grass that grew in the
verges. I knocked on the Currans' door. Their ancient Hiace was
here, so I knew they hadn't fled. There was no answer for several
minutes. I knocked again. Scuffling sounds came from inside, and
finally the door was opened by Gerry.

'Wha'?'

'Johnny is badly hurt,' I said to him. 'He may not recover fully.'

'He wasn't never righ', tha' one. Sumtin' bad 'bout 'im.'

'That's not true, Gerry. He just wanted to play. I don't think you
ever really played with him, did you?' I felt rage building again, and
pushed it down as far as I could. It was not productive — not now,
anyway. 'What you did today was wrong. You didn't just slap him this
morning; you beat him with your fist closed, and broke bones in his
head. The pressure to his brain could damage him permanently.'

Gerry Curran shook his head, annoyed and, I thought, maybe just
a little ashamed. 'I never hit 'im that hard. You're romancin', boy.'

'I wish I was. I've come to see Tilly and the rest of the children.
Are they here?'

I heard steps on the thin wooden floor of the trailer and another
man appeared behind Gerry. He had the familial likeness of a
brother, but may have been a cousin. Traveller families intermarry
and kinship ties can get very confusing. First cousins marrying and
subsequently having children is not considered out of the ordinary.

'You'll not see my girl or the babbies,' Gerry said, the shame having apparently passed. 'You move right along now, or you'll bring trouble down on yoursel'.'

I sighed deeply. These things are never easy.

'The police are outside. We are prepared to come in and take the children if we have to. It would be far less upsetting for everyone if you just handed them over.'

Gerry lunged out of the door at me, swinging his fists. His brother/ cousin was right behind. Gerry was around my size, but still looked tired and sick with his hangover — not really much of a threat. His brother was a head shorter, but I did not want to get into a physical confrontation with them in the halting site. I could sense the atmosphere getting nasty, and wished I had told the gardaí to stay back out of sight until I'd had a chance to see if we needed them or not. I dodged a blow, caught another on my right arm, and then turned tail and ran. I could already hear murmurs of unrest about me, and a couple of missiles came in my direction as I sprinted for the gate.

'I take it they were not amenable,' Ben said grimly when I reached him.

'Whatever gave you that idea?' I panted, as the first bottle of urine shattered on the ground just in front of us, exploding with the smell of ammonia. 'Tilly and the kids are in there, though, as far as I can tell.'

The police had already begun to line out, getting in a defensive formation.

'Keep behind the shields, you two,' Brophy barked. 'We're going to make straight for the Currans' trailer. If they're not there, we'll split into two columns. Mr Tyrrell, you go with the left flank, Mr Dunphy, you stay with the right. Possible bolt-holes have been identified, and we will search each one systematically. Are we clear?'

'Perfectly,' Ben said. 'There's no need to shout.'

'I'm sorry. I hate these fuckin' Section 12's,' Brophy admitted.

'We're not big fans of them ourselves, Detective,' Ben said. 'Shall we get it over with?'

Shields held above us, we advanced quickly through the gates. As soon as our line began to move, the shouts and jeers became louder and shriller, and the shower of projectiles fell thicker and faster. A boulder that looked as if it must have been thrown by King Kong crashed into us, almost knocking several of the gardaí backwards.

'Jesus! Do they have one of those giant fuckin' catapults or somethin'?' a young officer in front of me muttered.

When we were several yards inside the halting site, the mob got braver, running over, throwing things at closer range, hitting out with iron bars and sticks. The armoured gardaí moved into a loose circle to protect Ben and me. I found that I was sweating profusely, despite the fact that it was now very cold and sporadic bursts of rain had begun to fall. A pony whinnied in fear beside us, bucking in alarm. With a throaty roar, a huge man rushed the group from the left, a hurley in his hand. He crashed into the shields on Ben's side, and the force of the attack sent him through the gap between the men. I heard Ben swear as the giant collided with him, the two of them hurtling into me. I fell against the police on my own side, who pushed back, and the whole tangled mess of us staggered precariously. I tried to hang on to Ben, afraid that if he fell, we'd be in serious trouble. Ben, for his part, was desperately attempting to push the huge man away from him. The hurley was swinging all about, and connecting occasionally, accompanied by a furious string of invective. Suddenly, I felt another lurch at the front. Several men had charged from that direction. The shields were no longer offering any protection; a bottle whizzed past my ear and landed directly on the head of our burly antagonist. He went down in a shower of glass, and did not rise.

The gardaí were fighting to keep us together, but we were badly outnumbered. To my relief, I saw the Currans' shabby caravan just ahead. We came up tight beside it, surrounded now on all sides by a leering mob. I reached for the handle and pulled, fully aware that we could have Gerry and his brother to the front of us, as well as the spitting, shouting army behind.

The door swung open and I dashed straight up the steps. Inside it was dark and bitterly cold. Tilly sat on the couch facing me, her youngest child, Polly, on her knee and the next oldest, the eighteen-month old, Jimmy, on the rancid carpet at her feet. That left three children unaccounted for. Her husband and brother-in-law were nowhere to be seen.

'Hurry the fuck up,' I heard Brophy shout from outside.

Tilly looked at me with huge, terrified eyes.

'Don't take my babbies,' she choked, tears beginning to stream down her cheeks.

'Come with me,' I said urgently. 'I want to help you — all of you.'

'Gerry is my husband,' she sobbed. 'I can't leave him. No man would touch me again.'

'He nearly killed your son,' I said, casting a look over my shoulder at the mayhem outside the door. 'Does he hit you too?'

'Only when I makes him,' she said, clutching the baby to her breast. 'He's not bad. He's not!'

'Shane, we have to be on our way,' Ben called to me.

'Come with me, Tilly,' I implored. 'There's no other way out of this. We can teach you to look after the children, help you with money, get you somewhere nice to live, with electricity and hot and cold water and a decent kitchen . . .'

'Noooo!' she screamed. 'Leave us alone! You can't take them!'

In two quick steps Ben was in the room. He went straight to Tilly and, ignoring her protestations, pried the child from her. The baby began to wail, reaching out for her with its stubby, pocked arms.

'Take the other kid and come on,' he said calmly, and with the distressed baby ducked back into the deepening dark outside.

I couldn't bring myself to look at the distraught woman. I simply grabbed the tot on the floor and rushed after Ben. I was too slow, though, and as soon as I turned she grabbed the back of my long coat.

'No, my baby, my baby.' She was verging on hysteria, repeating the words again and again. She fell to the floor, wrapping her arms around my legs.

The child began to scream and thrash about, confused and frightened. I wrenched myself away from her and followed Ben, holding the infant.

The gardaí seemed to have had some success in dissuading our adversaries from their efforts; there was only a scattered group remaining. Ben handed me the younger child and with two of the police walked briskly over to the larger trailer that stood adjacent, where Tilly had been earlier that morning.

The children, close together now in my arms, seemed to be a comfort to one another. I squatted down on the grass and began to rock and sing gently to them: *Hush little baby, don't say a word, Daddy's gonna buy you a mockingbird.* They hiccoughed and sobbed, but watched me, wide-eyed, the tears making pale tracks down their dirt-stained cheeks. I could still hear Tilly screaming in misery inside the caravan, and, with my elbow, I pushed the rickety door closed. *And if that mockingbird don't sing, Daddy's gonna buy you a diamond ring.*

After much knocking and a declaration that the police were outside, the door of the big trailer opened. Gerry stood silhouetted against the light, three-year-old Miley in his arms.

'Ye can't have 'em,' he shouted at the gathered police, Ben and me. 'Ye're on my turf now. These are my people, so they are. Ye'll not take my wains, not never.'

'We can and will,' Ben said. He spoke so quietly, I could barely hear him. 'Now, please don't make this any more difficult than it has already been.'

Without warning, Gerry, from his elevated position on the caravan steps, kicked Ben squarely in the jaw with his mud-caked boot. Ben keeled over backwards, landing with an audible thud on the frigid ground. There was a roar of approval from the crowd still around us, and the police rushed Gerry as one. I put my arms around the children tightly, and kept singing: *And if that diamond ring turns brass, Daddy's gonna buy you a looking-glass.*

'For the love of God, don't hurt the youngsters,' I heard Ben cry above the shouts of the crowd and the barking of the dogs and the bellows of the gardaí.

The children had stopped crying now, and were leaning into me and against one another. Their breathing had become deep and regular, the fear and the unhappiness of the day pushing them remorselessly towards sleep. I continued to sing, as much for myself as for their benefit. The melody of the old lullaby seemed to act as a force field, insulating us from the fury and insanity of our surroundings. *And if that looking-glass gets broke, Daddy's gonna buy you a billy goat.*

Gerry Curran burst through the gauntlet of struggling gardaí and irate travellers and made a lunge for me. Still singing, I tried to angle myself so that he would land on my back. Brophy, a look of grim determination on his face, rugby-tackled him and held him in an arm-lock on the ground. I cast a look down at Polly and Jimmy, to see how they were coping with the sight of their father being so roughly handled. To my relief, both were sleeping. I continued to rock them and sing as their father was cuffed and led away, and Ben and a young garda carried the remaining three Curran children out of the trailer. No one came near us, even those who had been so aggressive moments before seeming to realise that the only ones being hurt now were these exhausted, fragile innocents.

Eventually Ben came up to me. He was mud-spattered and an enormous welt was already coming up on his cheek where Gerry had kicked him.

'Let's get these two to the van,' he said.

I stood and handed Polly to him. 'What about Tilly?'

'What about her?'

'Well, we can't just leave her here like this.'

He looked at me and sighed. 'Go on. Give it one last shot. But we need to move, Shane. The children are our primary concern.'

I passed Jimmy over to him and went back into the foul air of the cramped trailer.

Tilly was lying on the floor where I had left her. She did not move or speak. I sat down on the grubby carpet and took out a cigarette.

'Do you mind if I smoke, Tilly?'

She didn't answer.

'I'll take it that you don't.'

I realised as I sparked my Zippo that my hands were shaking badly. I closed my eyes, trying to wrest back some control.

'Would you like a cigarette?' I asked her, my eyes still closed. I felt my breathing start to regulate, and opened them.

I thought she was going to stay silent, but after a long pause, she muttered: 'What happened to my Gerry?'

'The cops took him. I'm sorry, Tilly.'

'And my babbies?'

'They're in a police van, outside. We're going to take them to hospital tonight, and then on to a residential unit tomorrow. If you were to come with them, though … well, after you get checked out by a doctor, you could all go to a refuge until we can sort out somewhere for you to live.'

She lifted her head and looked at me, pain etched into the dark lines on her face. Her eyes were red from crying, tears still running down her cheeks as if something had ruptured inside her. I suddenly realised that she wasn't much older than me. Life had not been kind to her, however. She was already old, despite her years.

'I can't go, don't you see that?'

I shook my head. 'No, I don't. Tell me.'

'I'm a traveller. I was born on the road. I've spent me whole life on the move, had all me wains that way. I *can't* live in a house. I don't know how.'

I reached over and put my hand on her shoulder.

'That's okay, Tilly. No one is saying you have to stop being a traveller. We can probably help you to get a decent trailer, one big enough for you and the children. You can't keep living in this one.'

'You'd do that?'

'Yes. There would have to be conditions, though. You'd need to stay put for a while, because the children are going to need some medical treatment. They're all too skinny, and there's the headlice and the psoriasis that have to be taken care of. And you'll need help too. I'd like to keep visiting, and we'll probably send someone — a traveller mind — out to help you to deal with the children. I mean, there's six of them, and that's a lot for anyone. There's no shame in having a little help.'

She laid her head back on the slick, greasy floor.

'You say it like it's so easy. To hand me life over to someone else. But then, why wouldn't you? Sure isn't everythin' easy for people like you?'

I sat in the bitter darkness of the ruined caravan, after what had been one of the most difficult, draining days of my life, anger and resentment emanating from the prone woman like a physical thing.

'No, Tilly,' I said quietly, 'everything is not easy for people like me. Circumstances can often prove to be very difficult indeed.'

When she finally came with me to the van, she sat among her children in silence, barely casting a glance in my direction. It would be weeks before she could bring herself to speak to me again.

Chapter 2 ∾

T he rain, accompanied by some golf-ball-sized hail, came down with such a fury I wondered if God had finally had enough of us and decided to finish the job. I stood in the lobby of a dying shopping mall on the outskirts of the city, my collar turned up against the cold, and wished I had a cup of coffee or maybe something stronger. It was 10.30 in the morning and the weather forecast for the day promised unpleasantness without respite or apology. I lit a cigarette and cast my eyes over the virtually empty car park. Behind me in the echoing, warehouse-like space, a few desultory shoppers were pushing trolleys while store managers desperately tried to stay afloat for one more day.

Just as I was about to give up hope, a small, red, Japanese hatchback with a huge fin on the rear turned in the gate and pulled up next to my Austin. I recognised the driver immediately, although I hadn't seen her for ten years.

I had been to college with Roberta Plummer, and I had not liked her. This probably said more about me than her, for she had been studious and reserved, while I had, at that stage, been less than attentive to my academic pursuits and more attuned to the social aspects of the college experience. We had never exactly clashed, but had managed to navigate the three years of our diploma without ever really talking to one another.

She was short and plump in a pleasant kind of way, dressed in a very conservative pant-suit, covered by a tan trenchcoat. Her hair was cut just as it had been when I'd known her, long with a thick fringe, and I saw none of the grey that peppered mine among the black. In fact, if you ignored the few pounds she had gained, she had not changed a bit.

She smiled as she saw me, and approached with her hand extended.

'Shane, thanks so much for coming.'

'Roberta, you look well.'

She didn't return the compliment. 'Let me buy you a cup of coffee. There's a place inside that's not bad.'

I suspected that was a euphemism, but kept the thought to myself.

We sat at the back of the empty café. She was right: the coffee was not bad at all, and I felt some life returning as the warmth began to seep back into my limbs.

'I was surprised to hear from you, Roberta,' I said after several minutes of dead air. 'What have you been up to?'

'I manage a crèche not far from here. *Little Tykes*. Have you heard of us?'

'The name's familiar.'

'You work for the Dunleavy Trust, I hear.'

I nodded.

'You were involved with the Walsh boys last summer.'

'Yes.'

'Micky Walsh was with us, for a time.'

I nodded again.

She looked out the window. Whatever was on her mind, she was taking her time. I took a cigarette from the pack and lit it. I didn't really want one, but it was something to do. I was thinking about giving them up. Maybe I could cut down. I'd heard that cold turkey was the best way to do it, but I wasn't convinced.

'My mother died when I was ten years old,' Roberta said.

'I'm sorry.'

She waved off the sentiment, seemingly vexed by it.

'She'd been sick for as long as I could remember. My father was the only real parent I'd known. Mother was always just a presence in the upstairs bedroom. It was cancer.'

'Yeah, I lost my own mother to it the year we graduated.'

'Yes, I remember.'

That surprised me, but I made no comment. We were getting to whatever it was that had moved her to call me, and I was curious.

'When I was seventeen, my father remarried. Cynthia her name was. She was a wonderful person. A lot younger than him, but sweet and warm, and she was the mother I'd never had. I adored her almost as much as he did. They were married a year when she became pregnant, and suddenly I had a brother, Clive. Do you have siblings, Shane?'

'Brother and a sister.'

'I bet you're the eldest.'

'I am,' I said, wondering what gave her that impression.

'It was strange at first. Up until then, my family had been my parents and me. Now there was this other person to think of. But it was sort of nice, actually. I had a brother. I had to get used to calling him that, you know. *Brother*. Felt odd. But I liked it.'

'Happy families.'

'Yes. I moved out, as you know, to go to college, and immediately after graduation, I went to work in London for a time. Besides coming home for holidays, I made my own life. I rang home regularly, and got letters and e-mails, but I was removed, I suppose, from what was happening. It was all over, really, before I even knew what was going on.'

'What?'

'Cynthia had become very ill. Cancer again — a rare form, incurable. There had been some warning signs, but the doctors hadn't noticed them. Thought she had an inner ear infection. She died last year.'

'Jesus, Roberta, I'm sorry. That really sucks.'

'Yes. It does.' She was silent again for a while.

'Um, Roberta. Why did you ask to meet me?'

She blinked and looked back at me.

'Oh. Yes. Well, it's about Clive, of course.'

'Your brother.'

'Yes. You recall I said that I had not been as involved with the family as maybe I should have been? Well, when I came home for the funeral, I realised immediately that something was not right with Clive.'

'He must have been devastated, Roberta. What age was he? Twelve, thirteen, maybe?'

She nodded briefly.

'That's a really bad age to lose your mother.'

'It was more than grief. He was like another person. He startled at loud noises, wouldn't look me in the eye. Would break down into tears and become inconsolable for no obvious reason. Dad couldn't cope with him, didn't know what to do. I resigned from my post in London, secured a job at the crèche and moved back permanently. But it made no difference. Clive seemed to get worse and worse.'

'Post-traumatic stress. Watching your mother waste away will do that to you.'

'That's what we thought initially. We went to the GP, who said as much, and suggested medication: sedatives. They knocked him out, but when he was conscious, despite being a bit groggy, he was still like a frightened child. Then the hallucinations began.'

'Hallucinations? Auditory or visual?'

'Both. He claimed to be seeing all kinds of things. The visions were demonic, mostly. He said that he believed he was being taken over by something, being controlled. Possessed, I suppose you'd call it.'

'It sounds a lot like schizophrenia. The symptoms often become apparent at the onset of adolescence. I've seen it in younger children, but it's most common with people of your brother's age.'

'Again, that's what I assumed. But isn't there usually a history of it in the family?'

'I haven't got a huge amount of training in working with psychiatric illness, Roberta, but as far as I know there does tend to be a hereditary aspect to it, though not always. I don't think you can really depend on any information on schizoid disorders as being standard, across the board. It's all a bit vague, I'm afraid.'

'Well, my father seemed to accept that the problem was indeed schizophrenia, and he had Clive committed.'

'Where?'

'St Vitus's.'

St Vitus's was the region's main psychiatric hospital, built at the end of the eighteenth century when the English were constructing them in all the major towns and cities in Ireland. I had been there from time to time to visit parents or relatives of clients. It was a cold, depressing building. I would not want a family member of mine to be there, if I could help it.

'I didn't know they had an adolescent psychiatry ward?'

'They don't. He's in with the general population.'

I had thought as much. It made any chance of a rapid recovery much more difficult. 'It's not a nice place, by any stretch of the imagination,' I said, 'but if your Dad can't cope with him, maybe it's for the best until they can regulate his behaviour. I don't really like the medical model of care, but I believe they can do wonders with drugs these days.'

'He's stoned out of his head all the time, Shane. He doesn't seem to be hallucinating any more, but he's begun to talk, and I don't understand what he's saying. He's rambling about being abducted, about being held under the ground, about being tortured. It's like he's living in a nightmare, and I don't know how to wake him up.'

'It's distressing for you, Roberta, but he'll come out of it, I'm sure.'

'What if he's telling the truth?'

'What?'

'I know my brother, Shane. When he wasn't in his full mind, I knew. These disclosures ... they seem to be coming from the real him, from my Clive. It's not like before.'

'Yeah, that's because he genuinely believes them. In his head, whatever delusion he's trapped in is very real. He's not lying. He's not existing on our plane of reality.'

'I understand all that. I just think there's more to this than dementia. I mean, what if he's telling the truth? What if all this came about because of some awful thing that happened to him while I was away?'

'Roberta, you can't blame yourself for your brother's illness or your mother's death. You had your own life to lead. It's not like you abandoned your brother, or anything.'

'I know, I know. I'm not consumed by guilt. Shane, this is my little brother. I accept the disclosures may be the ramblings of a disturbed mind — but then, they may not. I can't take the chance.'

'So you're telling me that you suspect that Clive was, at some point while you were living in London, abducted and abused? Have you asked your father about this? Surely he'd have noticed that your brother was missing.'

'My father won't talk about it. Which makes me even more suspicious.'

I nodded. If I were she, I'd feel the same way.

'So, what has this got to do with me?' I asked.

'You helped Micky when they'd written him off.'

'No one said Micky and his brother were schizophrenic.'

'The symptoms aren't that different.'

'They're hugely different!'

'Help me, Shane. Go out and talk to him, and then tell me you think he's insane.'

'Roberta, there are psychiatrists in St Vitus's that can do that. It's not my remit.'

'*Please.* One conversation. I know you don't owe me anything … that we're not friends. But I don't know who else to turn to. My Dad doesn't want to talk about it and the psychiatrists have already made up their minds. But I *know* there's more to this than they're seeing. Yes, Clive's distressed; yes, he's not well. But I cannot believe he's schizophrenic, and I'll go mad if I have to see him under the influence of all those drugs for much longer. Help him, please, Shane. I'm begging you.'

I sighed deeply and looked at Roberta Plummer. It must have taken a lot for her to call me. From what I knew of her she was a fiercely independent, centred person. In college she had always viewed me with a sense of disapproval. To have opened up to me as she had was a sign of how desperate she must be.

'I'll have to clear it with my boss, but if he's happy enough, I'll go out and talk to Clive. I can't promise anything, okay? I may well come back and tell you I think your brother is schizophrenic.'

She nodded, tears barely kept in check.

'Thank you. That's all I ask.'

Dr Eric Fleming was perhaps two years older than me and dressed in a denim shirt and paisley tie; his white lab coat was a little too big for his slim frame. He had a week's worth of stubble, and looked tired and nervy.

He walked me down the dark, high-ceilinged corridor of the psychiatric hospital towards the Occupational Therapy Unit, where Clive spent most of his days. Small windows had been set high up in the thick walls, and these were covered with grimy net curtains. The building smelt of bleach and semolina pudding. The cold outside did not penetrate within; large, metal radiator grilles were hung at regular intervals on each wall, and huge metal pipes, dripping with condensation, ran near the floor, heat pounding out of them in waves. Now and then, black, glistening cockroaches scuttled along the skirting boards before disappearing into cracks that seemed far too small to accommodate them.

Besides our footsteps echoing off the cracked stone walls and tiled floor, there wasn't a sound. I am always struck by how quiet psychiatric hospitals can be. I've heard the howls of despair — anyone who has spent any time within these crumbling dens of unhappiness has — but they are infrequent, as if the people condemned to serve time there just can't be bothered. As we walked, we passed an old lady in a cleaner's uniform mopping the stone tiles, but even she was silent.

'I agree with you, Mr Dunphy,' Dr Fleming said as we walked. 'Clive Plummer shouldn't be here. There just isn't anywhere else for him to go. We have a limited number of beds for children in need of institutional psychiatric care throughout the country, but they're all taken.'

'When can he go home?' I asked, knowing the answer but wanting to hear the doctor's version of things.

'I don't see him leaving us any time in the immediate future, I'm afraid. The hallucinations are being kept in check by large amounts of Nembutal at the moment, and when he has violent episodes, which happen all too frequently even with the medication, he can be very hard to manage.'

'Aren't you worried about him becoming addicted to the barbiturates? He's very young to be on such a heavy dosage.'

'It's that or let him ride out the delusions, and they're pretty horrible. He thinks he's being controlled by devils and evil spirits. As it stands, he's still in the throes of some kind of psychotic fantasy that we can't seem to shift.'

'What kind of fantasy?'

'He claims to have been abducted by monsters. He says they took him to their lair and tortured him.'

'What form of torture? Physical? Sexual?'

'Both.'

'Any chance he may be confusing this with a real event of abuse?' I decided to throw it out just to see what response I'd get.

'Why? Do you suspect something?'

'Seems reasonable to ask.'

'His father hasn't reported anything to us. If he *was* abused at some time in the past, of course, it would have a bearing on the psychosis.'

'Is there any physical evidence of such an event?'

'Impossible to tell. He injures himself to such an extent that he's covered with scars. His father was incoherent with grief for a time after his wife's death, and Clive had been left to his own devices. When Roberta, his older sister, arrived home from London for the funeral, she found Clive standing under the flow of a gutter-pipe from the roof. It was raining heavily that day, and there was a torrent of freezing water coming from the overflow. She reckoned he'd been there for hours. He was blue with cold, and covered with scratch marks and bruises even then. In the intervening time he has broken teeth biting at the walls, gouged himself with pencils, tried to drink bleach … this is a desperately unhappy boy.'

We reached a large wooden door, set in the centre of the interminably long corridor. The door was arch-shaped, and had been varnished a brown so dark it was almost black. Fleming pulled a huge bunch of keys from his belt.

'Have you ever been in an asylum before?' It was unusual to hear that word used: *asylum.* It seemed so old-fashioned. But in this place the word was disturbingly appropriate.

'I've visited from time to time.'

'Then you'll know what to expect. The duty nurse has been informed that you're here to see Clive. I warn you: he may simply refuse to talk to you.'

'I'll take my chances.'

Fleming nodded, turned the key, and opened the door. A narrow flight of stairs curved downwards, disappearing into the gloom, and a heavy smell of tobacco smoke wafted up. I nodded at the doctor and descended. I heard the door being closed, then locked behind me, and was for a moment in almost complete darkness. I felt a moment of panic, but then an arch of light appeared below me.

The Occupational Therapy Unit was a long room with a dirty vinyl floor and high windows, the lower panes of which were obscured by opaque plastic sheets. Tables were dotted about, with board games, magazines, newspapers and books laid out on them. Couches and soft armchairs lined the walls, and most of the people in the room sat or lounged limply on these. The games and reading material didn't seem to be attracting much attention. Smoke from a mix of cigarettes, cigars and pipes hung in the air like thick fog, and the ceiling was stained earwax yellow from it. I found myself becoming quite light-headed, and took shallow breaths to compensate. *Here's another reason for quitting*, I thought to myself.

'You're here to see Clive?' a portly, middle-aged woman in a nurse's smock (there were three on duty) asked.

'Please.'

'That's him.'

I squinted through the haze and saw a boy, who looked to be in early adolescence, seated alone by a low table of comic books.

'Thanks. How's he been today?'

'Same as every day,' she shrugged. 'He comes, he sits. That's about it. I hate to see youngsters in this place, but what can you do?'

'You told him I was coming?'

'I told him. I don't know if he heard or understood, but I told him.'

'Thanks.'

I pulled a chair over to Roberta's brother, and sat. He neither looked at me nor made any show of my being so physically close to him. I said nothing for a time, examining his appearance.

The familial resemblance was undeniable, but there was something else there too. Roberta had a stout, solid build that emanated stolid resolve. Clive was more slender and had a finer bone structure than his sister. His face hinted at a sensitive personality, a gentleness which some would construe as effeminate, but which had behind it a steely inner strength. I guessed that it was this hidden reservoir that had stopped him from killing himself.

He appeared to have lost a lot of weight quickly. The flesh hung on his bones and there were deep black smudges under his eyes. Bruising was visible on one side of his face, and a gash ran across his forehead. One eye was filled with blood. I saw that both hands were marked with self-inflicted wounds from picking and ripping. His hair, as dark as his sister's, was cut short. He wore an expression devoid of anything — fear, pain, unhappiness — and sat perfectly still, gazing unblinking into space.

I extended my hand.

'Clive, my name's Shane. I'm a friend of Roberta's, and she's asked me to come out and have a chat. I'm very pleased to meet you.'

No response. I left my hand there. Still nothing. A minute passed, and my arm was beginning to get tired. I was tempted to reach over and pick up his hand, shake it anyway, but was unsure how he'd react. It might make him violent, which could cause some of the other patients to get upset. I was aware of the tenuous balance maintained in places like St Vitus's, and did not want to disturb it unnecessarily. So I lowered my hand and moved my chair directly in front of him.

It seemed as if the drugs had slowed his reactions, because, after three or four minutes, his eyes rolled painfully up and fixed on me. His mouth opened slightly, and a string of saliva dribbled from the corner and hung, yo-yoing in the air for a moment before dropping off and landing on the leg of his jeans. He studied me slowly, fighting against the influence of the medication. Finally, after what seemed to be an age, he spoke. His voice was a rasp, barely above a whisper. I wondered if it was raw from shouting and screaming, because speaking seemed to cause him pain.

'I don't know you,' he said.

'I'm a friend of Roberta's. She asked me to come and see you.'

He considered my answer for many long moments.

'I know Roberta's friends. I've never seen you before. And you don't look like her friends do. You look weird. Like a … like a rock singer or something.'

I laughed. The sound seemed odd in the big, quiet, echoey room, and several of the patients turned to look at me. 'No, I'm not a rock singer. I went to college with your sister. I suppose we aren't really friends, but I've done some work with young people who've had problems a little like yours, and she asked me to see if I could help you.'

Slowly — everything he did was at a snail's pace — the expression on his face began to change. Like a film being played at the wrong speed, his features rearranged themselves. It took me almost a minute to realise that he was frightened of me. Not just a little nervous, either, but genuinely terrified.

'*They* sent you, didn't they?' he hissed at me, fighting to get the words out. 'You've come for me. Some of them looked like you, with the long hair and the beard. I should have known they'd come for me sooner or later.'

'Hey, relax, Clive. I promise you, I'm here because Roberta asked me to come.'

He was looking about the room now, as if he expected several more bearded assailants to emerge from the smog. His breathing became rapid, and I saw beads of perspiration dotted upon his brow.

'You can't fool me. I've been waiting for you. You're from them. I can tell.'

In an effort to calm him, I abandoned my previous caution, and put a hand on his arm.

'Who are *they*, Clive? Who do you think is trying to hurt you?'

My touch affected him like an electric prod. He stopped stock-still, his eyes boring into me like laser beams. He bared his teeth at me, and I saw that many were chipped and cracked, some little more than stumps where he had tried to gnaw his way out of his hospital room through the wall, delirious with panic and paranoia. His whole frame began to shake, and a cry that had been building up exploded from his lips, a hoarse, petrified wail that ripped his already raw voice box in its urgency. '*Them! You know them! You know!*'

And then he was on top of me, knocking me backwards off the chair onto the linoleum, screaming, spitting and snapping at me with those shattered teeth. For a boy of his size, Clive was powerfully strong, and it took every ounce of my weight and the momentum of our fall for me to roll over, so that I was on top of him. I pinned his arms to his sides and got my knees up onto his shoulders. It was not the recommended restraint position, but he was too strong, and the correct hold would simply not have worked. One of the nurses rushed over, straddled his mid-section and held his legs, as I moved around to the proper hold of his upper body. He was still howling, not words now, but panicked, animal noises.

'What did you say to him?' the woman asked through clenched teeth as Clive tried to throw her off and almost succeeded.

'Nothing. He seems to think I've been sent to hurt him.'

She nodded. 'He's not really with it at all, God love him.'

The other nurses removed the patients, many of whom had begun rocking or pacing in dismay, from the Unit, and Dr Fleming arrived and administered an injection to Clive. Even with the extra drugs, it took close to fifteen minutes for the boy to become still, and when he was lifted from the floor, he was still semi-conscious, his eyes rolling in his head, but seeming to focus on me for a few seconds.

As he was carried away by two male nurses, I hauled myself up. It had taken an enormous effort to hold Clive down. I was sore, soaked in sweat, and could not get my breath back in the smoky atmosphere. Feeling a terrible sense of claustrophobia, I walked to a door at the rear of the room.

'Does this open?' I asked, beginning to feel as if I was drowning.

Dr Fleming fumbled with his keys, and at last a welcome burst of cold, fresh air poured in. It was as if a veil had been lifted. I stepped outside and breathed deeply. The rain from earlier that morning had passed, but dark clouds that looked heavy with snow or sleet gathered above like a murder of crows. Fleming stood on the doorstep, blinking in the light. The hospital was set in several acres of land, on a hill near the western edge of the city. It contained a small farm, and the gardens, if a bit overgrown, were quite pretty. I sat on a frost-coated bench and looked up at the psychiatrist.

'So, that's Clive Plummer,' I said, savouring the air like fine whiskey.

'You can see why he's here.'

'Indeed. He mentioned *them*, a group of people he seems convinced want to hurt him.'

'Paranoid delusions. Very common with schizophrenics. Someone with Clive's condition can watch the news and become convinced that every single item is actually about them.'

'But he seems to be genuinely terrified.'

'Clive is hearing voices in his head telling him to hurt himself. He sees demons and their minions everywhere he looks. Sometimes, he thinks that there is a devil inside him trying to rip its way out through his stomach. Of course he's afraid.'

'I'd like to see him again. I'll bring his sister the next time, though. Maybe that will prove to him that I'm a good guy.'

The doctor laughed and stepped gingerly onto the grass. It was as if it had taken an effort for him to leave the confines of the hospital. 'I think that would be best. We could do with the help. To be honest, the more people we have on the case, the better. There isn't anyone on staff here who specialises in childhood psychiatric disorders.'

'Well, it's not my specialty either.'

'You work with children, at least, which puts you at more of an advantage than the rest of us.'

He stood a little away with his back to me, looking at an ornamental pond set in the lawn to our left, covered now in a thick sheet of ice, silver bulrushes standing like sentries here and there. A rickety metal fence surrounded it, apparently to stop patients flinging themselves in. It didn't look as if it would provide much of a challenge to a determinedly suicidal individual, but I kept the opinion to myself.

'Do you like working here, Doctor?'

'What?' he turned back to me, seemingly disturbed from private thoughts. 'I … I don't really know. I've been here since I finished college. Did my internship here too. I suppose I like it well enough. There are staff members who've worked here far longer than I have.'

'Really?'

'Oh, yes. I was at a retirement party last month for a nurse who'd practised here for fifty years.'

'That's quite an achievement.'

'It certainly is.' He paused, lost in his thoughts again. 'She booked herself in as a patient two weeks ago. Cited "creeping insanity" as her disorder. There's no such thing, of course.'

'Retirement obviously didn't suit her.'

'No.'

A flock of lapwings came in to feed on the crusted mud around the lake, their plaintive *pee-wit* cries punctuating the silence.

'Could we work towards getting Clive's medication lowered?' I asked after a while.

'I don't think that would be wise just at the moment. The drugs are all that's stopping him from imploding.'

'I know that, Doctor, but I think they're also stopping him from healing. The chemicals are creating a barrier between his consciousness and whatever happened to cause the problem in the first place. We can't help him if we can't get to that cause.'

'Shane, there is no real *cause* for schizophrenia. It just … happens.'

'Mmm. I accept that, but just suppose, for a moment, that there's something more to this. That perhaps Clive experienced something that scared him witless, something so awful he just can't countenance it. Then his mother, whom he worshipped, died, and the combined effect was a complete breakdown.'

'You're suggesting a stress-related condition?'

'Yes. Very severe post-traumatic-stress disorder.'

He turned to look at me, his hands deep in his pockets, shoulders bunched against the cold. 'Your entire premise hangs on Clive's claims that he was abused. There is absolutely no evidence to support that. I don't know that I'm willing to adjust our method of treatment on a hunch.'

'I've worked with a lot of children who've been abused, Doctor. I agree that Clive's reaction is extreme, but it's not that far removed from what I've seen in other cases.'

Doctor Fleming walked back to the door of his domain, and stood for a moment, contemplating his shoes. 'I'll tell you what. Come back with Roberta. Let him see you're not a monster. Befriend him — I think what he needs more than anything else is a friend. And then we'll see. My job is to heal. If you can facilitate that healing, I'll go along with you.' He began to close the door and then stopped. 'You know, part of me hopes you're right, because it means we can maybe help Clive. But there's a big part of me that wonders what exactly could scare a child so much they basically go mad?'

He closed the door, returning to sweltering corridors and patients with haunted eyes. I buttoned up my coat, flung my scarf around my neck and walked to my car, followed by the cry of lapwings all the way.

Chapter 3 ～

I met Marian, a colleague of mine from the Trust, for lunch in a small Italian restaurant in the city centre. She was already seated when I arrived, a soft-featured, pretty woman in her early thirties with short blonde hair. Using Dunleavy House — or Last Ditch House as the staff tended to call it — as a base of operations meant that we saw each other at the fortnightly team meetings, but seldom in between. It wasn't that we didn't like one another; we were just so busy and involved with our individual caseloads, there was little time left for socialising. An invitation to lunch, therefore, was unusual, and this one especially so, as the next team meeting was scheduled for the following day. Whatever it was that Marian had on her mind, it obviously couldn't wait.

I ordered minestrone soup, a basket of breads and coffee.

'So, why the invitation?' I asked as she poured me a glass of water from a carafe. 'I am, of course, flattered, but there's got to be a catch.'

'I don't see why a girl can't ask a guy out for lunch without there having to be an ulterior motive,' she smiled. She was from Limerick, and her accent was thick, though not unpleasant.

'There is one, though, isn't there?'

'Yes.'

My soup and her salad arrived, and we waited while parmesan cheese and black pepper were offered and applied. When the waiters had left us, Marian pulled a file from a bag at her feet. 'How much of a caseload have you got at the moment?'

'I'm fairly free, as it happens, for the first time since the summer. I have two cases on, a third I'm sort of partially involved with, and Ben tells me he has something else pencilled in, but we're discussing it at the meeting tomorrow. What are you trying to pawn off on me?'

'You'll thank me, I swear. This is a really easy case — nothing heavy-duty or hard-core. You'll have it wrapped up in no time.'

'So why pass it my way instead of finishing it up yourself?'

She mopped up a dollop of dressing with some bread and took a sip of water. 'I can't. I've got two cases at absolute crisis point. One's about to go super-nova as we speak. Ben bounced this one my way this morning, and it turns out, when I make a few calls, that there absolutely has to be a visit this afternoon, or seven different kinds of shit will hit the fan. Only, see, I have got to be in court, because we're going for an emergency care order on my super-nova case, and if I'm not there, it'll be adjourned for the second time, which would be bad, take my word for it. I really, really need for you to do me a favour on this one, Shane.'

I took a sip of coffee. The tribulations of my morning visit to St Vitus's seemed far away, now. I liked Marian, and the caffeine and soup had me feeling warm and at ease. I could help her out. Why not? I could do with an easy case for a change.

'Have you discussed this with Ben? I mean, if he only just allocated it to you this morning—'

'I rang him as soon as I'd spoken to Gertrude — she's the mother of the family involved. He suggested I talk to you about it.'

I pulled the file over to my side of the table. 'Well, let's hear the lowdown, then. What am I taking on?'

'Thank you *so* much. I owe you one, I swear.'

'It had better be as much of a breeze as you say, or I will be royally pissed.'

'It is, guaranteed. Patrick and Bethany, aged twelve and ten years. They're being fostered by Gertrude and Percy Bassett. The kids have been in foster care with them for the past seven years. They've never been in any other placement, in fact, and have not had any contact with their family of origin during that time. They actually use the Bassetts' name, which as you know is not the norm in fostering cases. Patrick is doing well at school and he's a whizz at sports. Bethany is the most beautiful, sweet-natured little girl you've ever set eyes on.'

I flipped open the file and looked at the photo tacked onto the inside cover. Patrick was a strong-featured, if not handsome, boy, gazing morosely at the camera. Bethany was a heart-breakingly pretty child with blonde ringlets and a ready smile.

'You could be describing the fucking Waltons, Marian. Why, pray tell, is an agency that deals only with children *in extremis* involved with this family?'

'The Health Executive, which placed the kids with the Bassetts, contacted us. It seems the placement is about to break down, and they have been powerless to do anything about it. Several social workers and a child psychologist have been involved, all to no avail. So they called us as a last resort.'

'As is their wont. And the cause of this impending disaster?'

'Gertrude claims that Patrick has become unmanageable. He has been going to football practice and not coming home until hours after he's supposed to. He's become verbally abusive. There has even been an incident of physical aggression. She says that unless he is pulled back into line, he's out.'

'But not the little girl?'

'No. Bethany is an angel apparently.'

I pushed my soup bowl aside and gestured for more coffee. 'You've spoken to Mrs Bassett then?'

Marian nodded. 'This morning.'

'And?'

'Hard to tell. She seemed a little hysterical. What struck me was that the list of complaints about Patrick … well … they just didn't seem that bad. I mean, we deal with all sorts of genuinely messed up kids, right? We've both seen some kids *really* going off the rails. The reason Gertrude Bassett absolutely has to see someone today, believe it or not, is that Patrick went to his swimming lesson last night, and didn't come back until nine o'clock.'

'What time was he supposed to be in at?'

'Eight.'

'Well, I suppose it's dark by that time. A mother would worry.'

'There's a bus-stop right outside their front door. And — get this

— he rang her and told her he was going to be late and where he was going!'

'Oh.'

'I've spoken to the social worker who was on the case — Hugh Rosney. You know him?'

'Yeah, I know Hugh.'

'He's worked with the Bassetts for the past three years, and he's at his wits' end with them. Gertrude, he says, is totally unreasonable. She has it in for Patrick and won't see sense.'

'And why do you think she'd be any more willing to listen to me than Hugh?'

'A fresh face?' Marian asked sheepishly.

'I'll visit and see what I can do. If it becomes high maintenance, I'll be calling on you for back-up, okay?'

She grinned, leaned over and kissed me on the forehead. 'Deal. I knew you'd take it.'

'I'm a pushover, you mean.'

'I wouldn't have chosen that word, but …'

'Why don't you quit while you're ahead?' I asked her as I nodded at the waiter for the bill. 'Lunch is on you, by the way.'

———

The Bassetts lived in a Georgian house on a crescent-shaped street just off the main city thoroughfare, near the People's Park. I knew from their file that Gertrude, the mother, was a homemaker, while Percy, her husband, worked for the city council. She met me at the door. The woman was wide and swarthy, with tightly permed hair of a colour probably not found in nature. She brought me into a lobby, a small room that was decorated with wallpaper that set my teeth on edge in its garishness — it was kind of a brown and orange zigzag that was breathtaking in all the wrong ways. An ornate coat and hat stand adorned the corner, beside a pot-plant that seemed to be in some way related to the Triffids. I gave it a wide berth for safety's sake.

'Ah, you're the young man they've sent to sort Patrick out,' she said, a smug smile playing on her flat features.

'I'm here to talk to you and your family,' I said, handing her my coat and scarf. 'It doesn't really help to apportion blame before we begin. These things are often no one's fault. Sometimes it's just a matter of learning to look at the situation in a different way.'

'Well,' she said, laughing, a peculiar little snigger deep in her throat. 'If you can get Patrick to see he's in the wrong, fair play to you. He's a very stubborn lad is our Patrick. I think it comes from his genes, you know. It's in his blood. He never learned it here, that's for sure.'

Before I could express my unhappiness with what she had just said, Gertrude pushed open a door behind her, and ushered me into another room. The look in this chamber seemed to be turn-of-the-century French bordello chic: deep-pile burgundy carpets, prints by Toulouse Lautrec on the walls, an old upright piano in the corner. I expected her to offer me a glass of absinthe.

'I'll get the others. You make yourself comfortable,' Gertrude said, and stumped out a door to the rear.

Five totally impractical metal-framed chairs with electric pink, frilly cushions had been arranged in a circle in the centre of the room, so I sat on one, and tried to relax while I waited for her to return. I discovered after a second that whatever the chairs' designers had in mind for their creations, being sat on was not part of the plan. I stood up and paced instead. The room was certainly spacious, with a large picture window looking out on a big back garden that was a remarkable sight to behold. The first thing I noticed was an alarming variety of garden gnomes, all engaged in different activities — fishing, digging, pushing wheelbarrows and other such gnomish pastimes. My eye was then drawn to about a dozen faux Greek statues, each with one limb or another missing, of course. There was also a finicky-looking rock feature with wooden robins and an eagle (which someone had decided to paint bright blue and red) perched on it. And in the centre of the entire bizarre panoply, the *pièce de résistance*: a monstrous cactus that would have looked right at home with The Man With No Name standing beneath it and striking a match against it to light his cheroot. It appeared utterly out of synch here, though, dusted as it was with the light snowfall the city had just experienced. A small path made from lime green paving stones wove in and out of the strange porcelain and plasterwork figures. I could imagine that the children would have found it all kind of fun at first, but would soon have learned that it was not a space mapped out with play in mind. The kind of person who created this garden was the type who collected troll figurines, with all their outfits and accessories, and left them in their boxes.

Voices interrupted my thoughts, and I turned to see Gertrude leading two children into the room, followed by a small, bald man with a fluff of white hair around his ears.

'Percy Bassett,' the man said, walking right up and shaking my hand nervously. He sat on one of the chairs and seemed to zone out, staring intensely at the floor.

'This is Patrick.' The boy was pushed towards me. I extended my hand, which he took limply.

'I'm happy to meet you, Patrick. My name is Shane—'

'I know. Mother told me.' His tone was dull and antagonistic. He had clearly been told that I was going to give him a hard time.

'Well, it's good to be prepared,' I smiled. 'And you must be Bethany.'

The girl stepped up and took my hand. Bethany was indeed a beautiful child. She wore a flouncy dress, probably chosen by Gertrude. It was far too light for the weather and totally out of fashion, but then she had the radiant presence to make it look natural and pretty. 'We're very pleased to have you as our guest,' the girl said. 'Could I offer you some tea?'

This was obviously rehearsed, designed to make Bethany seem the perfect daughter.

'No, thank you. Maybe later. Let's all sit, and get started.'

I perched on the edge of one of the ridiculous seats and waited for everyone to do likewise — Percy, who was already seated, continued examining the pile in the carpet as if his life depended on it.

'Now,' I said, 'what I'm going to do is called family mediation, but it's really just a discussion. To make it work as well as possible, there are some basic rules. Everyone gets to talk, no one can interrupt, and there can be no name-calling, shouting or rudeness. If you don't like what someone else has to say, you wait until they're finished, and then you get to respond, but you can't be mad about it. Part of what we're doing here is respecting one another's feelings. So —' I pulled a piece of pink amethyst from my pocket ('Ooo, pretty,' Bethany said) ' — this is a piece of crystal — it's a coloured stone, really. The rule is that while you are holding it, you have the right to speak, and no one else in the group can butt in or shout you down. When you're finished, the next person who wants to speak gets the stone, and it goes on like that. You ask for the stone by raising your hand, and if more than one person wants to talk, I'll decide who gets to speak. I know that's not fair, but I'm kind of the outside person here, and I'm neutral. The last rule is that whatever is said within this circle stays here. If one of you says something that causes pain or upset to some-one else, and you more than likely will, it is not discussed or gone back over once the session has finished. We leave all the hurt and the annoyance within these five chairs. Once the chairs are taken up and the circle broken, the unhappiness goes with it. Is everyone in agreement?'

There were nods and noises of assent. I took a small set of cards from the back pocket of my jeans.

'Okay. I'm going to put the stone in the centre of the group, and I'm going to give each of you a card. The cards each have a number between one and four written on them. I don't know who's getting which number.' I set the amethyst on the carpet and passed around the cards. 'Now I'm going to pick a number. Whoever has that number gets to go first. I choose number two.'

Percy very shakily held up his arm. 'I have that one, so I do.'

I picked up the stone and handed it to him. 'Good. So, Percy, why don't you tell us how you feel we've ended up sitting here, having this talk?'

'Don't you know?'

'I was handed a file an hour and a half ago, and I have gone through it. But I want to hear the story from all of you. And I think it helps to discuss things out in the open. Sometimes you can see aspects you never noticed before.'

Percy fiddled with his watch strap. Gertrude was practically bouncing up and down on her ample buttocks, her hand bolt upright like a very large schoolgirl. I ignored her.

'What do you want me to say?' Percy asked, looking as if he wished the ground would open up and swallow him.

'Tell me what you think has happened to cause your family to be unhappy.'

'Well,' again a swallow and some deep breaths, 'Patrick hasn't been behaving himself. Gertrude has been very upset, so she has. She's not a well woman, you know, and this hasn't been easy for her.'

'I've been patient. Anyone will tell you,' Gertrude smirked, her arms folded across her bosom.

'You'll get your turn in just a moment, Gertrude. I'd like Percy to finish.'

'Oh, I'm done,' Percy said, seeming to visibly sag.

'Me next then,' Gertrude reached over and took the stone. 'Percy and I have had great hardship with that boy. He was never easy to get on with, even when he was little and we had him first. But we knew that God had denied us the power to have children ourselves so we could take some poor, unloved waifs into our home and raise them as if they were our own flesh and blood. We persevered, and we did not cast him aside. Bethany — well, just look at her — she's special, and has been my pride and joy right from the moment I first set eyes on her. But Patrick was stubborn. I'd ask him to take his shoes off when he came into the house, but he never would; he'd just leave muddy tracks right across my lovely carpet. I'd tell him to have one biscuit from the tin, and he'd always snatch two. It took us time, Shane, years in fact, to train him to have some manners, and I thought these past few years that our training had finally stuck. But then, well, that stubborn streak came back worse than ever.'

'Gertrude, what you are describing sounds to me like the kinds of things any mother would speak of when discussing raising a boy,' I said gently. 'I can remember pulling similar stunts myself as a kid.'

'Oh, they're not the worst of it, not by far. He's disappeared on us, gone off into town and not come back for hours.'

'Okay, let's talk about that. Patrick, would you like to tell me about what your Mum has just said? Have you been going off without telling her?'

Patrick gingerly took the stone from Gertrude. 'I always call her.'

'Sometimes not until he's been gone a good while!'

'Gertrude, Patrick has the stone. Go on, Patrick, please.'

'Some of the kids in my class go to an arcade in Dawnfield, near the market.'

'Yeah, I know the place,' I said.

'They have a new game there: *Superfighter 3*. I'm really good at it, and we have competitions. I got the High Score last time.'

'But do you tell your Mum that you're going?'

'What's the point? She doesn't let me play video games, and she thinks criminals hang about in arcades.'

'Those games are awful things!' Gertrude burst out. 'And that place he goes to is full of a bad lot. I've been down there. I know.'

'Gertrude—'

'Alright, I know, not without the stone.'

'So you go and then call her when you get there?'

'Yeah. They have a payphone. She won't let me have a mobile.'

'Well, we have a clear breakdown in communication here,' I said, looking from Gertrude to Patrick and back again. 'Gertrude, you don't want Patrick to go to arcades or play video games. Patrick not only wants to play them, he's really good at them. From what I've heard, the way he's been going about it has actually been quite responsible. He hasn't been staying out all night, just an hour here and there after football or swimming, and he's been calling you to let you know where he is. I have to tell you, I think he's showing a great deal of respect towards you, all things considered.'

'He has me worried sick,' Gertrude snorted. 'You don't know who he's with down there.'

'I told you, I go there with Harry and Peter and Neil. You know them and their parents. What's the problem?'

'And those games are violent and disgusting!'

I sighed and nodded slowly. 'You're right, some video games can be violent and unpleasant. There are a few I really don't approve of myself. But like it or not, they are a part of the culture our young people have grown up with. Most of what's in the arcades is tame enough; it's more the ones for home use that are really bad, for the PC or the Playstation.'

'It's not right — young men spending their spare hours in those places. Snooker halls and places of gambling and iniquity.' Gertrude was on a roll now. 'I know what goes on; you can't pull the wool over my eyes.'

'We have fun, Mum,' Patrick said, his voice imploring. 'That's not wrong, is it?'

I needed to defuse things. Both Patrick and Gertrude were entrenched in their points of view. Percy was locked in exactly the same position, staring at the floor.

'Bethany,' I said, looking over at her as she sat, swinging her legs on one of the silly chairs. 'What do you make of all this?'

I took the stone from Patrick and passed it over to his sister.

'I don't know,' she said, giggling a little in embarrassment at having all our eyes on her. 'I just want everyone to be happy.'

'How does it make you feel when your Mum and Dad and Patrick are fighting?'

She screwed up her nose as she thought about the question. She was a cutie, no doubt about that. 'It's mostly Patrick and Mum. Daddy never really says much about it, except when Mum tells him to give out to Patrick. Even then he never shouts or anything. I think it makes Daddy sad.'

I looked over at Percy. He did not raise his eyes either to me or Bethany.

'Why don't you ask him?' I asked her.

'Ask him what?' Bethany giggled again.

'If it makes him sad.'

She shrugged. 'Okay.'

'Go on, then.'

'Daddy?'

Percy looked up suddenly, as if he'd just been poked. 'Yes, love?'

'Daddy,' she broke into a fit of giggles. 'This is silly.'

'No, please, Beth,' I said. 'It's important that we ask one another how we feel. If you were sad, you'd want someone to do something about it, wouldn't you, to try and help you feel happy again?'

'Yeah.'

'Well, how would I know you were sad?'

'I'd cry, or maybe I'd look sad.'

'How would that look?'

She did a gorgeous pantomime of looking unhappy, lips down-turned and eyes squinted.

'Well that would certainly tell me you were miserable. I'll watch out for that face.'

'I don't always look like that, though. Sometimes, when I'm just a little bit sad, I just don't smile as much as when I'm happy.'

'Ah,' I said, 'so that would be harder to spot. And y'know, grown-ups don't always show how they're feeling on the inside. When you're big, you've got work to go to, and a house to keep clean, and little kids to take care of, and those things have to get done, even if you're sad. So you know what grown-ups do?'

'What?'

'They keep it all tucked away, down near their boots somewhere. So the only way to know if they're happy or sad, sometimes, is to ask them.'

'Oh,' she nodded vigorously.

'So why don't you ask your Dad?'

'Daddy,' she said. 'Does it make you sad when Patrick fights with Mum all the time?'

Percy looked at the child, and then back down at his shoes. They were shiny, made from black patent leather. He stared at them for maybe a minute without answering. I wanted to reach over and shake him, but this was obviously his custom, because the other three just sat and waited.

'Yes, Bethany,' he said finally. 'I suppose it does. Yes, it makes me very sad indeed.'

'What about you, Gertrude?' I asked. 'Does it make you sad to fight?'

'Of course it does. I've had Patrick for seven years. I don't want to be at odds with him from dawn till dusk.'

'And Patrick?'

'I want things to be normal. Like they were before.'

I nodded. 'I think we've made some progress.'

'Do you?' Gertrude asked incredulously.

'Yes, I do. You have all agreed that your behaviour is making you unhappy. That's a big thing to admit. We've identified the main thing you're disagreeing over, and that's an important step too.'

'There's a hell of a lot more than that going on,' Gertrude said. 'Percy, tell Shane about when he got violent!'

Percy took a breath, as if to start talking, but I held up my hand. 'I'm going to deal with one thing at a time. If we start looking at every single angry interaction, we'll end up going around in circles all evening. It will not be productive. No, we've done enough for today. I want to give you all some homework.'

'The other fella never left us any work to do,' Gertrude said, not looking happy.

'The other fella's gone, Gertrude, at your request, I believe. I'm going to come back in two days to talk to you again. Patrick, I want you to agree not to go out to the arcade between now and then, and to make an honest effort not to annoy your mother — try and take off your muddy boots, don't hog the biscuits — you know the drill. Gertrude, I want you to agree to try not to get into unnecessary confrontations with Patrick. There's a saying of mine that I tend to use in situations like these: "Don't sweat the small stuff." Ask yourself if whatever he's done is really worth a row. All I'm looking for is two days where you both really try to get on. Does that sound reasonable?'

Both parties nodded reluctantly.

'Now that's just for starters. I want each of you to write something too. Patrick, I want you to write down for me what you would like out of your relationship with your parents, if we had a magic wand and could make everything right. A wish list.'

'Okay,' Patrick said. 'I can do that.'

'Gertrude and Percy, the same, only about your relationship with Patrick. But I want each of you to do it separately, in private — I don't want you to show this to one another until the next meeting — alright?'

More nods.

'And Bethany, I want you to write about how you'd like your home to be, if we could use magic to make it all better.'

'Cool! Can I pretend to be a fairy? I could pretend I'm a fairy and write about how I'd make everyone happy again.'

'You're as pretty as a fairy, darling,' Gertrude simpered.

'Sure you can,' I said. I looked around at the family. 'Are we okay to finish? I want you all to agree that you will not discuss what has been said until I see you again, and that you'll all try really hard to get on with each other. Do we have a deal?'

'Yes,' in a chorus.

'Good. I'll see you at the same time on Thursday. That's two days from now.'

Gertrude walked me to the door.

'I hope we'll see a real improvement now,' she said as I stood on her doorstep. 'But he always says he'll try, and he never does.'

'Now, we said no talking about it, Gertrude, and I'm part of that agreement. You have a lovely family. Both the children seem well adjusted and normal — and I want to stress that word — *normal*. They're a credit to you. I don't think that the problems you're having are insurmountable at all. And you tell me that you all really want to work together to sort them out …'

'Oh, we do. We surely do.'

'Alright then,' I said, stamping my feet against the cold. A heavy frost was coming down as the evening descended rapidly. 'I'll see you soon. I think things will iron themselves out soon enough.'

I walked briskly back to my car, thinking that Marian was right: I'd be closing the file on the Bassetts in a week or so, and looking forward to Christmas.

I should have known better.

Chapter 4 ⌒

Through a two-way mirror, I watched as two women held a dark-haired girl in the same kind of restraint the nurse and I had used on Clive Plummer the day before. My eyes were fixed on the prone child. She was fighting desperately: screaming, threatening and struggling for all she was worth. Beside me, Dorothy Carey, the manager of the unit, stood silently. The girl's name was Katie Rhodes. At that morning's team meeting, Ben had asked me to meet her. His information had been sketchy: 'She's the archetypal Last Ditch Kid,' was all he'd tell me.

The residential unit Katie called home was a three-bedroomed dormer situated on a recent development in the quiet suburb of Rocksbridge. The estate was so new that many of the houses were still vacant.

I got the impression that the team had moved into the house in a great hurry. The front garden of the unit had not been properly seeded, and X's of duct tape still adorned the windows. The blinds were all pulled down, and it was only the cars out front that led me to believe anyone was at home.

Katie was fourteen, and had spent most of her young life in one care institution or another. I had rarely seen a face more etched with anger, resentment and pain. Here was a child close to the end of her endurance.

'And this is pretty much a daily occurrence?' I asked after fifteen minutes of unremitting fury had passed in what the staff at the unit euphemistically called the 'Time-Out Room'.

'Usually more than once a day,' Dorothy said. She was a petite woman in her early forties, her light brown hair shot through with grey. 'It's exhausting for the team. I can only imagine how tiring it must be for her, but whatever's driving her just keeps her going. She never sleeps through the night without some kind of episode, and she's up each day at cock-crow.'

'Have you tried medication — Ritalin maybe?'

'I've suggested it. I don't like using drugs on the children, but I'll be honest with you: anything that brings her some relief at this stage would be welcome. I'm not convinced she's hyperactive, though. We're waiting to have her assessed by the psychologists.'

'Hasn't she been in care for almost a decade?'

'Yes, but this … ferocity is a new behaviour. She was a quiet child up until ten months ago. Then she changed. It was like something just broke inside her.'

'She began to get violent?'

'Yes, but if it were only that, it wouldn't be so bad. Her whole personality changed.'

Katie was starting to exhaust herself, now. I could see by the faces of the workers that they knew she was approaching burnout. Her limbs finally relaxed and her head came to rest on the mat. The woman who was at her top end released a hand to stroke the jet-black hair that was now a tangle of sweat and knots, speaking to her in soothing tones all the while. Immediately the prostrate girl saw her opportunity, and her hand snaked out. Before either of the women knew what was happening, Katie had dug her nails into the nearest limb, which happened to be the leg of the woman who had just let go. Using this as an anchor, she started to lever herself free. The staff members suddenly found themselves struggling, both to keep her restrained, and to pry loose that vice-like grip. Captive had become captor in a split-second.

'That was a stupid thing to do,' I observed as the three grappled with each other anew. 'It was way too early to let go.'

'It was,' Dorothy agreed, shaking her head. 'Martina's new to the team. She'll learn.'

'So, what do you see me doing here?' I asked, turning away from the battle. 'Are you thinking of putting together a tag-team?'

She looked at me blankly. 'I don't follow.'

'Wrestling?' I said sheepishly, gesturing at the scene in the Time-Out Room, realising as I did so that Dorothy's sense of humour was probably pretty blunted from the relentless aggression she and her team were facing daily.

'Ah, you think you're a comedian.'

'I'm still working on the act.'

She laughed without enthusiasm. 'Tag-team. I'll have to use that one myself.'

'Feel free. I've got a limitless supply.'

She forced a smile again. 'Let me show you the playroom.'

Katie had been 'specialed', meaning she was the only child in a fully equipped house, with her own skilled team of staff. This is something that happens only in cases of absolute necessity. It is expensive and there is almost always a rapid staff turnover, since dealing with only one child, day-in/day-out, has a peculiar effect on workers: burnout happens quickly, because you tend to either become unprofessionally attached to the child in question or start to detest the very sight of him or her.

Special units work intensively. Their goal is to deal with whatever issues are causing such extreme behaviour in their subjects, and bring that child to a point where he or she can return to mainstream care. And they try to achieve this as quickly as possible. In Katie's case the plan had gone somewhat awry — she was wild and unpredictable when she had arrived at the unit, and continued in the same vein almost a year later without improvement.

A decision about Katie's future had to be made within the next few months, but no one seemed to know what to do with her. Several possibilities had been touted: perhaps a more secure placement was necessary; but then, what could be more secure than having her isolated? Maybe her problem was physiological rather than emotional, and a medical unit was more appropriate? Unfortunately, however, there wasn't a hospital in the world that could cope with her erratic moods and physical outbursts — except, of course, for a psychiatric setting, and she was certainly not insane; on the contrary, she seemed to know precisely what she was doing. If she *was* to return to communal living (and she would have to eventually), a population had to be found that could absorb her anti-social behaviour. That meant looking to settings that catered for juvenile offenders of the most hardened kind.

Dorothy was unhappy with all these eventualities, and suggested that Katie be given one final chance before she was condemned either to endless exploratory operations or spending what remained of her childhood in a children's prison. I was that last chance.

The playroom Dorothy brought me to contained just what a therapeutic play facility should. There was a good-sized doll's house, complete with furniture and figures the right size to fit it; a miniature town and a supply of cars and shops and houses; a sand-pit and water tray; paint, brushes and an easel; a set of bookshelves stocked with a variety of children's books; a cheap, nylon-strung guitar, a small, two-octave keyboard and some percussion instruments; and a stereo, with a selection of CDs. Large, comfortable-looking beanbags were placed here and there, and soft safety mats, of the same kind as those in the Time-Out Room, were rolled up against the wall. The room was decorated in bright, primary colours, and a mural depicting a sunny day, green fields and a house with smoke coming out of the chimney adorned one wall. High up, near the ceiling, two video cameras watched us with their electric eyes. It was a bright, pleasant space, and it didn't look as if it had been used more than once. The smell of fresh paint hung in the air, and there was still plastic wrap on some of the toys.

I wandered over and picked up the guitar. It was, of course, badly out of tune, and I switched on the keyboard, got the G note, and began tuning the strings absently.

'So,' I said as I turned the pins and plucked with my thumb. 'What d'you think is really wrong with Katie?'

Dorothy settled herself wearily onto a saggy, purple beanbag. 'I haven't got the foggiest idea. There was no build-up, no signs of disintegration. One morning she just woke up and was as she is today.'

'Are there any particular idiosyncrasies, anything unusual about what she does that might give us a clue as to what's motivating her?'

'Well …', Dorothy looked uncomfortable. 'There is one thing, but I don't know if it's relevant or not.'

'Okay. Let's hear it.'

'Well,' Dorothy took a deep breath. 'She has an absolutely virulent hatred of men. We have no men whatsoever on the team here … can't have, to tell you the truth. Her last social worker was a guy, and Katie put him in hospital, almost took his eye out with a pencil. Her attacks here are bad, but they don't have the same sense of purpose and, well, meanness as when she's around men.'

'Brilliant,' I said, strumming the chord of C — it wasn't great, but it was close enough. 'That'll make my job a lot easier.'

Dorothy laughed, a little manically, I thought. 'Won't it,' she said.

I began to pick a jaunty Cajun tune. It may appear rude, my continuing to play the guitar while talking to Dorothy about Katie and her problems. I had a feeling, however, that the manager was struggling to tell me something, and I thought that a small diversion may help her. Psychologists refer to it as the 'third party' method — putting something between you and the person you are hoping will disclose.

'There were male staff at her previous setting, though?' I asked.

Dorothy stopped laughing. 'Yes. One.'

'And this change occurred suddenly — all this terrible rage and hatred of the male of the species?'

'It did.'

'It must have occurred to you that this male staff member could have had something to do with the transformation.'

Dorothy said nothing for a few moments. I continued to play the guitar, improvising around the melody line.

'You're quite good, aren't you?' she said, her eyes fixed on the mural.

'I can carry a tune.'

'The male staff member at Katie's last setting is my husband.'

I nodded. I hadn't expected that, but tried not to let my surprise show. I'd been around childcare workers for long enough to know how absolutely devastated she must have been by what I'd just said, and was about to say. I took a deep breath, and continued. 'I'm not the first one to suggest a connection, am I?'

'No. But Katie has never indicated any interference, and she has been given ample opportunity to disclose. There was a half-hearted investigation — of course there had to be — but Claude was never even suspended from active duty.'

'With the greatest of respect, Dorothy — he should have been, regardless of whether anyone believed Katie or not.'

'I know. It's just that, well, no one *really* thought he'd done anything, and Katie never for a minute actually *said* he'd touched her. She just … just seemed to start hating him. I know it was the most obvious thing to think. I didn't and don't blame anyone for wondering about it.'

'The allegation still hurts, though, doesn't it?' I asked.

The biggest risk for any male working in child protection is that a child will allege that you have molested, abused or otherwise interfered with them. I have been incredibly lucky that in my fifteen years of practice I have never had a single charge brought against me. Part of the reason for this is that I am extremely careful in the way I interact with each child I encounter: I try to ensure that I am never in a room alone with them unless there is a window through which I can be seen, or the door is left open; I keep my tone of voice moderate; I try to avoid touching a child until a relationship has been built up, and then only when permission is given; I never raise my hand to a child in anger; when I hug a child, I keep my waist away from them, leaning into the hug with my shoulders to avoid any inadvertent genital contact. And there are countless other things I do that are instinctive — they've been drummed into me by people like Ben Tyrrell and other teachers, colleagues and professionals. They are a survival mechanism, and important for the safety and security of the kids as much as for my own.

Children get confused very easily. The line between reality and fantasy is never more vague than during the years of childhood. For children who have been abused, this blurring is even more intense. The imagination is often used as a tool for survival; children will pretend to themselves that the abuse never happened, or that someone other than a beloved father, mother, uncle or brother was the perpetrator, because that is easier than accepting the truth. False allegations are, unfortunately, common, but are rarely meant maliciously. And of course each one must be taken seriously and investigated thoroughly. The problem is that once a complaint has been made, suspicion hangs in the air about the accused like a fog. Even when the investigation has been carried out and the individual's name has been cleared, there is always doubt: *maybe there wasn't enough evidence; suppose the child was confused and certain dates got mixed up; perhaps the alleged abuser was careful and covered his tracks — after all, who knows how to manipulate the system better than someone working within that system?*

'Yes,' Dorothy said, the pain evident in her voice and posture. 'The suggestion that he might have done anything to hurt her is deeply upsetting.'

'I'm going to ask you something, and please understand that I'm only asking because I have to. My job is to try and help Katie, and that means I have to look at every possible line of investigation.'

'I know that.'

'Do *you* have any suspicion whatsoever that your husband may have actually abused her while she was in his care? Is there any doubt in *your* mind?'

Dorothy rubbed her eyes vigorously. I knew she had asked herself that same question countless times over the past ten months. But I needed her to look at the possibility again.

'Of course I have doubts,' she said. 'You know as well as I do that abusers don't look like monsters, and that this type of work sometimes attracts people for the wrong reasons. But in my heart, I know Claude could never, ever do anything to hurt a child. I trust him.'

'Okay then.' I put down the guitar. 'It's as likely to have been that social worker you mentioned, anyway.'

'No. She attacked him the first day she met him. Her old social worker had been transferred to the disability section.'

There wasn't much to say to that, so I let it go. 'What's Katie's background then?'

'It's pretty ordinary, really, for a child in care. She's an orphan. Her parents were killed in a house-fire when she was six years old.

She had been in and out of care before their deaths. They were both young, barely out of their teens, and she was always a neglected, frightened little thing. The first time she came to the attention of Social Services was when she was three. She had been abused by a babysitter, a friend of her mother's—'

'A female?'

'Yes, unfortunately. It would have answered a lot of questions. Katie's mother placed her in care voluntarily, but applied to have her back after six months. There were regular complaints to the health services from neighbours and pre-school workers that had her on and off the books for the next couple of years. Then the fire occurred — Katie was staying over at an aunt's house when it happened; otherwise she'd have died too. And that's it, really.'

'Nothing else unusual happened to her between then and now?'

'Nope. I wish something did.'

'Well, I have only one other question.'

'Yes?'

'Do you have any decent coffee in this place, because I am hanging out for a cup.'

She smiled, looking decidedly relieved. 'I'll see what I can do.'

———

They only had instant, as it happened, so I opted for tea instead. Dorothy and I chatted about everything and nothing, most of our conversation revolving around this strange thing we did for a living. I went out of my way to keep things light, and threw in as many inane jokes as I could. She appeared to need a laugh and to cut loose. The job of running this house was proving to be a heavy burden for her. I guessed that she had taken it on out of some twisted sense of responsibility for what her husband had been accused of — it was like a penance. I did not know at this stage whether he was guilty or not, but I guessed that, for Dorothy, working with Katie must have been like having a splinter that was causing her constant pain, but was embedded so deeply she couldn't pry it out. I felt sorry for her. She seemed a genuine person, and I sensed no anger or hatred towards the child, which might have been understandable under the circumstances.

Around forty-five minutes later, an exhausted-looking woman came in and plonked herself into a chair at the table with us. I recognised her as Martina, the woman who had, to her detriment, loosened her grip on Katie before it was safe to do so. Dorothy introduced us.

'She's in the playroom,' Martina said to me, pouring herself a cup from the teapot. 'You will get absolutely no good out of her, but on the positive side, she's too knackered to go for you.'

'Thanks for the vote of confidence,' I said, and stood up. To Dorothy, I said: 'Would you mind switching on the cameras, microphones and whatnot in the playroom, and keeping an eye on things? Particularly with her attitude to men …'

'Of course. I meant to record your sessions with her anyway.'

When I went into the playroom the child was sprawled on two beanbags that she had pulled together to make a kind of couch. I came in and pushed the door closed, then stood leaning against the wall, far enough away that I was not posing a physical threat to her, but still in her line of vision.

'Hello, Katie,' I said. 'I'm Shane. I know you were told I was coming today. Is that why you got so angry?'

She turned her head to look directly at me. The girl held my gaze without flinching. People with intellectual disabilities and psychiatric problems find making eye contact difficult, but not Katie. She had a strong, handsome face, with prominent cheekbones and an almost oriental slant to her eyes. Combined with coal-black hair and a dark complexion, this gave her an exotic look.

'You can fuckin' stand there and talk. I'm all shagged out; otherwise I'd goddamn well friggin' have you. But take one step closer, and I swear to fuck that I will ram my fist right down your Christ almighty shite-spoutin' throat. Right?'

I shrugged and stayed where I was. She had a colourful and imaginative talent with profanity. I've been around people who use expletives liberally, and am not adverse to the odd outburst myself. But Katie's command of vulgarity was almost poetic. I was impressed.

'I get the feeling you're kind of pissed off I'm here.'

She returned to staring at the ceiling. 'Jaysus. How'd you pick that one up, you snot-arsed cunt?'

'Call it intuition.'

'I tell you what,' she pushed herself up onto an elbow. 'You shut the fuckin' hell up, and I'll chill out over here. I suggest you stay for a little while and then feck off, and we'll let on you did your bit of whatever arseholin' nonsense you're meant to be doin'. How's that sound to ya?'

'Can I sit down?' I asked, pointing to the beanbag nearest to me.

'Suit yourself.'

I sat. 'Look, I'm not going to ask you any questions. I'm not a shrink. All I'm here to do is to give you some time to play with the stuff that's in this room. If during the time I'm with you, you want to lie on beanbags, that's your call. I think it'll get pretty boring, but this is your time.'

'You talk so nice. All these wonderful bastardin' promises. You're just like all the others. You want to find out why I'm such a human wreckage.'

'You know they're talking about where to send you next, don't you? None of the places they're looking at are very good. I'd like to be able to give them some options. And Katie, you're unhappy. I mean, you're really miserable. If I can change that, I'll have done *something* worthwhile.'

'Yeah, okay. Whatever. I'm going to have a rest now. You can see yourself out when you're ready.'

She feigned being asleep, but I knew she wasn't. She was like a coiled spring, ready to snap into action the moment I got too close. I sat for a few minutes, watching her.

'Look, I'm going to sort through some of the toys,' I said. 'You don't have to do anything. I just want to see what's here.'

'Come near me and I'll burst ye.'

'You are quite safe, believe me.'

'But are you?'

I ignored her and began to look through the cars and figures for the miniature town. I set them out in rows, and began to quietly play a game, moving a couple of cars around the little streets and making some quiet sound effects to accompany what I was doing. From the corner of my eye I could see Katie watching me. I made no sign that I had spotted her, and continued to play. After five or six minutes, it all got too much for her.

'What the skankin' hell are you doin'?'

'I thought you were asleep.'

'How the fuck can I sleep when you're playin' Bob the mother-fuckin' Builder over there?'

'Sorry. I didn't mean to disturb you. Just got a bit carried away.'

'You're a fuckin' wank stain.'

She rolled over so her back was to me. I picked up a Tonka Truck and started to make the loudest, most offensive engine noises I could muster. That, as I had hoped, was as much as she could endure.

'What in the name of Bill's bollix are you playin' at?'

She rolled off the beanbags and stormed over, snatching the truck from me and giving me a punch that was so half-hearted it was more of a gentle shove.

'I'm playing. What's the problem?'

'You boys are all the cuntin' same. Cars and trucks're all you're into. Stupid, sucky, shitty-arsed baby games.'

'What's stupid about them?'

'They don't mean anythin'. Diggers and dumpers and concrete mixers. Empty-brained, fuckin' bollix skid-mark stuff.'

She threw the truck as hard as she could against the wall. It bounced off and hit the floor with a thud. She picked up another car, a model of a Ford Fiesta, and began pushing it aggressively around the narrow streets, smashing it into some of the buildings and knocking them off kilter. She made a car noise that was even more vulgar than the one I had been emitting. Suddenly she swerved the car off the road and knocked down two little plastic figures. She paused for a split-second, before reaching over and picking them up, putting them into the back of the car. She moved it off again, push-ing it around the track a couple of times, then parked it outside the model of the hotel.

'Come on, Barbie, let's go party,' she said in a loud, mock jovial voice. The two figures were taken out of the car and moved into the hotel. 'Drink, barman. Loads of drink for me 'n' Barbie.

'Yes sir, Mr Ken, sir.'

I sat back, saying nothing. I had picked up on the 'Barbie Girl' reference (years working with children has left me, regrettably, with an above average knowledge of novelty pop), but I could already see that there was something deeper afoot.

'More drink, Mr Barman.

'No problem, Mr Ken. Here's more pints for you and your good lady. Don't be getting drunk now.

'Oh, we won't get too drunk, barman. Sure haven't we a baby at home to mind?'

This continued for ten minutes. The baby was mentioned several times more, but only as being 'at home'. Whether this child was at home with a sitter or alone was not, at this point, made clear.

'Come on, Barbie girl. Let's go home in our car.

'Okay, Ken. You'd better drive. I'm too scuttered.

'Sure amn't I flootered as well? You drive.

'Oh, alright. Stop fuckin' naggin' me, woman. I'll drive.

'Tha's no way to talk to the woman of your dreams.

'Shutup, you fuckin' whore's cunt or I'll stick you with one right in the gob!'

The two figures were placed back in the car, which then recklessly careened about the roads, smashing into whatever happened to be in the vicinity. It finally pulled up outside a little house. The two figures got out and were put inside.

'Oh baby? Come to Mammy.

'No, come to Daddy.

'She doesn't love you; she loves me, you fucker.

'You don't know what love means, you rotten tart.

'Shutup for a minute — can you hear somethin'?'

Katie took a police car and began to make a piercing siren sound.

'Nee-naw! Nee-naw! Nee-naw!

'Oh shit! The cops are coming. Now we're in for it.

'Quick, let's get out of here.

'But the baby —

'Fuck the baby. What's she ever done for us except shit and eat and bawl?

'You're right, Ken. Let's split this joint.'

The two figures piled out of the house and back into the little car, which tore off, followed tenaciously by the police car, siren sounding all the way. Inevitably, the Fiesta was caught.

'Step out of the vehicle. You have the right to remain silent. Off to jail with you both for drinking and driving into stuff. You are very bold people.

'No, please garda, not prison. I'm too young and beautiful.

'And I'll end up as someone's bitch.

'Too late for that. You're going away for a *looong* time.'

A building was chosen (the miniature town didn't have a 'jail' as such) and the two tiny figures were placed inside. Katie fell silent for a minute, looking at the prison. Suddenly, from deep within her, came a mournful cry. Then another, and another. Tears actually began to stream down her face.

'Mammy, Daddy, why did you leave me? I'm only little, and I've been left all alone in this big old house. I can't get out … and there's not enough food … and no one knows I'm here. I'm so alone and so frightened.'

She stood up, her face wet with tears, and walked back to the beanbags. 'Stupid miserable cock-suckin' games,' she muttered, and lying down, fell asleep.

I sat in the now silent playroom under the electronic stare of the camera, with the wails of the plastic child still echoing in my mind.

Chapter 5 ~

Salt Island, referred to as 'the Shaker' by the men and women sentenced to serve time there, is a chunk of rock sitting in the middle of Seal Harbour, about three-quarters of a mile from shore. It is as godforsaken a piece of land as you will ever see. Winds heavy with salt spray lash it constantly. Vicious currents and raging riptides, treacherous underwater shelves and silt beds, make it inaccessible to all but the most competent sailors; the only transport on or off the Shaker is a small ferry that carries guards, prisoners, a few visitors and supplies to the prison twice a day.

Aside from the grey stone buildings that make up the prison itself, the island offers no shelter from the elements. It is, literally, a reef of granite sticking out of the ocean. In the late eighteenth century, the British built a small military fort on it, and a custom house for ships coming in and out of the city's wide harbour. The soldiers did not linger on the Shaker for long, finding it too depressing and inhospitable, so the Board of Guardians ordered that the buildings be made into a prison. Inmates were initially political detainees and military deserters, and the gaol rapidly developed a reputation as one of the harshest penal institutions in the country.

The chances of surviving a twelve-month stint on Salt Island during its first hundred years of service were 50/50. The guards were ex-soldiers and mercenaries, renowned for their brutality. Hygiene, diet and basic comforts such as warmth and even having enough space to lie down were secondary considerations to the primary function of keeping dangerous criminals and rebels contained. When British troops finally left the city in 1922, the prison, seen by the citizens of the new Republic as an abiding image of the tyranny of the crown, was closed. However, practicality sometimes wins out over such luxuries as patriotic outrage, and in 1935 the Shaker reopened, with a promise from Eamon de Valera that it would, henceforth, be a model prison, catering with equanimity to male, female and juvenile convicts.

Prisoners today are certainly free from the beatings, cold-water baths and other tortures of the bad old days, and lecturers from the City University donate their time to go out and teach a variety of academic courses to the prisoners, but the Shaker still sends a chill through many hearts. I can only imagine what it must be like standing on the deck of that ferry, watching the island getting closer and closer, the low buildings of the prison visible against the dark skyline; watching this and knowing that the gull-shit-caked lump of rock amid the heaving waves is to be your home for the next month, year or decade.

I must confess that I have a phobia of prisons. I have, through the course of my work, seen the inside of most of the correctional facilities in Ireland. Some, like Mountjoy or Spike Island, are gothic dens that assail you with the smell of faeces and panic the moment you walk through the door. Others, like Wheatfield or the Curragh, are newish, clean and brightly lit. The surroundings make little difference to me. I fear that locked door. I don't know whether it's some kind of latent claustrophobia, or that therapy might reveal that at some point in my childhood I was accidentally locked in a cupboard, but as soon as I'm inside a prison and that key turns behind me, I suffer a moment of white-knuckle panic. I find it hard to breathe, I break out in a sweat that soaks through my shirt and runs down my face in sheets. My heart pounds as if it wants to leap out of my chest. I rationalise that I am there as a visitor, that the guards are in fact my colleagues, that as soon as I wish I can get back out again; I go over all this in my head, and after a second or two I can proceed, but there is always that brief explosion of irrational terror. I'm used to the panic attacks by now, and before visiting a prison I prepare myself, but the experience is no less potent for all that. The funny thing is it never happens in psychiatric hospitals, where doors must be locked, or juvenile detention centres, where doors are also kept secure. Only in prisons. I know, now, that there is a chink in my psychological armour, but I can still do my job, even when it takes me to places like the Shaker.

———

The first sailing to Salt Island was at ten in the morning, and I was on it, clutching a cup of coffee I'd picked up at a dockside café. Rain, so heavy with ice it was more like snow, fell intermittently; the sea was a grim, muddy grey, topped with yellow froth, and the small metal boat tossed and bobbed as it chugged into the roiling trough before us. By the bow three uniformed guards were smoking and chatting quietly. I sipped my coffee and looked out to sea towards our destination, then just a black smudge on the horizon line.

I had, despite the discomfort it caused me, been visiting the Shaker quite a bit over the previous couple of months. The reason for these trips was that Malachi Byrne, the father of two children I was working with, was serving time there. Malachi and his wife, Vera, had systematically tortured, abused and brutalised their twin children, Larry and Francey, in the most appalling and degenerate manner. The twins, when they were finally rescued from their miserable existence in the vast, crumbling house their family owned, were more like animals than children, running on all fours, snarling and growling, and using a peculiar dialect when they did speak. It finally emerged that, though Malachi had been extremely violent and abusive both physically and sexually to the children, Vera had really been the instigator, and had, if anything, been even more sadistic and vindictive than her lumbering partner. Malachi, a towering troll of a man, was mean and unpredictable, but he was also slow and indolent. When the police were informed and a report of disclosures the children had made was filed with Social Services, Vera had some-how persuaded Malachi to take responsibility for it all, claiming that he had coerced and frightened her into taking part.

So, while Malachi languished in an eight by ten cell, Vera was in regular contact with the twins, and had set about improving her appearance and general demeanour. Gone was the wild, frightening countenance to which I was so accustomed. She had been to the dentist and had her teeth straightened and whitened. Her long, stringy hair was now styled and full-bodied. The ill-matching, worn clothes had been cast aside for fashionable, carefully chosen couture. Vera Byrne was now extremely presentable. And this metamorphosis had brought about the desired effect: the social workers she was in contact with seemed to have altered their opinion of her. Surely, they suggested, this carefully groomed, sweet-smelling woman could not have done the terrible things alleged against her. Now that she was free from the stifling influence of her husband, she was positively blossoming into a gentle person.

I was not so easily swayed. I knew Vera, and had been keeping a close watch. My surveillance had yielded one particularly disturbing piece of news. The Byrne house, an almost derelict brick structure in the heart of Oldtown, was being renovated by degrees. Vera was not stupid enough to have workers tackle the mammoth task of repairing years of neglect all at once. But gradually the house was being rebuilt. The shed, where the twins had been kept as prisoners for so much of their childhood, was now gleaming with new paint, and the broken board through which they had sometimes plucked up the courage to escape had been firmly secured back in place. The front path, which was cracked and subsided, had been relaid and levelled, and most of the windows given new glass and frames. There had been countless other jobs, some small and some quite large, carried out on the property, and it made me extremely worried. Vera informed me that, despite the reports and disclosures that had been passed on to the authorities, she would be getting her children back sooner rather than later. And this house was a deeply symbolic part of her sense of power and dominion over, not just her family, but Oldtown and the city itself. The Byrnes, whom she had married into, were once wealthy, and had employed large numbers of local people in the nineteenth century in a steel mill they had run. But through numerous problems — economic, social and psychiatric — the family had fallen on difficult times, and lost its foothold in the upper echelons of city society. Vera, in her cold, calculating and self-serving manner, had developed the notion that she may have been able to scale the heights of opulence once more, if she had Larry and Francey back, and if the Byrne homestead was returned to something of its former glory.

The boat docked at the wooden pier and we disembarked. A narrow pathway, cutting through damp, green-tinged stone, brought us up to the main entrance, a metal door that was held open by a hook in the wall. I could feel the heat emanating from inside, and this almost offset my rapidly growing sense of panic.

The room inside was a long, spacious, dark reception area, with a high counter at the top, where visitors signed in, emptied their pockets and went through a metal detector. I submitted my bag for inspection. It contained five packs of cigarettes, a pile of comic books and some fruit. The guard nodded me through, and I walked down the long corridor towards the visitors' room. I knocked on the door, and it swung open. I stepped inside, and the door was closed and locked behind me. I leaned my back against the wall, and felt the cold numbness of the panic attack wash over me. I gritted my teeth, breathed deeply, counted down from ten, and finally pushed the sensation as far back into my subconscious as possible. Then I opened my eyes and cast about for the bulk of Malachi Byrne, who was sitting at a table in the centre of the room, looking simply too big and unwieldy for the space we were in.

Malachi was forty years old, over six feet tall, and weighed nearly four hundred pounds. In the few months he had been in prison, he had probably gained seventy of those pounds, simply through refusing to engage in exercise of any kind. While actively involved in the case, I had believed Malachi to be intellectually disabled, probably with an IQ somewhere around the borderline between normalcy and dysfunction, in the region of 75–80. When I started to visit him in the Shaker, and saw him away from his wife's malign and domineering influence, I realised that he was in fact far less functional than I had thought. He could not, for example, tie his own shoelaces. He was functionally illiterate. His moods changed like those of a child, tears following laughter with little warning. An assessment by the prison's visiting psychologist showed that Malachi's IQ was in fact 60, placing him in the lower end of Mild Intellectual Disability, and in need of a tremendous amount of support to achieve even the simplest day-to-day tasks.

The violence endemic to his personality was still very much in evidence — he had almost killed a fellow prisoner during his first week on Salt Island. As is so often the case with prison brawls, the provocation was slight, and probably unintentional. The attack happened because an unfortunate fellow inmate had taken the dessert tray on which Malachi had his eye at mealtime. And the behemoth seemed surprised when he discovered that his victim was hurt so badly he could have died. Cause and effect appeared to be beyond his limited capacity for understanding.

Prison visiting rooms, in Ireland at least, are nothing like what you see on television. There are no glass partitions, no telephones through which you must conduct your conversations, no prison uniforms with little arrow patterns sewn into them. The room in which I met Malachi Byrne was wide, bright and airy, painted a pleasant yellow, the walls adorned with framed pictures that had been drawn by the children of the inmates. It was far from comfortable — the chairs on which we sat to talk were straight, wooden kitchen chairs, and Malachi seemed barely able to get his legs under the table — but it was as pleasant and accommodating as it was possible to make it under the circumstances.

I sat down opposite the huge man. His hair had grown out a little — he was bald on top, but his natural growth was curly, and a kind of reddish brown colour, which sat in a peculiar frizz around his ears. He was grossly overweight, the flab hanging out in great rolls over the waist of his elasticated tracksuit bottoms. He had a small face, with tiny, piggish eyes and a nose that had been broken at least half-a-dozen times, and was now at an odd angle, so that Malachi whistled when he breathed through it. With him being so enormous, and so ugly, it was hard to remember that he was, to all intents and purposes, just a child. A potentially lethal one, and one capable of great cruelty to boot, but a child for all that.

'How are you, Malachi?' I asked him, putting the bag on the table between us.

He was almost hopping up and down to see what I had brought him.

'What's in the bag, Mister, what have you got for me?' His voice was deep, almost baritone.

'You can call me Shane, Malachi. I've told you that. Take a look.'

He pulled over the bag, almost taking my arm with it.

'Cool! *The Beano* and *The Dandy* and …' he paused, trying to make out the title of the comic he held in his hands. '… the Sss … the …'

'Can you sound out the letters?' I asked him. The literacy tutor in the prison had been using a form of phonetics with Malachi, not unlike the Letterland system children use in schools, which focused on the sounds the letter made, and how they interacted with one another.

'I can't get it!' He tossed the comic onto the tabletop in frustration.

'Okay, look at the pictures, then, and see if you can work it out that way. That's why comics are good when you're learning to read — the pictures tell the story too.'

He sighed and looked at the cover of the comic. A smile spread across his face.

'That's Homer and Chief Wiggum!'

'It sure is.'

'The Simpsons! It's a Simpsons comic! Thanks, Mister.'

'You're welcome. There's some fruit there too, which I would really like you to eat instead of sweets as snacks, okay? You're getting really, really fat, Malachi. You'll have a heart attack if you don't start to do some exercise and cut back on the junk food.'

'Yeah, okay. It's just that I don't like fruit too well.'

'I know that, but you might find you'll get to like it if you just try to eat some instead of crisps or bars of chocolate. You don't want to be so fat, do you?'

He shrugged. 'Dunno.'

I sighed and decided just to cut to the chase. 'Has Vera been out to see you?' I was hoping that she may have told Malachi her plans.

So far she was playing her cards very close to her chest with me. She couldn't keep it up; she would have to snap and brag to someone about how clever she was and how she was fooling us all.

Malachi cast down his eyes, suddenly seeming to shrink quite dramatically in size, as if someone had stuck a pin into him and let all the air out.

'What's wrong, Malachi?'

'Nuthin'.'

'I don't believe you. What's the problem?'

He shuffled uncomfortably on the creaking chair, glancing nervously up at me and then back at his hands, which he had pressed together and was wringing, seemingly in the depths of despair.

'She said she din' want me seein' you no more. That I was to tell ya … tell ya not to be comin' out here.'

I nodded and took out my cigarettes. I knew that he didn't smoke, so didn't offer him one.

'You know, Malachi, you don't always have to do what she says. I mean, you're locked up in here because you told the judge and the police that everything that happened at home was your fault. I know that Vera made you take all the blame.'

Again, the eyes, with surprisingly long and feminine lashes for such a huge man, flicked in my direction, a spark of anger alive in them now.

'She tole me not to ever — *ever* — talk 'bout that to *nobody*.'

'I know, I know, Malachi. It's okay, I'm not going to go into it right now. It's just, well … do you like it in here?'

He leaned back on the chair, sighing deeply. 'No. I don' like it here.'

'Well, it was doing what Vera told you that got you locked up in the first place, wasn't it?'

He nodded, and, to my surprise, a tear rolled down his corpulent cheek. 'Mister, d'you think they'll let me go home soon? I gets awful scairt here at night. There's voices all over and people cries and when I has bad dreams, no one will sit and talk to me 'till I ain' scairt no more.'

I reached over and patted him on one of his shovel-like hands. 'I'll talk to one of the guards about that, Malachi, okay? I'm sure we can arrange someone to talk to you if you get frightened.'

He nodded, sniffing, and squeezed my hand so hard I winced involuntarily in pain.

'Would you ask them to leave the light on in my room, too? I can' get to sleep in the dark, see? Would y' ask them for me, Mister?'

'Sure, Malachi. I'll arrange that for you.'

'Thanks.'

I lit the cigarette, which had been hanging, unlit, from my lower lip during Malachi's unexpected outburst. 'So Vera doesn't want me to visit you.'

He shook his head vigorously, and ripped open the net covering on the punnet of mandarin oranges I had brought him. 'I'm no good at peelin' these,' he said, sheepishly.

I pulled the plastic box over and took one out, quickly removing the skin and passing him the fruit. I peeled another while he swallowed the first in two mouthfuls.

'Would you like me to continue coming out to see you?'

He nodded again. 'You bring me stuff, and you talk to me and you don't look at me like some of the guards do, like I'm a right bad fella.'

I started to peel a third mandarin. 'Mind if I have one?'

'No, go ahead. They're not bad — for fruit.' He laughed as if he had made a great joke.

I grinned. 'See? It's not so terrible when you give it a go, is it?'

His face took on a sullen expression. 'I shouldna done some o' that stuff to Larry and Francey, should I?'

'No, Malachi. It was very, very wrong to do what you and Vera did to the twins.'

'I din' know,' his voice broke with emotion, and then the tears flowed down his cheeks like water from a tap. 'My Daddy, he done them things to me, an' he told me it was what parents done wit' their childers, to make them good and to show them how to act when they gets married. An' Vera, she said the same thing when we had them twins. "You has to show 'em who is the boss of the house," she said.

I din' know we was hurtin' 'em. I wouldn'a' done it if I knewed it was a wrong way to go on.'

'Well,' I said, unsure how to respond. There was a part of me that found it almost impossible to believe there wasn't a place deep inside Malachi Byrne where he knew damn well that his actions towards his children, actions that encompassed physical, sexual and psychological abuse in their most sadistic and extreme forms, were appallingly wrong. Yet he was a childish, unformed personality, and perhaps his own abusive and tormented childhood had left him without the capacity to know right from wrong. I chose my words carefully, and continued. 'It's good you know that what you did was wrong, Malachi. I want you to think about that. Part of the reason you're in here is to think about what you've done, and try to work out how to put some of it right.'

'Maybe I could tell Larry and Francey that I'm really, really sorry.'

'That would be a start, I think. I reckon they'd like to hear that. But there's more you could do. Have you ever told anyone else about what your Dad did to you, when you were little?'

'No. 'Cept Vera.'

'When you get scared at night, and have bad dreams, have they sometimes got to do with things that happened when you were little?'

'Sometimes. Not always.'

'I think that a really good way of helping to make things better would be to make *you* feel better. Remember the man who came in and played those games with you, with the cards and the pictures and the words?'

'Mr Giles?'

'Yeah. Mr Giles is what's called a psychologist, and his job is to talk to people, and help them to make sense of things that happened to them and might be making them sad. Now I think that it would be really good for you to chat with Mr Giles.'

He handed me another mandarin. 'Okay,' he said. 'I'll talk to him.'

'And you want me to keep coming, even though Vera doesn't?'

He took the peeled fruit, and put the whole thing into his mouth. 'She doesn' need t' know, does she?' he said around the juicy segments.

I grinned, patting that massive hand again. 'I won't tell if you don't.'

———

I walked slowly back down the stone steps that led to the dock, wind lashing my coat about my legs and the sleety rain coming in at a 45-degree angle. The nausea and drenching sweat of the repressed panic attack held me tightly and refused to give me up. I took a deep gulp of salty, moist sea air, and felt somewhat better. Despite my sickness, I was pleased with the results of the visit. If Malachi would start seeing Giles, the psychologist, and was prepared to flout Vera's wishes and continue seeing me, I thought we might just be on the verge of getting him on our side. His gradual realisation of the innate wrongness of the abuse of the twins was monumental, and, I hoped, meant that Vera's days of freedom might be numbered.

I put an unsteady foot onto the wooden platform of the dock, and saw that I was not alone. Standing with his back to me, looking out to sea, was a figure I recognised immediately from the long dark hair and angular, lean build. Today he was swathed in a long, brown leather trenchcoat.

'You took your time,' he said, without turning. 'I thought you didn't like prisons.'

'I don't. But Malachi was feeling talkative today.'

Karl Devereux turned, a grim smile on his thin lips. 'Sit down before you fall,' he said, steering me to a metal bollard. 'Why are you still pursuing the Byrne case? I thought it was closed.'

'It's supposed to be. It's just that I'm not finished with it yet.'

Devereux nodded and, in a single fluid motion, squatted on his haunches beside me. Somehow he actually looked comfortable in the position. 'I need your advice.'

I raised an eyebrow. I had, from time to time, approached this slim, quiet man for help or a guiding hand, but I was unaware of *him* ever having gone to anyone for assistance.

Karl Devereux was an ex-career criminal: an assassin, leg-breaker and occasional explosives expert who had eventually been framed by his own organisation and had served an eight-year sentence in Dublin's Mountjoy Jail, the toughest and most unpleasant penal institution in the country. He had emerged a seemingly reformed man, and dedicated his life to voluntary social-care work, basing himself in a small office in the community centre in Blackalley, the ghetto where he grew up, the child of an abusive, alcoholic single mother who had never wanted him and had no qualms about letting him know it. Devereux was still spectacularly unorthodox, and a lot of professionals gave him a wide berth, unable to put aside the latent threat his past carried. I was convinced of his commitment to his clients, however, and knew that he had done a tremendous amount of good since his release. I also had reason to have been glad of his assistance on more than one occasion, in particular when, three months earlier, he had helped me locate a client, a young lady with Down's Syndrome, who had been abducted by some very unpleasant individuals.

'How can I help?' I asked.

'Do you know St Callow's Home?'

'The residential unit? It's an assessment centre for young offenders, isn't it?'

'It used to be. It has become a community-based facility for mainstream clients over the past twelve months.'

Assessment units were established to take in young people, usually through the courts, for short terms of observation, to establish which kind of treatment would best suit their needs. There had been a move over the past five years or so to base most residential child-care within the community — a normal house on a normal street, where the children could take part in local activities and, with luck, be accepted — and rather than group problem children together and stigmatise them, the plan had been to disperse them among less troubled populations, and use existing staff teams to carry out observation and assessment.

'Most places are moving that way now,' I said. 'There's only a few real juvenile detention centres left. It's probably for the best, I suppose.' I paused. 'How does this involve you, Karl? I thought you worked mostly with youth clubs and voluntary outreach programmes. You're not involved in residential work now too, are you?'

Devereux wandered over to the waterside again, gazing back across the dark expanse of water at the city.

'You know that I was born and raised in Blackalley.'

'Yeah.'

'*Bleak Alley* we used to call it,' he said, laughing dryly. 'And it was. There was nothing there for any of us, no hope of ever getting out, of making a life for yourself.'

'I don't think it's changed much,' I said. It was turning out to be a strange morning: Malachi Byrne opening up to me, and now Karl Devereux. I was on a roll. 'Blackalley is still pretty much run by the gangs, as far as I can tell.'

'Yes,' he said, his eyes still on the horizon. 'They offer something education, or religion or an apprenticeship can't: money, power, and better than that — better than anything else — *respect*. When I was young, you just had to prove that you were as tough as nails and prepared to do anything. I was. I was meaner, angrier, tougher and more vicious than any of the kids my age, more so than even a lot of the adults.'

'A young man destined for greatness,' I said.

'Oh, most certainly. When I was fifteen, the gang I ran with asked me to become an enforcer. A professional bully is all that is, really, but I jumped at the opportunity. If they wanted someone to give them money, or stop dealing drugs in a particular area, and that person refused, I'd be sent over there to persuade them. I was tall for my age and had no problem with inflicting hurt on others, and I was furious with the world for the hand it'd dealt me. If I arrived at your door and asked you to do something, you didn't argue for very long. I was good at my job.'

'It's nice to have a skill.'

'I learned how to hurt people, but I also learned not to have to. Don't get me wrong, it wasn't about mercy — beating people up is hard work. I was simply saving energy. I worked out how to use my voice, my eyes, or the way I moved, to scare people so much I never even had to hit them.'

'I can imagine there are circumstances where that could be very useful.'

'Oh, there are. But you see, there is always a danger when you're used to being met with fear and awe, that you'll come across some-one who won't be scared; someone who has good reason not to be scared. I came across just such a person, a few months before my six-teenth birthday, in a betting shop in the Oldtown. Did you ever hear of Benjy MacDonagh?'

'No.'

'He's dead now. Killed in a feud. But in his time he was one of the toughest gentlemen in this or any other city. Benjy was a member of the travelling community, and a bare-knuckle boxing champion. A little guy, not more than five feet six or seven, but every single inch of it muscle and bad attitude. The owner of this particular betting shop was aware that my superiors would be sending someone around, because he just flat refused to pay us a nominal fee for pro-tection and insurance. He happened to know Benjy, probably through running a book on some of his matches. So Benjy, at his request, took to hanging around the shop, just in case someone like me should show up.'

'Did you know he'd be there?'

'Of course I did. But I was young, cocky, full of my own self-importance, and believed I was the baddest gangster in town. Benjy MacDonagh was forty-five, an old man, as far as I was concerned, and a scruffy tinker. I thought I'd have him on his back seeing stars in less than a minute.'

'I take it Mr MacDonagh did not go quietly.'

'No. The second I walked in, all the customers in the place walked out, but they stayed hanging around outside, trying to peep in through the windows to see what would happen. Benjy just stood there, leaning against one of the counters. He looked to be as broad as he was tall. He had the longest arms I've ever seen, and his knuckles were all knobbly and covered in scar tissue. He had the look of someone who'd been in a lot of fights, but, then, I'd seen plenty of people who looked like that, and I thought nothing of it. I told him that I knew who he was, and that he should step aside and let me do my job. He smiled at me, friendly as you please, and very politely advised me to turn around and walk back out the way I'd come in. He said . . .' Devereux stifled a laugh, 'he said he didn't want to have to hurt me. Well, that was it. I charged him.' Devereux turned back to face me, a wistful smile on his lips. 'Big mistake.'

'What happened?'

'I received the soundest beating I have ever gotten. He broke both my arms, three of my ribs, my jaw. Loosened most of the teeth in my head. Cracked my left eye-socket. Punctured one of my lungs. And he did it with such . . . sympathy! He kept begging me to stay down, he was almost in tears by the end of it, caught me as I fell and laid me down, cradling me like a baby as I passed out. But I couldn't stay down, you see. There was quite a crowd outside now, and someone had wedged the door open to see the fight. I had a reputation to maintain. I knew after he'd landed his second punch, which knocked out three of my teeth and fractured one side of my jaw, that there was no way I could beat him. The only way for me to come away with any dignity was to take the beating like a man, and try to give somewhere near as good as I got. Oh, I planted one or two on him, but I honestly believe that he allowed me to, to save me some face. He had barely a hair out of place when he finally knocked me unconscious.'

'I suppose it's true what they say: no matter how tough you think you are, there's always someone tougher. A painful way to learn the lesson though.'

'Oh, the lesson didn't end there. Benjy and the bookie loaded me into the back of a Hiace van, and brought me around to the local priest's house. The bookie wanted to leave me on the green in the middle of Oldtown, let the police pick me up, but Benjy wouldn't hear of it. So Father Niall McDrumm found me on his doorstep, beaten to a pulp and bleeding all over his crazy paving. He brought me to the hospital, where it was established that I was actually still fifteen, and therefore under the laws of the time still a minor. My mother, the old bitch, was uncontactable. I was placed in care, for the first and last time.'

'St Callow's Home.'

Devereux nodded.

'It was an industrial school, in those days, and every boy in the place was aware which priests or brothers were to be avoided, but I was lucky enough to be taken under the wing of one of the more enlightened clerics, Brother Finn. I was there for less than a year — once I was sixteen I was an adult, and they were never going to keep me for long — but he was the first person I ever encountered who treated me with kindness and asked for nothing in return. At the time, I was too young and damaged to understand, but later, during the long nights in the Joy, I remembered. It made a difference.'

'Sometimes that's all we can hope for in this work: that a short period of real care can make enough of a difference to change the trajectory of a life. Even years later.'

'I looked him up, Brother Finn, when I got out of prison. He still works at St Callow's. We stayed in touch. I received a call from him yesterday. The problem he's facing, it's not really my area of expertise. I thought you might have some thoughts.'

The boat pulled up beside us, bringing with it more visitors, and we climbed aboard for the return trip.

'How'd you know I was here?' I asked him as we pulled back out into the foam.

'No one else in the city drives a bright red 1981 Austin Allegro. It's distinctive, to say the least. You're not hard to track down.'

I nodded. 'So what's up at St Callow's?'

Devereux took a tube of mints from the pocket of his trenchcoat and put one in his mouth. He offered the tube to me, and I took one from it before handing it back. 'Since the changeover to purely therapeutic work, Brother Finn has been intent upon creating as safe an environment as he possibly can. Settings for young offenders, as I'm sure you know, are often as much about containment as they are about healing, and Finn wished very much to move away from that.

At his request, he was sent an almost completely new contingent of children ten months ago: early adolescents, a mixed group of males and females. They have come from a wide variety of backgrounds: for some, this is their first care placement, others have been in the system for years. He was very mindful not to ghettoise them in any way. The problem is that, almost immediately, they began sexually abusing one another.'

'Peer abuse is extremely common in residential settings, Karl. Some statistics I've read suggest that as much as sixty percent of all sexual abuse perpetrated upon children is carried out by other children.'

'I'm aware of the studies. Finn feels, and I agree with him, that children in care should be free from such activities. He just isn't sure how to go about eradicating the problem.'

I lit a cigarette and considered.

'First thing you need to understand: it just isn't possible to stop peer abuse completely. If a child is determined, he or she will bide their time, and that one second you're not watching will be the time they strike. Also, calling it abuse is not strictly accurate. It is often consensual experimentation between peers. The tone of it is probably what makes it abusive. Children who have been abused approach normal, adolescent sexual exploration in a violent and aggressive manner, because that's how they have experienced it themselves.'

'Understood.'

'The obvious thing I'd do is to ensure that all children have their own room, increase staff-to-child ratios and, if there isn't already one, introduce a live night-shift, with regular patrols to safeguard against bed-hopping. I've read of places that have installed closed-circuit television systems, but that might be a little over-the-top.'

'It's a thought,' Devereux said. 'I could get one quite cheaply.'

'I'll bet you could.'

The little boat dipped and bobbed through the water, and the skyline of the city we both loved and, sometimes, loathed, got ever closer through the rain and salt and freezing wind.

It was four weeks until Christmas.

PART TWO

Piggy in the Middle

They laid me in the prison and they threw away the
*   key.*
I heard a young boy screaming as the night came
*   down on me.*
I swore they wouldn't break me, that I would still be
*   strong*
But last night I woke up crying — I guess that I was
*   wrong.*

'PRISONER'S BLUES', TRADITIONAL BLUES SONG

Chapter 6 ∽

They parked the shiny, metallic-coloured mobile-home right beside a cracked, subsided footpath not far from the thunderous docks, the brown, stinking River Torc flowing in a rippling, seemingly alive torrent of eddies and treacherous currents below it. I was far from happy with the geographical placement — this was not a safe place for Tilly's children. Yet she was insistent. They were in danger from Gerry, her husband's relations now, and she had family parked nearby. This was the best site for them to set up camp.

The young woman was still treating me with a liberal dose of distaste, but my delivering a brand, spanking new four-bedroom trailer with its own electrical generator certainly raised me in her estimation. She stood at my side by a low metal railing that was supposed to prevent people from falling into the river, shivering against the biting, sleet-sodden wind, and watched as new furniture was loaded into the mobile home.

Since the awful night I took her and the children from the halting site, there had been a gradual, almost painful rebuilding of trust between us, spurred on by the fact that the children all seemed to like me — and they were, in many ways, all she had left.

I had long since learned that, in situations such as this, tenacity was my greatest asset. Tilly could try to freeze me out by leaving every time I came into the room, or by totally ignoring me if she had to stay; she could make every effort to thwart me by not bringing the children to see me at prearranged times. But I kept on coming back, and continued to talk to her with a pleasant, easy tone. When she blanked me, I made a point of responding as if she had answered, filling in the gaps in the conversation myself if I needed to.

However, I also knew that, in reality, this type of interaction (or lack thereof) could not go on forever. If I were to ever really help this family, the bridges I had been forced to burn would have to be reconstructed. I figured that there was only one sure-fire way of getting that started — bribery.

I have always said that there is no shame in resorting to a good, old-fashioned bribe if all else fails. I needed Tilly to start interacting with me, and although I was beginning to sense a thawing, it was happening far too slowly. So, the previous Monday, I arrived to the shelter where she and the kids (all except Johnny, who was still in hospital) were staying with a catalogue for new mobile homes. Ben had already approved the purchase, so I knew I had the financial wherewithal to back up my promises.

Tilly was still refusing to deal with me in all but the most super-ficial manner, so I simply came into the sitting room where she was absently watching television, sat opposite her and began to leaf through the brochure, ensuring she could see the large pictures of trailers that adorned each page. I watched her out of the corner of my eye and waited for her to make some comment. She held out for ten pained minutes, until, finally, she could take no more.

'What're ya doin' with that?'

'I told you that we'd get you a new trailer, didn't I?'

'Yeah …'

'Well, you'll need to pick one out. I figured you'd want to look in some catalogues first, and then you, me, and the kids can go and see some. This company has a yard not too far from here. You could try a few out for size.'

She eyed me warily. 'You're really gonna buy me a new caravan.'

'I am. The money's been cleared. We have five thousand to spend on the mobile home, some new furniture, an electrical generator, and whatever else you all need.'

She shook her head and looked down at her knees. There was that internal struggle again. How could she trust me? I was male, from the settled community, a representative of Social Services — there were so many reasons to refuse to play ball with me. But the prom-ise of a new home for her and the children was simply too good to pass up.

'Here, throw that over,' she said at last, looking at me openly for the first time in many days. 'I bet you don't know the first thing about trailers.'

And so the particular model (a tube-shaped creation that reminded me of some kind of spaceship) had been settled upon, and a purchase was made.

By the river, the wind picked up with renewed ferocity. Tilly glanced over at me as I brushed a wet strand of hair from my face and stamped my feet to reintroduce some sensation. 'This is a nice thing,' she said, suddenly unable to hold my gaze. 'No one never done anything like this for me nor the childers 'fore.'

I grinned, and nodded at the side of her head. 'You're welcome, Tilly. I hope ye're all happy here. You might find that hard to believe, but I genuinely do.'

——

I dropped in on the Curran children, who were at the refuge while their mother and her brothers moved furniture and possessions. The kids were either in bed, or having their suppers before going to their respective rooms. Those still up were ebullient, excited at the prospect of having their own place again. I got roped into reading Miley and Becky a couple of chapters of Roald Dahl's *The Twits*, which we had been working our way through, and then had a hurried cup of coffee before driving to the hospital to see Johnny.

The thing that always affected me the most when I visited Tilly's son was just how helpless and delicate he looked, bundled up in a bed that seemed far too big for him, his head still covered in bandages, the swelling and scar tissue visible about his eyes and nose. I found, each and every time I entered the ward, that I was, for a moment, almost overwhelmed by a rush of sadness and anger at this child's plight. Children never bring abuse upon themselves, but somehow, the injuries done to this little boy seemed to me to illustrate perfectly just how cruel, random and thoroughly unfair the world can be. Johnny should have been out playing, having birthday parties and collecting *Yu-Gi-Oh* cards. Now, it seemed, he was unlikely to be doing any of those things for a very long time.

Travellers, as a rule, do not like hospitals, the old adage that you enter them to be born or to die causing a good deal of discomfort for Tilly each time she visited Johnny. So she came only about once a week. I tried to see the little boy every day, often flouting normal visiting hours and seeing him early in the morning before work if I knew I'd be clocking off too late that night to make it worth my while coming over (sitting by the boy's bedside while he slept seemed a bit daft).

When I arrived that evening, Johnny did seem to be sleeping, but as I pulled the heavy, uncomfortable chair over to him, his eyes flickered open, and a wan smile spread across his pale face.

'Hey, there,' I said. His tiny hand reached out for mine. I took it, and we sat like that for a while.

The prognosis for Johnny Curran was bleak. Two days after he was admitted, I had dragged a seething Tilly to talk to the doctors who had operated on the child, in an effort to limit the already grave harm done to him. Tilly stood beside me, her body taut and trembling, as a young intern explained that Johnny would, in all probability, never make a full recovery. I waited for her to ask questions, to respond to this news, to even express disbelief or horror, but she never moved or uttered a sound. The doctor looked uncomfortable, shuffling from one foot to another, and finally made an excuse and left. Tilly had walked slowly to a side-door, pushing it open and descending the steps to the car park, where she crumbled into a heap, sobbing uncontrollably. I watched her for a time, wanting to go out and put my arm around her, but instead I went to sit with her son. My comfort would, at that stage, have been unwelcome.

The swelling around Johnny's brain had subsided, but he was still gravely weakened by his ordeal, and unable to do anything except lie in bed. I had brought in games, some big, colourful picture books, and a few basic, tactile activities, like large beads that could be threaded onto strings. Other than the stories, which he seemed to love, the equipment ended up sitting on his bedside table untouched. It was all just too much for him. It broke my heart, and I continued to bring in something new every day, but so far, he had only looked at the toys and learning materials with a vacant expression.

I was promised that he would be receiving physiotherapy, but that he needed to regain some strength first. In fact, the physiotherapist, a muscular, short-haired woman, told me we should not expect too much from this child. 'In all likelihood,' she said, 'he'll need to learn how to walk and talk all over again. It will be a painfully slow process, and I'm not convinced his mother will stand the long haul. Without a huge amount of support, children like this can often just stagnate. I've seen them waste away, regress. That woman won't be able to provide that kind of consistency. Mark my words.'

I felt myself bristling at this. 'He'll get whatever help he needs,' I said.

'What?' the large woman had scoffed. 'From you? You'll get bored and move on. You'll have other cases. And when he starts to get frustrated and maybe violent, he won't appear half so cute. They do, you know. A year or two stuck in bed, and even the sweetest ones start to get narky.'

Was she testing my resolve? Was she trying to see if I'd run right then and there? I was agog at a medic speaking in such a negative manner, but her facial expression was still jovial as she patted me on the shoulder and wandered off down the corridor, humming the theme tune to *The Archers*.

My mind wandered back to that conversation as I sat with Johnny. With his huge, liquid eyes, his skin improving under the sterile conditions of the hospital, aided by the improved diet, he certainly was cute, and I could not deny that the trauma of his injuries and my involvement in getting him into hospital in the first place had possibly caused me to become even more attached than I normally would. But, after much soul-searching, I decided that no, regardless of cynicism, I was not by this kid's bedside out of some inflated sense of duty or an over-romanticised belief in the healing power of love. I was there because I knew he needed me. And I would be there as long as that need remained. I hoped that, eventually, Tilly would rise to the challenge, but until she was in a position to, I would continue to visit and do what I could.

And anyway, it was not like he was just lying there staring at me. Despite his immobility and silence, there was a huge amount of interaction. He had responded from the moment he regained consciousness. What I sensed from Johnny, and I will admit that this was based on nothing but my own instincts, was that the child I had encountered before the injury was locked up inside. What we needed to do was untangle the wiring, and find a way to let him out. As a childcare worker, I had little understanding of the physiology of Johnny's condition. I'd done Biology in school, and a year of what had been referred to as Child Health Studies when I was in college. Combined with one or two First Aid courses over the course of my professional career, I was as far from a medic as it was possible to get. I did, however, have a wealth of experience with hurt and damaged children. I had learned to trust my gut feelings. Somewhere, within the shattered body that lay before me, holding on for dear life, was a child crying out to be helped, begging us not to give up on him. The little hand squeezed mine tightly.

'What would you like to do this evening, Johnny?' I asked him. I knew he couldn't answer, but I always chatted to him anyway, trying to read his responses as best I could.

The boy seemed to squirm in the bed, moving his chin slightly, rolling his eyes, a stream of saliva running down his chin. I took a tissue from a box on his bedside locker, and cleaned the drool off.

'Would you like to play a game?' I asked as I wiped the spittle away.

No response.

'What about threading some beads together? I've got lots of different colours.'

Again, no change.

'Alright then, how about a story?'

A huge smile, like the sun coming our from behind a cloud, erupted across Johnny's bruised and battered face.

'A story it is then. Y'know, I've been reading this one to your brother and sister. It's very funny, about a mean old man and woman, and a family of monkeys that live in their garden.'

His eyes opened wide at this information. It was as if he was saying: 'A family of monkeys! I want to hear more about that.'

'Shove over in the bed so I can show you the pictures, then.'

I helped him to slide over a little, and perched beside him, leaning over so he could get a good view of Quentin Blake's wonderful, grotesque depictions of Mr and Mrs Twit, and their terrible house.

One of the things I love about Roald Dahl's books is that they tap into aspects of children's psyches the way that very few other children's writers have ever dared to do. Other than the old, traditional fairy tales, I don't think there is another relatively contemporary writer who ploughs such a rich, dark furrow, while maintaining a sense of wonder, fun and outright joy within the fabric of each book. His tales also present simple and recognisable, but complex, characters, which children can latch onto immediately.

In the case of *The Twits*, there is a long sequence about bearded men. Mr Twit is a filthy, ill-tempered old grouch, with a spiky, bristly beard that covers most of his face. Dahl proposes the idea that bearded men are inherently dirty and duplicitous, as they cannot possibly wash their faces properly (there is a truly glorious picture of all the food Mr Twit has managed to get stuck in his moustache, which is worth getting the book for alone) and wish to hide behind something.

I am, of course, a bearded man myself (although nowhere near as impressively adorned as Mr Twit), which means that, when I read *The Twits* to a child, I always come in for a fair amount of ribbing. I was interested to see how Johnny would react — if he would be able to respond at all. I could see right off that he was carefully watching the pictures, and there were a couple of rapid intakes of breath as we read the first pages. Finally, as the beard sequence got into full swing, I suddenly felt a sharp nudge into my ribs. I looked down, and there was little Johnny, grinning broadly, pointing up at my face.

'What?' I said, unable to contain a smile myself. 'You don't think I'm like Mr Twit, do you?'

Still pointing, Johnny nodded, and suddenly, bubbling from within him like a fresh spring: a laugh. It was full of merriment and innocent joy, and I thought I would almost burst with happiness myself. This was a major breakthrough. A sense of humour, as unimportant as it might at first appear, is a clear indication of intellect. If you can understand that something is funny, then you can *reason*. What this meant was that, mentally at least, Johnny was not as badly injured as we had feared. There was still much work to do physically, but his mind, and his spirit, remained intact. Laughing along with him, I gave him a tight hug, and then continued on with the story. And we laughed again and again, as Mr and Mrs Twit waged a war of practical jokes against one another — putting worms into each other's spaghetti, frogs in one another's beds, and glass eyes in glasses of beer. The rain and snow beat on the window, but on the ward it was warm and I was never so glad to be able to do the work I did.

——

Roberta Plummer unlocked the door, and stood back to allow me inside her brother's old bedroom. I turned to her before going in.

'Are you sure you're okay with this? If you'd prefer I didn't, I'll understand.'

She took a deep breath, and tried to smile. 'You must do what you have to, Shane. I want him to get better. If this will help, I'm all for it.'

'But you think it's an invasion of privacy.'

She laughed. 'As you pointed out to me when we met some weeks ago: we are not friends. It is not easy to bring you into my home, and let you into my little brother's private quarters like this. I admit to feeling slightly … violated is perhaps too strong a word, but it nevertheless feels a little like that. However, I know that you are very good at what you do, and I also realise that you are not so insensitive as to have made the request to see his room unless you deemed it absolutely necessary.'

'I need a way to get through to him. It would be good to know what he likes, what his interests are. This is the best way to do that. He's not able to tell me, right now, so I have to use another approach. I promise you that I will not remove anything — the room will be just as if I was never there.'

She nodded, and walked past me down the hall. 'I'll be downstairs.'

'You don't want to wait while I look around?'

That sad little laugh again. 'One of the main reasons I am finding it so hard to let you in there is that I can't go in myself just at the moment.' I heard tears enter her voice. 'Clive is very, um, *present*, in that room. It hurts too much to spend time where he slept and studied and lived. I'll wait for you in the kitchen. Come down when you're ready.' She took a couple of steps down, then stopped. 'Please don't think me rude,' she said, and continued her descent.

I stood in the doorway and surveyed the small room before me. I had been dubious about asking Roberta to let me come here, but the truth was, I was getting nowhere with Clive, and I was growing desperate.

He was no longer trying to kill me when I visited, and his overall behaviour seemed to have levelled out quite considerably, but I had the impression he was putting on a performance, and that the role-play was brought on by sheer terror. He spoke to me, during my visits, with that same, slow, deliberate manner, but his answers to my questions were mechanical, and he rarely sustained eye contact for more than a second. I had come to suspect that Clive still believed me to be one of his tormentors, and even Roberta coming in with me on my second meeting, to reassure him that I was there at her request, had done nothing to dispel that belief. I was at a loss. This was the only course of action I could think to follow.

Clive Plummer's room was small, the slope of the roof causing it to have very little actual useable floor space. The walls were painted in a pastel green, and the carpet was a mix of floral pink and purple. I knew immediately that Clive had not chosen these colours, or even been consulted on them. I went and sat down on the bed, which had been made with a duvet cover and pillowcase that matched the room's colour scheme. I closed my eyes and breathed in the dusty air, trying to tap into that 'presence' Roberta had described. Try as I might, I was unsuccessful. The room had that slightly edgy atmosphere other people's spaces tend to have — that feeling that you are an intruder — but otherwise it was, to me, just a room. I looked about to see where Clive had left his mark, as teenage boys will. There was a poster of *The Killers* on one wall, and a very small and (comparatively) moderate one of an almost fully clothed Britney Spears on another, but they were the only references to his age, and I found no CDs of either among the small collection on the shelves that had been put up beside his desk. The music Clive enjoyed seemed, like the décor in his room, to have been chosen by his parents: there was an album of well-known classical music (the Moonlight Sonata, the Four Seasons, that sort of thing), Daniel O'Donnell's greatest hits, a Neil Diamond collection and a boxed set of Christian rock. I put them back into their neat pile. There was nothing to be learned about Clive as a person from those.

Languishing beside the Britney poster, there was a wall chart. It was a large, A2-sized sheet containing colour prints of all the common, and some of the not so common, Irish wild birds. On closer inspection, I could see that a small x had been written in pencil beside many of the pictures. It seemed to me that he had been marking off the species he had seen. I knew that birdwatchers are inclined to do this: it is, to the twitcher, a little bit like having a collection — here are all the birds I've spotted, and here are the ones I'm still hoping to catch.

Judging from those he had ticked off, Clive was no casual observer, either. Several of the more elusive birds of prey were marked, as was the avocet, that delicate wader with its strange, upwardly curved beak. I noticed that he seemed to have moved across all the habitats, with mountain, sea, lake, hedgerow, woodland and pastoral dwellers all being represented among those he had seen. This meant that Clive was either a liar, or had gone to some effort to pursue his hobby. I turned my attention to his books. Alongside school volumes

and a couple of encyclopaedias, Clive's books were all about wildlife
and natural history. A cursory search of the room's only wardrobe
turned up a small, but powerful, pair of rather expensive binoculars.
It appeared that I had found what I was looking for.

———

The grounds around St Vitus's covered several acres, and were made
up largely of farmland. One hundred years ago, the hospital had
been self-sufficient, growing its own vegetables, butchering its own
meat and even going so far as to grind flour for bread. While many
of these activities had been discontinued over the years, a small farm
still operated, worked largely by the patients of the hospital, and a
walk around the full expanse of the hospital's estate took a good
forty-five minutes.

Clive was no longer violent, and was not seen as a flight risk, so
when I suggested to Dr Fleming that I bring the boy for a walk about
the grounds, he shrugged and said: 'Why not?' So on a cracklingly
cold afternoon I helped Clive into a heavy anorak, and handed him
a pair of binoculars, which, though quite serviceable, were much
lighter and cheaper than his own. I had left those in his wardrobe,
keeping my promise to Roberta not to remove any of the contents of
the bedroom.

He looked at them confusedly. The words, as always, seemed to
come after a delay, as if he had willed them to be said a good thirty
seconds before they emitted from his mouth.

'What are these for?'

'I thought you might get some use out of them. You're interested
in wildlife, aren't you?'

For a moment I thought he would not answer me, but suddenly, it
was as if a veil had been lifted from him, and he smiled sheepishly.
For the first time since I had known him, I saw who Clive Plummer
had been before the demons began to haunt him. Rather than a hag-
gard, tired creature, wracked with fears he could scarcely articulate,

here stood a young boy, suddenly excited at the prospect of doing something he really loved, but slightly embarrassed at sharing this uncool hobby with someone else.

'Yeah,' he finally said, holding the binoculars loosely by the strap. 'Kinda.'

'Well, let's get going then. There's a lot to see.'

I pushed open the door, and held it for him. He didn't move. 'We're going outside?'

'You won't see many birds inside, Clive.'

The uncertainty became almost paralysing, for him. I had read articles about battery hens who, when their cages were opened by animal rights activists, would not leave the place of their confine-ment. They just sat there in their own filth, staring at the space through which their escape could be accessed, but too scared to move the few steps required to grasp it. Clive reminded me of them, now, frozen to the spot, wearing a coat that was several sizes too large for him, barely healed scars criss-crossing his face. I could feel the cold air drifting in like frigid mist, and then I heard it: *pee-wit, pee-wit.* I knew that Clive could hear the sound, too, and I met his eyes, cupping my ear with my free hand. The lapwings were calling him, and I knew it. Slowly, painfully, he took step after faltering step towards the door. The birds continued to cry to one another, and, with each call, Clive moved with a little more purpose, until he was standing on the steps outside the door, gazing in the direction of the frozen field where the crested birds gathered to feed.

'They're from Scandinavia,' he said, to himself as much as to me. 'The weather here is milder, even in winter, so it's easier for them to find food.'

He moved ponderously down the steps, and, on reaching the bottom, suddenly seemed to realise that he had the binoculars in his hand. Awkwardly, he raised them to his eyes and adjusted the focus. It was painstaking. He was rediscovering a part of himself that had been buried, unearthing it a tiny piece at a time.

'Lapwings are a kind of plover, you know,' he said. I was straining to hear him, so quietly was this dialogue happening. It seemed that it didn't matter to him if I engaged or not. He was exploring being outdoors again, experiencing the birds and the feel of the air on his skin.

'I saw a really lovely heron, and a couple of egrets the other day close to that pond,' I said, going up beside him and pointing at the small, partially frozen expanse of water. 'Why don't we go for a walk and see what else we can see?'

Clive stood there, blinking at me in the brightness. His breath came out in clouds, and some colour was seeping into his cheeks. Turning to the flock of lapwings, he meekly mimicked their call: '*Peewit, pewit.*' It should have sounded ridiculous, but there was something so sad about it, I could find no reason to laugh or be amused.

'There's a kestrel that hunts above a cornfield behind the hospital,' I tried again. 'You can see it hovering, most days, about this time.'

'Sure,' he said at last. 'Yeah, okay. Let's go and see.'

I grinned. 'Good. Follow me.'

And so began a new phase in my relationship with Clive Plummer. Birds and wild animals became our medium for communication. I had, as a child, been greatly interested in the natural world, and still indulged the diversion from time to time when the mood took me. Now that Clive and I spent several sessions a week either outdoors among the flora and fauna, or poring over books on the subject, I found the names, markings and calls flooding back. I brought in a new chart for the wall of his room, where we ticked off our latest sightings. He was delighted with this, and often, when I arrived for a visit, would have prepared a list of which birds he expected to see that day on our walk, suggesting parts of the grounds we might head for in the hopes of finding a curlew, or a hen harrier.

As the numbers of birds and animals we encountered grew, so did my comprehension of just how monumental the changes in this child had been as depression, paranoia and mania took root in his personality. Clive, as he continued to emerge and allow himself to be seen by me, was a sweet, gentle, soft-spoken and self-effacing boy. He was also piercingly intelligent, and possessed a razor-sharp sense of humour, which caused us to laugh a lot of the time. The plight of his fellow patients, as tragic as these stories so often were, turned out to be a constant source of funereally dark mirth for Clive.

One day, as we walked along the narrow lane that led to the stubble fields, he recounted a story he found particularly amusing, and in the telling drove home to me how even the most bizarre of circumstances can become normal in time.

We were watching a flock of fieldfares, large thrushes which migrate to Ireland during the winter months. They were a good distance from us, so we were chatting quietly, comparing these birds to our resident song and mistle thrushes.

'They really do have a padded cell, you know,' Clive said, out of the blue.

I had my own bins trained on the birds, so was able to hide my surprise at this sudden change in the subject matter.

'Yeah, I heard that,' I said. 'Well, I suppose that when someone is really wound up, and in danger of hurting themselves, a place like that is the best place to be.'

I lowered the lenses, and looked at him. 'Did they ever put you in there?'

He laughed, showing me his chipped, jagged teeth for a moment. 'No. They always just doped me up and strapped me to the bed. I've seen the room, though. They leave the door of it open, sometimes. It's all white in there. And you can see the places where people have ripped through the lining on the wall, and all the foam's coming out.'

'Probably best that they have that mended,' I said. 'Not much point having a padded cell if all the padding's gone. Kind of defeats the purpose.'

He guffawed at that, then was quiet again for a moment. 'Do you know Jemima?'

He was referring to a fellow patient.

'The old lady?'

'The fat one, yeah.'

Jemima was hard to miss. She somehow managed to combine spectacular obesity with a wizened, prune-like face. Despite her odd appearance, though, her moments of lucidity showed her to be a kind-hearted woman, and Clive had taken a shine to her. Unfortunately, those moments of calm were punctuated by violent outbursts, and it did not do to get caught in the firing line when one of these was erupting.

'They put her in there the other day.'

'Did they?'

'Yeah. We were all on the Occupational Therapy ward, playing cards. And this new woman, Betty, she wasn't playing by the rules.'

'She was cheating?'

Clive considered this for a second. 'No, I think she was just used to a different system. Like, in poker there's a lot of ways to play it.'

'I see.'

'Jemima had warned her three or four times that this was the way we played, but Betty wouldn't listen. So Jemima threw a chair at her.'

'I'm sure that got her point across.'

'Betty is only an old woman herself, and she's skinny. The chair hit her in the head.'

'Ouch.'

'Yeah, she went down as if … well, as if someone had hit her in the head with a chair.'

'So, they put Jemima in the padded cell?'

'Well, they had to catch her first. See, the nurse made to grab her, and she went behind the table. The nurse kept coming after her, so Jemima said to me: "Would you mind giving up your chair for an old lady?" I moved, and she threw my chair. Everyone else had scattered at that stage, so she just kept on throwing chairs until there was none left. She tried to chuck the table, but that was a bit too heavy, even for her.'

'Mmm. Tough woman.'

'She sure is. By then, a load of male nurses and a couple of doctors had arrived, and they all jumped her. That's when she was sent down.'

'Did they keep her in there for long?'

'I'm not sure. She was out, and back playing cards the next day. She told me that, when she was put in the padded room first, there was a chair in there for her to sit on. When a nurse came in to check on her after a while, Jemima threw *that* chair at her.'

'I would have thought they might have seen that coming.'

'Yeah. So, they took it away. She told me she didn't care, though, because the floor was nice and padded, like a mattress, so she just lay down and had a snooze.'

Clive's face creased up at this, and he laughed and laughed. It was infectious, and within moments I had joined him. The fieldfares, alarmed at our outburst, took off in a cloud of slate-blue and brown.

'Sometimes,' he said eventually, tears rolling down his cheeks, 'sometimes, you just have to laugh.'

'Yeah, it's strange what can seem funny when you think about it,' I agreed, trying to catch my breath. 'I reckon almost anything can raise a smile, no matter how sad it actually is.'

As soon as I said it, I realised how thoughtless and wrong I was. There had been so many things I had encountered, through my work and, truth be told, in my life in general, that I knew I would never, ever find amusing. But the fatuous statement was out before I could do anything about it.

Clive's face dropped and he seemed to sag, almost shrinking in height.

'There's a lot that's not funny,' he said. 'I mean, being locked up in here isn't really a joke, is it, but I can sort of laugh about it some-times. When I'm out here, it's like I'm not in a madhouse, y'know? It's easier to see the funny side of things. But the stuff that happened to me ... the stuff I *think* happened to me ... I'll never, ever be able to laugh at that.'

'I know that, Clive. I'm sorry about what I said. I wasn't thinking. It was really stupid of me.'

'Lately I haven't been as scared. The days have been good. Getting out into the countryside, seeing the birds, I almost feel like the old me again. But when I sleep, the dreams come.'

'Bad dreams?'

'I'm here, in the hospital, and it's night-time. I'm the only one on the ward. Everyone else is gone, and when I go to the door, it's open. I walk out into the corridor, and start to go down it. I know I shouldn't, and in my head, I'm screaming at myself to just go back inside and close the door, but I keep going. I can see a light away in the distance, and I can hear something, like voices praying or chanting. The sound sort of pulls me forward. As I get closer, I can see that there's someone — some*thing* — standing at the end of the passage.'

His voice was cracking, as if his very being did not wish for him to continue this narrative, but he seemed determined to purge himself of it. I reached out and put a hand on his shoulder.

'You don't have to tell me this if you don't want to, Clive.'

'I need to. I have to tell someone.' He looked at me, and the terror was etched into every line in his face; I thought, as I watched him, that fourteen-year-old boys shouldn't have lines on their faces, but Clive did. 'You believe me, don't you, Shane? I thought you were one of them at first, but I know you're not. You understand I'm telling the truth.'

'I know something awful happened to you, Clive. I'm certain of that much. I can see you're in terrible pain, and I know that you're scared out of your mind.' I paused, squeezing his shoulder in an attempt to anchor him here with me, with the smell of grass and trees and frozen earth. 'What's at the end of the corridor, Clive? Can you tell me what you see?'

'One of them.'

'Who? Who are they?'

'Not who. What.'

'I don't understand.'

'See, Shane, they're not men. Standing at the end of the hallway is their leader. He's tall, much taller than you. His body is like a man, but the head is like a goat or a bull. It has horns and eyes like a cat, and smoke and fire come from the nose when he breathes. The monster wants me back. More than anything else, he desires me, and must have me. He'll find me. In my dreams, he tells me he's coming.'

I turned him to face me fully. 'Listen to me, Clive. I don't doubt someone did something really awful to you. But whoever did those things, whoever hurt you so badly, was a man or a woman. There are

Chapter 7 ~

It became obvious within a week that the family mediation sessions with the Bassetts were a waste of everyone's time and energy. Despite the tasks I had left them to carry out, the second visit I made to their bizarrely decorated house proved to me that this was not going to be the simple, open-and-shut case Marian had led me to believe I was taking on. In fact, I began to suspect things had the potential to get very challenging indeed.

The first sign that my hopes for a constructive and productive session were ridiculously optimistic came when I sat down and suggested everyone take out the written work I'd asked them to prepare — their wish lists: how they would like things to be if we had a magic wand and could miraculously make everything perfect. Gertrude was so excited that I decided to just let her go first. I thought that having her express a desire to make things right and achieve a sense of harmony would be a nice way to set the tone for the rest of the session. With a contented smile, she opened her notebook — a pink, hardbound volume, with some kind of purple fluffy trim about the edges.

'If a fairy could come and make our lives right again,' she began, 'the first thing I would like would be for Patrick to realise what an awful time he has given us all this past twelve months, and give a heartfelt apology. Then I would like him, for the first time, to keep to his word and never raise his hand to me again, never stay out long into the night hanging out with juvenile delinquents in gambling houses and dens of iniquity—'

'—Gertrude, I have to stop you there,' I said, trying to keep the temper out of my voice. 'That is not what I asked you to do. This was meant to be an exercise in being positive. It certainly wasn't meant to be about attacking Patrick.'

Gertrude stopped and looked at me in surprise.

'But you said that we were to write about what we would like to see happen if everything was made good. That's what I did.'

There was a palpable sense of tension in the room. I was focused on the matriarch, but could feel the eyes of Percy and the two children glued on Gertrude and me. I knew exactly what she was doing — I had established myself in the previous session as being in charge, as the authority within the realms of these meetings. She could not have that. Gertrude Bassett's entire persona was wrapped around being the supreme leader within her home. She could not bear to share that position, even in a situation where she had actually asked for help. Perhaps that was what had caused her to complain about, and finally to usurp, the previous social worker. At any rate, she had decided to conclusively knock me back down to size, and her tool was the very task I had set her to do.

'Gertrude,' I smiled, ensuring that I was being as unthreatening as I could be. 'Maybe I didn't explain myself adequately. What I wanted was for you to picture your relationships if all the problems you are now experiencing were gone. Now, for us to get to that point, there may, or indeed may not, have to be apologies and expressions of regret. But I don't want to focus on that. I want us to get a good, clear picture of how you would all be — of how you *could be.*'

Gertrude did not return my smile. Instead she closed her fluffy pink notebook and crossed her arms across her ample bosoms. 'I am sure, Shane, that you have plenty of training and experience in these types of situations.'

I shrugged. I wasn't going to be baited into a discussion on my qualifications.

'Well, what I have is a degree in motherhood. Do you have any children, Shane?'

I shook my head. I could see where this was going, but wasn't yet sure how I was going to respond. Interactions like this require a deftness of touch — I had to get Gertrude to understand the necessity for working with me if we were to save her family, but I didn't want to embarrass her or make her lose face in front of her husband and kids to achieve that. I let her continue to talk while I considered my next move.

'I can't say I'm surprised. You people never do. You think you know it all, that you can come into people's houses and lay down the law. Let me tell you — I know Patrick. For there to be any hope of us getting to a place where we're in good shape as a family again, he will need to admit that he has been totally in the wrong, and that the absolute misery he has put us all through for the past year will never happen again. Then, for me to be satisfied that he has truly turned over a new leaf, there will have to be a consistent period of exemplary conduct. I cannot see beyond those things just now. I'm sorry, but I can't.'

I looked over at Patrick. He was, as I expected him to be, gazing down at his hands, rigid and impassive. Percy was staring at the carpet. Bethany looked as if she were about to start crying. Gertrude's annoyance radiated from her like heat. She sat like an angry Buddha, challenging me to defy her.

While I was definitely aggravated by Gertrude's determination not to cooperate, I felt genuine sympathy for her. Despite the silly, girlish demeanour and the nonsensical furniture, Gertrude was inherently a good person, and far from stupid. I decided to take a leaf from Patrick's book, and adopt a passive-aggressive response. I would pretend I was completely unaware of the challenge, and continue the session as if nothing had happened.

'Okay, thanks, Gertrude, for that, and for your honesty. Percy, how about sharing what you wrote?'

I wished that I had the time, and the gumption, to enjoy the expression of disgust that spread across Gertrude's face. I heard Bethany gasp, and Patrick suddenly looked up, as if someone had kicked him. Percy started, and sat bolt upright.

'Oh, ummm … okay, so. Yes, I'll read my essay. Where are we, now …' He noisily unfolded a little wad of paper he had been holding in his hand. 'Right. Now: What I would like to see happen if our family was to get better would be for Patrick to say he was very sorry for what he's done. I would like for him to understand that he has been a great strain on his mother—'

'—Percy, this bears a shocking resemblance to what Gertrude has just read.'

Percy stopped and flushed a deep scarlet.

'Did you and Gertrude collaborate on your wish lists?'

'Yes, we worked on them together,' Gertrude was not even trying to contain herself. 'I thought that it was important we were all singing from the same hymn-sheet.'

I nodded. 'And was Bethany involved in this group effort also?'

'We worked on it together, like on a project in school,' Bethany beamed. 'Mammy told us what to write.'

'Now, sweetie, I wouldn't go so far as to say that …'

I held up a hand to silence her. 'Please, Gertrude, I get the picture.' I could not suppress a sigh. I was getting a sinking feeling, a sense I was in quicksand, and that struggling would only cause me to submerge faster. 'Patrick, let's hear what you wrote.'

'I didn't write anything.'

Patrick sat hunched over, seemingly trying to protect himself from the barrage of antagonism that had been directed at him since we sat down.

'Why didn't you do the exercise, Patrick? You seemed fairly enthusiastic the last time I was here.'

The boy shrugged, a barely perceptible movement of his right shoulder. 'What's the point? I knew they were all getting stuck into me in the kitchen. I could hear her giving orders. It didn't matter what I wrote or didn't write.'

I couldn't argue with him. Somewhere, in a distant part of my mind, I could hear Gertrude declaring that this proved, conclusively, that Patrick was a hopeless case, but I was scarcely listening. Gertrude had beaten me. Despite my best efforts, she had shown that she was, in reality, in control of the family mediation sessions.

———

I gave it one more chance, but the following meeting was even worse. I had set no tasks, and went in with an open agenda, but this time I was treated to a lesson in all the ways that Bethany was a much superior child to her errant brother. I was, once again, powerless to intervene. Every time I pointed out that such negative comment was out of bounds, and that all that was being achieved was an even further alienation of Patrick, Gertrude or Percy stopped momentarily, only to continue moments later, as if I had not spoken.

I did the only reasonable thing, and discontinued mediation. Gertrude was delighted, although she pretended to be irate when I phoned her the following day to give her the news.

'So, he's too much for you, too, then. Leaving us in the lurch, are you, just like that other fella? Well, don't concern yourself. We'll struggle on, somehow.'

'I'm not giving up on Patrick, or you, for that matter, Gertrude. I'm just going to try another tack for a bit. I'd like to see Patrick and Bethany, together, outside the house.'

Silence emanated from the other end of the line. 'Bethany doesn't need any work, Shane. What do you want to see her for?'

'She's Patrick's sister — they're both fostered. She's been living with you all during these difficult times. She's bound to have a perspective on what's been going on, but without the politics the power struggle has imbued between you and Patrick. So, I'll pick them up tomorrow, after school, if that's alright.'

Gertrude seemed lost for words: the only response I received was a grunt before the receiver was slammed down.

Both children were waiting when I arrived at the house, already out of their school uniforms and with coats and hats on. Gertrude had recovered, and quietly (but loud enough for Patrick to hear, of course) told me that she thought I was absolutely right to adopt this approach, as I could experience just how bad the boy was for myself, without the protective barriers of her, Percy and their home. I thanked her, and left, feeling a sense of untold freedom as we closed the gate at the end of the drive, and walked to the Austin.

I am ashamed to admit that I had an overwhelming urge to take the kids to an arcade to play video-games, but knew that to do so would be an unforgivable flouting of Gertrude's rules, and would send a clear message to the children that I had picked sides. So, at Bethany's suggestion, we went for ice-creams instead.

I've taken countless children out for countless sundaes throughout my career, and the experience never fails to make me smile. It also causes me to wonder at the perversity of ice-cream parlour owners. When a kid goes into one of these establishments, he or she is always met with photographs of the different confections on offer — it is as much a visual experience as one of flavour. The rooms themselves are usually pretty much the same: black and white tiled floors; wooden ceiling fans; booths with red seats; a jukebox with music from the fifties and sixties. To the front is a tall counter, and above it, the menu, beside which are the pictures of what you can buy — food pornography, in other words.

These photos depict enormous, towering glasses filled with cream — both iced and whipped, fruit, chocolate syrup, cake, biscuit, jelly and all sorts of other delectable edibles. The child ogles these works of frozen art with barely concealed covetousness, and finally chooses one. Most kids go for a Knickerbocker Glory on their first visit. It is, after all, the ice-cream of myth and legend, the one you see children in movies and on television shows digging into. When the waitress brings this monstrosity of a dessert to the table, there is always a gasp of surprise and anticipation — it looked big in the photo, but in reality it is *huge*. Impossibly big, way too much for any adult, let alone a child, to finish.

The psychology behind taking the first spoonful from your virgin Knickerbocker Glory would fill a thousand tomes on Freudian psychoanalysis. Do you simply take a shallow portion of whipped cream from the top? Do you plunge the long-handled spoon deep into the glass, getting a mix of all the contents? Do you take the cherry from the top first and eat it? The possibilities are many and varied — I probably haven't even seen them all yet.

One thing, however, is certain. By the time that glass is half-empty, the child will be covered in a sticky mess of jelly and cream, and will have developed a greenish tinge. Yet the challenge of the Knickerbocker Glory for a child is something akin to the unspoken draw of the Antarctic to Ernest Shackleton — despite massive odds and untold adversity, they just cannot abandon their goal.

I have long since stopped suggesting kids leave the glass midway, and just allow them to gorge themselves into oblivion. I have also stopped marvelling at the fact that on subsequent visits, they will actually order another Knickerbocker Glory, and have a second attempt at reaching the Pole — with the same results. I always have an image of a 1950s era ice-cream vendor, striped apron, paper hat and all, somewhere at the back of the shop, poring over closed-circuit TV monitors, laughing maniacally: 'Eat, eat, my pretties!'

My visit with Patrick and Bethany was no different. I had some-how expected that Bethany would avoid getting covered in food, but she didn't. To my surprise, she threw herself into the experience with whole-hearted gusto, and actually ate more than Patrick.

Our conversation was light and pleasant. I purposely steered away from anything heavy — we'd had enough of that during the oppres-sive, abortive family mediation. So we talked about school, about sports (Patrick was a huge Manchester United fan, I discovered), about toys (Bethany was a closet *Bratz* fan — she admitted to me that she was a little afraid to tell Gertrude, who she felt, probably correctly, would not approve of the sexually precocious dolls) and, finally, about the children's birth family.

It was Bethany who brought up the latter subject. There had never really been any mention of the kids' previous lives before this, and I was unprepared for it. She had finally conceded defeat to the ice-cream, and sat back, looking exceptionally cute with her face now almost completely obscured by the amount of food she had managed to attach to it.

'I cannot eat another thing!' she said, sitting back and holding her distended belly. 'If I do, I think I'll explode.' She seemed to find this hilariously funny, but was too stuffed to be able to laugh, so she ended up groaning instead.

'You'll be sick,' Patrick said.

Throughout the hour we had spent in the café, he had been polite and had responded perfectly appropriately to any questions addressed to him, but I still felt there was something missing. It was as if he was just not fully there with us: some part of him was cordoned off and inaccessible, possibly even to him. He never smiled, never laughed, and his eyes were dull and lifeless. The pressure he was living under in the Bassett household was taking its toll on him.

'I'll be sick all over you,' Bethany retorted, still half-laughing, half-moaning.

Patrick snorted at that, and looked out the window at the crowds of Christmas shoppers that barged past one another outside.

'How come Mammy never brings us here?' Bethany asked.

'*Gertrude* doesn't think we should eat sweet things,' Patrick said.

'Stop calling her that,' Bethany said, her tone changing quickly from fun to anger. 'She's your mother.'

'No she's not.'

'Is too! You can't remember our real mother, so you can't.'

Patrick sighed and glanced at his sister, who had tears in her eyes now and was gazing at him with a hurt expression.

'I can remember her,' he said, and returned to his people watching.

I knew that this was an opportunity to learn something about the children's lives before they were fostered, but I could also see that it was a hugely sensitive issue for Bethany. I didn't want to upset her, or to kill the happy mood we had managed to maintain so far, so I laughed and patted the girl on the hand.

'Hey, it's alright that Patrick remembers his birth mother, Beth. It doesn't mean he loves Gertrude any less. Your lives before you went to live with her and Percy are still a part of who you are. You shouldn't just forget about them.'

Bethany looked uncertain. 'Mammy says we're lucky to have been chosen by a good family,' she said. 'She says God wanted her and Daddy to bring us up.'

'That's nice to think, isn't it?' I said. 'That you were all meant to be together.'

The little girl nodded. 'She says that I was always her daughter, we just had to find one another.' She paused, seemingly unsure of how to continue. 'Sometimes, I wonder what my other Mammy was like, though. *I* don't remember her, even a little bit.'

Patrick smiled wistfully to himself.

'She was the most beautiful woman I've ever seen,' he said, and I knew immediately that they had been over this many times together, probably during the dark of night in whispered conversations. The words I was hearing were well rehearsed. 'She had long blonde hair, and the sweetest, kindest face. She looked just like you, Beth, and, just like you, everyone who knew her loved her.'

'Tell me about my other Daddy.'

'Our Daddy was a motorcycle stuntman in a circus. He wore an amazing costume, with stars all over it and a bright red helmet, and the sound of his bike was so loud, you could hear it ten miles away. He was so brave, even the ringmaster got scared sometimes by the stunts he'd do, but our Dad was the best there was. He knew what he could do, and how far he could push that motorcycle.'

'And my little sister?'

I began to make rapid mental notes. There had been no mention of a sister on the children's file. Could Patrick be mistaken? Was this whole thing a fantasy the children had concocted in the first days of their being fostered, to make the experience easier?

'She looked like you too, Beth. She had a head full of golden curls, and she used to sit on my knee and laugh when I told her stories. She was just lovely.'

'What was her name, Patrick?' I asked, unable to remain silent any longer.

Patrick sighed, and fiddled with the strap of his watch absently. 'I can't remember. It was so long ago, and we haven't seen any of them since we were fostered. Gertrude won't allow it. But that's okay, 'cause as soon as I'm old enough, I'm gonna find them. She won't be able to stop me forever.'

———

Dorothy Carey watched uncertainly as I pushed back all the toys to clear a space in the centre of the playroom, and then unrolled soft exercise mats, to create a wide, cushioned area. I was dressed in my workout gear: a large, loose-fitting T-shirt, tracksuit bottoms and trainers, and my hair was tied back in a ponytail.

'Explain this to me one more time,' Dorothy said.

I stood up, brushing myself down. The room was long and wide, and Katie and I would have plenty of space, now.

'Katie spends as much time being restrained during our play sessions as she does playing, agreed?'

Dorothy shrugged. 'I would have said she spends more time being restrained than she does doing anything.'

'Let's not split hairs. Have you ever heard of "The Rumble in the Jungle"?'

Dorothy shook her head. 'Is it a song?'

I paused. 'Now that you mention it, I think Creedence Clearwater Revival did have a song with a similar name … but that's not what I'm talking about, now. Muhammad Ali and George Foreman fought each other for the heavyweight title in Zaire in nineteen seventy-four, and the promoters called it "The Rumble in the Jungle".'

'Boxing? You're telling me about boxing now? Men. I don't understand ye at all.'

'Bear with me. Ali knew that Foreman was stronger than he was, and that, in an open, face to face bout, he couldn't win. So he had to develop a strategy. He called it "rope-a-dope". In each round, he leaned back against the ropes, and let Foreman hit him. In fact, he taunted him, told him he boxed like a girl, encouraged old George to punch harder and faster.'

'I still don't follow.'

'Each round, Foreman got more and more tired. In the end, Ali started to fight back, and when he did, George was so exhausted, he had nothing left. He was beaten by knockout.'

'And your point is …'

'I'm getting nowhere with Katie because more often than not, I come in here and she attacks me. I've tried reasoning with her, I've tried bribing her, I've tried ignoring her. Makes no difference. So, that leaves us with one option. If she wants to fight, we'll fight.'

Dorothy's mouth dropped open. 'You have got to be joking.'

'Nope. I'm not going to exactly restrain her. I'm just not going to let her hurt me. So, there's going to be a lot of thrashing about, and probably a lot of sweating and swearing. At the end of the day, she's a fourteen-year-old girl. I know she's deeply disturbed, but I think I can just about handle her. Anyway, you'll be watching in the observation room, so if I do get into trouble, you can send reinforcements.'

'And what do you hope to achieve?'

'When she finally realises that she can't scare me off, that I'm perfectly happy to let her vent, I'm betting she stops trying, and we can get on with the play.'

'You're going to let her wear herself out, basically.'

'Yep.'

Dorothy shook her head. 'This, I have to see,' she said, and went to get Katie.

I am not ashamed to admit that Katie Rhodes, that diminutive fourteen-year-old whom I was convinced I could 'handle', pushed me to the limit of my endurance over the next three sessions. I decided I would meet her daily until she ran out of steam and understood that I was not a threat and would, regardless of provocation, never hurt her.

As I had discovered at our previous meeting, Katie was not slow on the uptake. She understood my intent as soon as she saw the mats and the cleared space in the playroom, and it enraged her beyond anything I might have expected.

She stood in the doorway, looking at me and the proposed battleground, aghast.

'You stupid cocksucker,' she hissed. 'I'll put your sorry, cuntin' arse in the fucking hospital.'

With a roar, her hands like claws, she rushed me.

I have little recollection of what followed. I seem to recall a sense of surprise at how strong she actually was, and of having to constantly use my greater weight to gain an advantage. I have a memory of her struggling and wriggling like an eel. I remember being terrified of hurting her, and of calling on all the training I had in restraint to hold her without doing harm. Her unnatural speed is also emblazoned upon my psyche. Within the first three minutes she had raked me across the forehead with her nails, leaving four deep gashes, and I realised there and then that I might have bitten off much more than I could chew.

The real problem was that, once I had committed to this course of physical therapy — because that is, inherently, what it was, I had no choice but to continue until it had reached its conclusion. I was acutely aware that if Katie got the better of me, and sensed that I was weakening, then our relationship would be damaged beyond repair. She had to see that I was the one in control, and that, not only was I able to withstand her rage, but I could also keep her from harming herself. Where she was spiralling into chaos, I would maintain order and help her do the same. A large part of this, as odd as it may seem, was about making her feel safe with me.

That first day, it took an hour and fifteen minutes for her to stop struggling. By the end of this period, I was drenched in sweat and aching in every muscle. Katie wasn't much better. Her black hair hung in strands, and she breathed in ragged gasps. When I was sure she was spent, I picked her up and carried her to a beanbag, where I left her lying, inert, then left the room to clean out my wounds.

Dorothy was waiting for me down the corridor, the first-aid box in her hand.

'Jesus, Shane. Are you alright?'

'I've felt better to be honest.'

The following day, I woke up stiff and aching, with the overwhelming urge to stay in bed and ring into work sick. I spent almost an hour in the shower, with the temperature as high as I could stand it. Then I made coffee and a light breakfast, smoked three cigarettes and finally felt like I might actually be able to get through another eighteen rounds. Just.

Katie entered that day without a word, and circled the room before leading her attack with an attempted kick to my groin, followed by a head-butt I barely protected myself from. It took an hour to wear her out, and I almost didn't make it. There was a point when she elbowed me in the throat with such force I almost lost my grip, and couldn't breathe for close to thirty seconds.

The most significant thing about this second day was that she was silent throughout. The previous session had been punctuated by Katie's now customary flow of colourfully arranged obscenity. This day, however, she fought without a word, her whole being focused on her fury, her drive to hurt.

Day three ended, thankfully, after forty minutes. I sensed a renewed desperation in the girl's attacks, a real draining of her available energy resources. Panic was setting in. No one else had endured her venom like this, and she wasn't sure how to react. So she fell back on even greater cruelty. She tried to bite me, which she had not done before, and in the end broke away and spent two whole minutes casting about the room for a weapon. She settled on throwing toy cars at me, before collapsing in a heap on the floor in tears. I fell to my knees on the mats, close to breaking point myself, and watched her sobbing silently. This was what I had been waiting for. The rage was gone. Only sadness remained.

It took two further days of Katie ignoring me completely for her to begin to play again. I expected this — she, understandably, felt she had lost face. Katie's persona, when she was with me, was of the tough, unrelenting warrior. I had shown her that I was not afraid of her, that I could, repeatedly, take all she could dish out, and would keep coming back for more. I let her work it out for herself. Sitting in silence in the playroom, after three days of unremitting rage, was actually quite pleasant. I did not want to force the issue. She had to work it out for herself.

Then, one morning, I arrived to be told she was already in the playroom, and that I'd better hurry.

'She said to tell you she's waiting and you'd better move your arse or you'll miss the show,' Dorothy informed me. 'Looks like she might be coming around.'

'Don't count your chickens,' I said, but ran up the stairs.

I heard her before I even got to the door. It was the strange little game she had played before, about Ken and Barbie getting drunk and abandoning their child. In the days that followed, this was all she played. It didn't matter what toys or equipment I brought in or suggested, it was always the same sad psychodrama. Occasionally there would be a variation, where the police arrived to the house unbidden, and arrested the two drunken dolls, but even in this version, the baby was left behind when the parents were sent to prison. Not even the gardaí cared about that lonely, plastic baby.

A week of this made me realise that a change of scenery might be called for. I had been toying with the idea of taking Katie out of the house anyway, but wanted to ensure it was safe to do so. Seven days without an outburst (and it wasn't just me — the staff had reported a cessation of all but the most half-hearted violence) assured me that things were as safe as they were likely to get. I discussed my plans with Dorothy, who approved them.

So it was that, despite the freezing weather and occasional flurries of snow, Katie and I arrived at the beach one Monday morning. I wanted to try something new with her, a technique called 'sand-and-water' play, a method developed by the visionary psychologist Carl Jung. Jung is believed by many to be part of the lunatic fringe of childcare theorists. He is the person who came up with the idea of the collective unconscious (the concept that we are all psychically linked), wrote his doctoral thesis on spirit mediums (he actually took some of them perfectly seriously) and believed he had a prophetic dream warning him of the outbreak of World War I. Like his friend and mentor, Sigmund Freud, he was an inveterate womaniser, and wrote books on everything from personality types (he developed the by now widely accepted description of introverted and extroverted personalities) to Tarot cards and the I Ching.

My interest in him, however, stemmed from his work with the deeply traumatised. Jung was fascinated by the plight of children who had been so abused as to effectively shut down — children who were elective mutes, who were catatonic, or who had become desensitised to pain and other physical stimuli. To work with such children, Jung developed a barrage of methodologies that were completely based on primal sensation: touch, taste, sound and smell. He

used natural media, such as sand, water and clay, believing that these
are the basic materials of life. Jung rationalised that catastrophic
experiences can cause children to dissociate, to shut themselves off
from all feeling and sensation. Children who have regularly been
beaten, for example, cease to allow themselves to sense pain, while
those who have been rejected by a loved one will not permit friend-
ships or close relationships to develop, purposely sabotaging such
interactions. Yet, virtually everyone can identify the feelings you
experience on plunging your foot into a pool of freezing water. The
words 'wet' and 'cold' are perfectly apt descriptions. Such physical
experiences are then used to begin a process of reconnecting the
person with his or her more elusive emotions.

I have used this technique several times with really disturbed children, and am always bowled over by the rapid responses I experience
from the kids. I don't know why such a simple play exercise is so
powerful — but it is.

I purposely brought Katie a little after ten in the morning. I
decided to come early, so that there would be few people about other
than the usual assortment of hard-core joggers and dog-walkers.
If Katie did disclose or become upset, I wanted there to be as few
witnesses as possible.

The child was uncharacteristically quiet as we walked along the
sand. It was almost like she knew something serious was afoot. I was
looking for something specific, and after we had gone around
500 yards, I found it: a rock pool, right on the water line, so that
there was wet sand on one side, and dry on the other. All about were
shells, stone, bits of seaweed and driftwood. Katie was carrying a
bucket and spade we'd bought at a little shop on the waterfront.

'What're we gonna do here?' she asked.

'Well, that's up to you,' I said. 'I thought this might make a nice
change from the playroom in the house. I know you haven't been
out in a little while, and I reckoned the open space would be good
for you. It's cold, but it's pleasant. I like to come here and walk and
think sometimes. There's a kind of peace to the place, isn't there?'

But Katie wasn't listening. She was on her knees, in the dry sand by the pool, the plastic spade in her hands, digging a shallow hole. I squatted a little away from her, and lit a cigarette.

At first, Katie dug delicately: little, loose shovelfuls of sand were tossed into a pile by her side. But as she continued, the action adopted a frenetic energy. Deeper and deeper she went, until she had made a trough around three feet deep. For a moment she stopped, sliding on her knees into the hole. Then, grunting with the exertion, she continued. The sand was cold and hard, damp and difficult to cut through, but she worked on regardless.

I badly wanted to intervene, but knew from experience that to do so would only be detrimental. Katie was acting out her own, private game here, and I was not part of it. We had, painfully and haltingly, built up a kind of trust over the past week, and I did not want to do anything to break that. I had told Katie that her play was her own, and that I could only get involved at her invitation. She had, as yet, never asked me to join in. She seemed hyper-aware that I was watching, and her 'Ken and Barbie' games were certainly performances for my benefit, but she had never asked me what I thought of them, or what they might mean. She had come to accept my presence, but seemed not to quite know what to make of me.

Katie's excavation was now at least four feet deep, and as long as she was. All of a sudden, I realised what she was doing. Finally, her work finished, she lay down in the freshly dug grave.

I stayed where I was, feeling the wind push at my back, smelling and tasting the salt spray beneath the tobacco as I smoked. For several minutes, she lay in the hole in silence, then I heard her call me: 'Shane.'

'Yes, Katie.'

She was lying flat on her back, he dark hair spread about her, he hands crossed over her flat chest. I had never looked at her and seen vulnerability before, but just then, I did. My heart went out to her. 'Bury me,' she said.

I took the spade and began to fill the sand in, until all but her face was covered, to a thickness of maybe five inches. She closed her eyes while I worked, seemingly relaxed, enjoying the feeling.

'There you go,' I said, after I had patted the sand down.

'You're not finished,' she said. 'I want you to bury me. All of me. Fill in the fuckin' hole.'

'I can't do that, Katie. You'll suffocate.'

'I don't care! Bury me, you fucker. You said you'd do whatever I asked. I want you to bury me and leave me here.'

'I also said that I wouldn't let you hurt me or yourself. Filling in this hole because you asked me to would be the same as letting you hurt yourself.'

She looked up at me from the deathbed she had made, and I saw the anger drain from her as quickly as it had appeared. 'Don't you see, Shane? I want to die. I don't like being what I am, any more. I'm too tired.'

'Let me help you, then. Together we can work something out.'

Tears dribbled out of the corners of her eyes and ran into the sand. Her hand suddenly appeared from where I had covered it. I took it, and pulled her out. She cursorily brushed herself down, but most of the stuff, which was pretty wet, remained stuck to her clothes. Picking up a stick, she walked a few yards below the water-line and began to draw something. I followed, and saw that she was sketching the shape of a simple house:

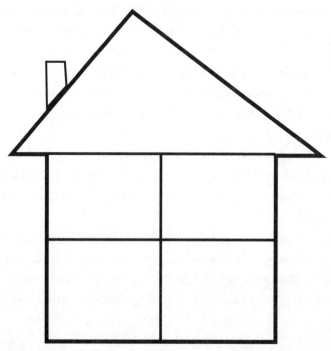

She hunted about until she'd found a scallop shell, and placed it in one of the rooms she had outlined in the ground floor of the structure. 'This is Katie,' she said. 'Katie lives in this house with her Mammy and Daddy. Katie is four years old. This is the kitchen. Katie would sit here sometimes, when Mammy and Daddy were so drunk they fell asleep. She would stay there, because there was bread and milk, and her Daddy would usually have passed out in the living room, so she was scared to go in there. She felt alone and afraid, and wished her Mammy would wake up and come and talk to her. Even though her Mammy was not always nice to her, Katie still loved her.'

She moved the shell to an upstairs room. 'This is Katie's room.' She took a black stone from the rock pool, and placed it beside the shell. 'This is Katie's Mammy. She used to come to Katie's room, sometimes, after Katie was asleep. "Get up," she'd say. "Come downstairs and help me with the cleaning," and Katie would have to get up and do housework — washing the dishes or sweeping the floor. Mammy'd be drunk, and when Katie couldn't work fast enough, or when she dropped a plate because she was so tired, Mammy'd sometimes beat Katie until Katie was too sore and scared to go back asleep.'

She moved the shell to the other upstairs room, and took a dried piece of seaweed from the sand, placing it in the room also. 'This is Katie's Daddy, and this is Katie's parents' room. When Katie's Mammy was at work, Daddy would take Katie up to his bed, and make her do things to him. Sex things. If she didn't do them, he'd hit her until she did. Sometimes the things he forced her to do would make her cry, but he didn't care. Once, he shoved his thing into her, and she thought she would die, it hurt her so much. She screamed and screamed, and he stopped, but he was mad, and even though she begged him not to, he put it in her mouth instead and made her do him like that.'

The shell was moved again, this time to the remaining downstairs room. A little piece of wood was placed beside it, and a crab claw. 'This is the living room, and this is Una and Jumbo. Una was Daddy's friend, and she came to babysit Katie when Mammy and Daddy went out to the pub. Katie thought Una was really nice. She let her stay up late, and they sometimes watched scary movies together, and when Katie got afraid, Una would hold her real tight. Una always brought sweets and crisps, and fizzy drinks with her, and Katie looked forward to her Mammy and Daddy going out, 'cause she liked being with Una so much. One night, Katie told Una what her Daddy had been doing, and Una listened, and told Katie she believed her, and that she'd help. Katie was so happy. She dreamed about Una coming and taking her away, and being her new Mammy. Only that didn't happen. Katie's Daddy kept on doing bad things. Her Mammy still beat her, and the next time Una came to babysit, she brought her boyfriend, Jumbo. Jumbo seemed nice, too, but he wasn't. He made Una put Katie to bed early, and in the night, he came into her room and did worse things than her Daddy had ever done. Katie was bleeding after he was finished, and he gave her things to put into her knickers to stop the blood — sanitary towels, Katie knows now. She was too little to know what they were then. After that, he always came when Una was babysitting, and in the end, Una used to come with him to Katie's room and they both did horrible sex things to Katie.'

Using the shovel, she slowly and deliberately scratched out the picture of the house, erasing its image from the surface of the beach in deft, wide strokes. I watched her, feeling sick and empty.

'I'd like to go back to the centre now, please,' she said, when all that was left where the house had been was rough sand. 'I don't think I like the beach very much.'

Chapter 8 ~

Tilly sat in the back seat of my Austin. She was holding her son Johnny's hand. If I had not insisted against it, on grounds of safety, she would have had him on her knee, with her arms wrapped around him. Johnny accepted her affections with good grace, but seemed more interested in watching the cityscape drift past as we drove from the hospital to the Currans' new trailer. He was going home for Christmas, and both his mother and I were elated. Beyond all but my naïve, stubborn hopes, it seemed that Johnny would recover, perhaps not all, but much of his previous faculties.

The little boy's progress had been nothing short of remarkable, testimony to his amazing strength of character and the skills of the various medical staff who had worked with him during his time in hospital.

While a bandage still adorned his head, and his face still bore marks of injury, he was speaking a few words now, and, with the aid of crutches, was walking very short distances. The greatest miracle, though, was Johnny's obvious intelligence and glowing personality. The nurses who came into contact with him were all affected by this little boy, still mostly silent, but with the most expressive eyes any of them had ever seen, who managed to communicate so much without words. A laugh seemed to always be touching his lips, a smile never far away.

The other children on the ward responded to him with boundless affection, too. One or more of them was always at his bedside, reading a comic, playing with one of the games I had left, or just talking. Johnny didn't need to be able to speak back. He had rapidly developed a system of body language that served him perfectly well as a method of communication.

Despite all of this, however, the reality was that Johnny was still not forming sentences, and the odd words he did attempt were indistinct. He was walking only with assistance. I continued to harbour the belief that, over time, he could effect a full recovery, but the medics insisted this was unlikely. Johnny Curran was, they informed me, permanently brain damaged.

Tilly had started to visit a little more, but it was painfully obvious that she hated spending any time in the hospital. I knew that she found the doctors deeply intimidating, and for their part, they made absolutely no effort to speak to her in a language she could understand. On the couple of occasions they had taken time out of their busy schedules to condescend to her, I had seen her eyes glaze over as they told her about Johnny in terms I had to struggle to follow — cranial fractures, cerebral fluid, neural pathways — these were words from a foreign language as far as Tilly was concerned. She was a proud enough woman to be embarrassed by this, and it only added to her reluctance to enter the hospital at all.

When I was given the news that Johnny could go home, I drove straight to Tilly's caravan to tell her, and to explain the parameters of Johnny's prognosis. I was still unsure if the young woman realised just how slim Johnny's chances of, for example, ever playing football, were. My relationship with Tilly was improving daily, and, to my delight, her new home was always sparklingly clean, and her children maintained the healthy state they had been in when they left the refuge. There had never been the necessity to appoint a family support worker — Tilly's extended family had rallied round and helped her adjust to her newly single life.

She opened the door to me with a smile. It was a miserable night, and by the river, where her trailer still sat like a grounded space capsule, the wind howled, as if in protest. I was glad to climb up the steps into the warmth.

The children all shouted greetings to me, then continued watching a video of a wedding on the TV, commenting on this person's clothes and that person's hairstyle.

'My cousin, Josie,' Tilly explained, as she put on the kettle. 'She got married to one of the Staple Street Connors.'

I nodded, and unwound my scarf.

Tilly had changed, in the fortnight she had been out of the refuge. The harried, bitter woman I had met in the halting site was gone. In her place was a capable, strong-minded mother, much more at peace with herself, and therefore with others. She seemed less tired, more confident, and better able to express what she wanted from life. I felt that she found dealing with me far less wearing than she had at first. I knew part of that was my coming through for her with the trailer, but it was also her own growing sense of self, and perhaps I, too, was being more open with her, and less judgmental. I am always conscious that, no matter how hard we try, prejudices can, and do, creep in.

'I have good news, Tilly,' I said.

'You take your tea black, don't you?' Tilly asked, as she took mugs from a cupboard.

'Oh, yeah.'

Travellers have a way of making tea that differs from the usual, recommended procedure. They put water, teabags, milk and sugar into the kettle, and boil the whole concoction together. The result-ant liquor, a dark brown, thick mixture, is then put into the teapot and served. I admit that I have sat and nursed cups of this foul stuff many times, but even having it in my hand makes me feel so ill, I had eventually just told Tilly I could not stomach it, and asked her to stick a teabag in a mug for me, and pour over boiling water. To my relief, she was not in the least bit offended — she in fact seemed to find my tea-drinking preference quite amusing, smiling at me as if to say: 'You settled folk and your eccentricities.'

'Johnny can come home, Tilly,' I said when we were both seated with our drinks. 'The ward sister told me this evening.'

'That's great,' Tilly said, beaming. 'When?'

'Tomorrow,' I said. 'Listen, there's something we have to talk about. You know he's not fully better yet, don't you?'

Tilly sipped her tea and looked out the window, which revealed an inky blackness. From where the caravan was parked, we could hear, in the distance, the roaring of machinery from the docks. It created a kind of ambient background noise, which was not, actually, unpleasant.

'I know he's not able to walk right, if that's what you mean,' Tilly said at last.

'He's barely talking either, Tilly. He might not ever. Therapists … doctors are working with him every day, but he's still making very slow progress. He might have to go back into hospital for a bit after Christmas. And he'll probably need regular check-ups, maybe for the rest of his life.'

'I know,' Tilly said. 'I know what you're trying to tell me, Shane.'

'Do you, Tilly? Do you really?'

'My Johnny is goin' to be special. A special child.'

I smiled at her, and suddenly felt like crying. It was a cliché, but it was probably the best way to express who Johnny was.

'Yes,' I said, and my voice sounded hoarse. 'He is special.'

That had been the previous day. Tilly's brother, Tom, met us at the door of the trailer, and Johnny's brothers and sisters were gathered in a guard of honour outside, despite the inclement weather. Johnny became visibly more excited as I parked, and refused to accept help from either me or his mother as he struggled out of the low seat and onto the frost-hardened ground. There was silence from the gathered crowd as he tottered uncertainly, balancing his weight between the crutches and his spindly little legs, and then awkwardly climbed the steps into his home. At the top, he turned, a huge, proud grin on his face. Tom led a cheer, and Johnny revelled in the applause. Polly, his smallest sister, overcome with excitement, almost undid all her brother's hard work by knocking him over with a hug.

'All he needs is love, Shane,' Tilly said, standing beside me.

'I wish that were true,' I said, unable to keep the pain from my voice.

'I know what you've been doing for him,' Tilly went on. 'The nurses have told me you've been in there day and night, sitting with him, talking to him. Well, I can take over now.'

'Johnny is going to need a lot of time, and a lot of patience,' I said. 'He might never be able to walk without crutches. And his speech might not come back either.'

'But then, it might,' Tilly said. 'And y'know, it doesn't matter. He'll be home. If he needs a little more love than the others, well we've all got plenty of that to spare. Let's just be thankful he's back with his family. It's goin' to be baby Jesus's birthday. Who knows what might happen?'

Those words would return to haunt me, but that evening we laughed and looked forward to the oncoming season, and life seemed rich and full of hope.

———

I was in the office, just after lunch the following day, catching up on paperwork when the call came from Roberta Plummer.

'Clive's had an episode.'

I paused in pushing a piece of paper into a plastic folder, the phone cradled between my chin and shoulder. 'What kind of episode?'

A pause, then: 'He attacked a nurse and almost killed her. He … he tried to rip her throat out. Scratched her with his nails. Broke her arm. They said he almost tore her cheek off with his teeth.'

I was horrified. How could this have happened? He had been so calm when I'd spoken to him last. The doctors had been discussing sending him home for a couple of days.

'I suppose that qualifies as an episode. What brought it on?'

She was crying now, barely able to speak. 'I don't know. Jesus, Shane, he'd come on so well. I thought he'd be discharged soon.'

I sighed and lit a cigarette. The window of the office I shared with a behaviour management expert called Loretta looked out on an overgrown garden, which Ben insisted be allowed to run wild. It seemed to mirror my mental state as I looked at it now, the trees and shrubs thrashing in the wind. 'Me too. Look, I'll go over and see what we can do, okay?'

This was met with even greater sobbing. 'Okay. Thank you. I'm sorry to ring you in this state.'

'I'll call soon, Roberta.'

———

Clive had been placed in a private room, where, to restrain him, he had been fastened to the bed with leather straps. Dr Fleming had informed me that the boy had been sedated, but the drugs seemed to have had little effect: Clive was fully conscious and raving when we entered. He was struggling with all his might against the shackles, and screaming a hoarse, painful cry. On seeing me he fell silent for a moment, peering through lidded eyes.

I had seen Clive two days before, but the intervening time had much altered him. He looked, to be honest, as if he had received a severe beating. One of his eyes was swollen shut, a long gash ran down his left cheek, and his lips were cracked and damaged. I noticed that two of his front teeth had been knocked out. I looked at Dr Fleming. No one had told me to expect this, and I was shocked and angry.

'You led them to me,' Clive said, suddenly, glowering at me from the bed. 'You tricked me into being your friend, and then you brought them here.'

'Who, Clive?'

I moved to go over to him, but the doctor held me back. 'It'll only make him worse, and he might hurt you. He's deeply distressed and dangerously delusional.'

'The monsters,' Clive said, and then laughed maniacally. 'One of them came, oh yes, he came to me. They'll have me back, he said. They will come and take me to them and that'll be the end of me.'

'No one is taking you anywhere, Clive. Listen to me,' I broke away from Fleming and grabbed the boy's arm tightly. He thrashed even more wildly to get at me, but the straps were too strong. 'I *am* your friend. I haven't spoken about you to anyone but Roberta. I would *never* knowingly allow anyone to hurt you. You have to believe me.'

He leaned forward as far as he could, craning his neck, and hissed in a cracked whisper through his ravaged teeth: '*They dress as men of the cloth, but they are not men, Shane. They walk among mortals, and they prey on the unwitting. You cannot help me …*'

His voice trailed off, and he began to bang his head back against the bed. The mattress and pillow softened the blows, but the force

with which he lashed himself got more and more aggressive. I tried
to stop him, to hold him down, but he bit me as soon as I got close
enough, my thick jacket being the only thing that saved me. I drew
back, and saw that he was crying now uncontrollably. I glanced over,
and Dr Fleming already had a syringe out, filling it from a phial of
clear fluid.

'Hold his arm still,' he said, and moments later Clive was unconscious.

I sank to the floor, my head in my hands. 'Jesus Christ, Doctor.
What the fuck happened? How did he get into that condition?'

'He … he put up quite a struggle, I believe.'

'I've restrained kids who put up quite a struggle, Doctor. None of
them ended up looking like that.'

'The nurse he attacked … he almost killed her. She must have
fought back.'

'No female nurse did that,' I said, forgetting, in my anger, that an
angry and threatened woman can be just as dangerous as a man.

'I don't know! He was in that condition when I arrived on the
ward. He might have done it to himself, God knows he has in the past.'

I stood up feeling exhausted and impotently angry. It was possible
Clive's wounds were self-inflicted, but I had a notion some of the staff
who had come to the rescue of his unfortunate victim may have
gotten a shade over-zealous. I'd seen such things on rare occasions in
the past. Dr Fleming seemed as upset as me at what had happened,
though, so I took a deep breath, and ran my hands through my hair.

'I'm going to file a complaint, Doctor, just to let you know. Come
on, let's get a cup of coffee, and you can tell me just how this whole
shitty mess happened.'

————

The canteen in St Vitus's looked just like one of the wards, except
with wooden tables and plastic chairs instead of beds. The coffee was
weak, and the only thing they had to eat were Marietta biscuits.

There was an old lady, the cleaner I'd seen several times, drinking tea and smoking at the other end of the room. She cast a hurried glance at Fleming and me now and again. I nodded at her, and she quickly looked away. I lit a cigarette and took a long pull.

'Would you mind if I have one of those?' Dr Fleming asked.

I pushed the box over, and he lit one with a shaking hand.

'So, what happened?' I asked when we had smoked in silence for several minutes.

'The simple answer is that I don't really know,' Dr Fleming answered. 'I'd been really pleased with Clive's progress. Taking him out birdwatching was inspired — we've actually started a nature walk programme with some of the acute patients, and it's working really well with a lot of them, too. We'd lowered Clive's medication, and I had planned to begin gradually weaning him off it altogether. Then … this. I'm at something of a loss, really.'

'Where was he when the episode occurred?'

'On the OT ward — Occupational Therapy.'

'The games room.'

'Precisely.'

'Was he with any other patients? Was this nurse — Yvette, didn't you call her — talking to him? Had he been agitated earlier in the day?'

'I'm not sure who was around him earlier, but from what I've been told, Clive was sitting alone when Yvette went up to him to just check if he was alright. He responded by grabbing her and, well, you know the rest.'

'Was there any other nurse in the room at the time?'

'Yes, Claudia Harris was there, too.'

'Where is she now?'

'Still on the OT ward, as far as I know.'

I stood up, stubbing out my cigarette. 'I'll go and have a chat with her.'

Dr Fleming nodded. 'You know the way.'

———

Claudia Harris, dressed in plain clothes, was seated at a desk at the top of the Occupational Therapy room, which had only a smattering of patients, mostly seated on their own at various points about the room, reading magazines. Claudia was writing an incident report. She was around five foot one or two, and muscularly built, with shoulder-length brown hair.

'Yeah, I was here,' she said. 'If I've said it once, I've said it a thousand times, kids of that age should just not be in this place. Is it any wonder he snapped? Poor Yvette. She's going to be scarred, God love her.'

'Is that how it happened? He just lost the head with no warning whatsoever?'

'I'm telling you. He'd been in great form when he came down. I played snap with him, and then he was reading one of those bird books of his, and going through some of the nature magazines we've ordered in for him — he loves those — oh, and he had a visitor.'

'A visitor? Who?'

'I didn't know him, now. Some priest — '

'The chaplain?'

'No, not Father Aodhán, I'd never seen this guy before. He was with Clive for twenty minutes or so, then he was gone. Never said goodbye.'

'And you didn't catch his name?'

'No, I just called him "father", as you do.'

'Has he been in to see Clive before, do you know?'

'Well, you'd have to check with the weekend staff, but he certainly hasn't been in while I've been on shift.'

I nodded. *They dress as men of the cloth,* Clive had said to me. Had the cleric upset him in some way?

'Did Clive seem agitated when the priest was with him?'

'He got a bit quiet alright, but I thought he was just shy.'

'And the attack happened after this visit?'

'Well, almost an hour and a half after it. And he'd been chatting to a few other people in that time.'

I thought for a moment. 'What about the visitor's book? Did he sign that?'

Claudia pushed it over to me across the desk. 'He did, actually.'

I opened the page for that day, and ran my finger down the list of names. There were only three: one was my own, and the other two were women. I read their names out to Claudia, and she confirmed they had indeed been in that morning.

'You must be mistaken.'

'Sure I was standing right here. He wrote something down. Maybe he got the wrong day.'

I checked the pages before and after, but to no avail.

'I'm telling you, he definitely wrote his name,' Claudia said irritably (I was interrupting her report writing now). 'I heard the pen scratching.'

'Okay, chill out. I'll have one more look, then I'll get out of your hair.'

Looking a little more closely, I saw that, other than the three names, something had indeed been written on the page. There, in the margin, was a doodle, something that a person might draw absent-mindedly while talking on the telephone. This, however, seemed to have been sketched with purpose. The picture was small, but had been rendered with an economy of pen strokes, giving the impression that the artist had practised it until the act of drawing it had become second nature — almost like a signature. It was a picture of a goat's head.

Chapter 9 ～

Vera Byrne laughed, a sound that never failed to make me want to cringe.

'So, I said to Helena, I said: "Sure, those children will be home with me before the New Year." She looked like she didn't believe me, but I told her to mark my words. They know where they belong, and the social workers know it too.' She turned to smile smugly at me. 'Isn't that right, Shane?'

I forced a smile. Larry and Francey Byrne, grown several inches in the six months since I'd begun working with them, were seated on either side of their mother in the access room of Dunleavy House, a comfortably decorated sitting room that had been fitted with a camera and sound recording technology to capture all supervised access visits. I had been accompanying the Byrne twins to these visits, initiated at their request, since their father, Malachi, had been imprisoned, and I had come to dread them.

The children were not the only ones to have changed, but with their mother, the aging process seemed to have gone into reverse. Vera looked ten years younger than when I had first met her. Dental work had straightened and whitened her teeth. Her hair, once stringy, constantly thick with grease and speckled with dandruff, was now full-bodied and carefully coiffured. Vera's early, stumbling attempts at make-up had developed into skilled application, which enhanced her visage enough to have caused several male social workers who had come in contact with her to mention to me that they found her quite attractive.

Vera was a consummate actor. She presented as a caring, sensitive parent, working desperately hard to prove to the authorities that she deserved to have her children returned to her care. I was not fooled. I knew that she had horrendously abused Larry and Francey, and had somehow persuaded Malachi to take the blame for everything. Her lumbering husband had been Vera's weapon, and even though I knew prison was causing his reserve to crack, I was aware that he could still be wielded by her, a blunt instrument largely unaware of the damage he was capable of.

'Well, we'll have to wait and see how things develop, Vera,' I said, feigning the friendliness that had become our mask during the access visits.

In truth, there was no love lost between the twins' mother and me. She was in no doubt that I was aware of her true intent, and it galled her. Yet she, in her twisted, tormented way, *was* determined to have the children back. And her force of will was such that she was quite capable of doing it.

Something that bothered me a great deal about these visits was the fact that Vera could distress the twins right under my nose, with a look, a tone of voice or an apparently harmless gesture. It had taken me almost a month to work out why Larry and Francey were often so disturbed after the meetings that they reverted to their old, semi-feral patterns of behaviour: running about on all fours, losing control of their bladder or bowels, and disappearing for hours into the wilderness behind their residential home.

The real problem, of course, was that I couldn't prove what Vera was up to. I tried to make myself hyper-aware during the visits, taking note of each nuance of verbal and physical interaction, but I quickly began to feel as if I was viewing a movie in Japanese without the benefit of subtitles. What was clear was that there was a deep, complex bond between this woman and these two youngsters, dimensions of which would always be hidden from me.

However, I gradually began to pick up subtle changes in tone, followed by one of the twins lapsing into silence with a cowed expression. There would be a flick of the wrist that would make Francey start in alarm, or a word would be used in an odd, out of context manner that caused both of the twins to blanche.

I spoke to Ben about it.

'It's not unusual for children in care to act out after an access visit with their parents,' he told me. We were sitting in the kitchen at 'Last Ditch House', and he was nursing a cup of green tea. 'It's a pretty harsh reminder of what has been taken away from them. I mean, they're brought from their new, residential home, with its team of staff whom they've bonded with, and who are, to all intents and purposes, acting as parents. They're brought to a cold, clinical building where a social worker sits in while they're "visiting" with the person who gave birth to them, who shares their DNA. It's a very cruel, artificial environment, really. Should we really be surprised that Larry and Francey regress a bit afterwards?'

'I suppose not — I just reckon there's something happening that I'm not picking up on. There seems to be a hidden code of communication going on. It's not even body language, it's almost telepathic.'

'Look, you were close to your mother, right?'

'Yeah.'

'Did you ever notice she was in bad form, but, if you really thought about it, couldn't say *how* you knew? It could have been a facial expression, the way she stood, something about her eyes … d'you know what I mean?'

'I think so.'

'What's going on between the children and Vera — and I know you don't like her, so we have to take that into consideration, too — is a perfectly natural thing. It's the kind of telepathy all families share, and it comes from growing up together, living in the same house, having meals at the communal dinner table. Now, throw into the mix the fact that this was a very isolated, introverted family. Larry and Francey weren't seeing any other children, and had no other adult role models. Malachi and Vera didn't associate with anyone outside the home either, so far as we can tell. They had one another. For years, their world was the family and their awful, frightening house. You've formed a very strong relationship with those children, and I can see they're very fond of you. But you'll never have the intensity they share with Vera. How could you?'

Ben had a way of cutting to the core of an issue, and making me look at it from perspectives I might not have seen otherwise. Was I allowing my negative feelings about Vera to colour my interpretation of the access visits? I had supervised countless such meetings throughout my career, and had seen many children respond badly. I had never been so bothered by it before, and usually only attempted to stop the children seeing their parents where there was alcohol or drugs involved: the parents arriving either drunk, stoned or both.

I was of the committed belief that children *should* live with their biological families if at all possible. I had done my level best, over the years, to work with parents in dire circumstances, in attempts to enable them to continue caring for their children. What was different about all those cases, I asked myself, as I sat in my chair, looking out at that entangled, untamed garden. The difference, I finally decided, was that in every other instance, I firmly believed that the parents involved truly loved their children, and ultimately wanted the best for them. No matter which way I turned it over in my head, I could not bring myself to accept that Vera Byrne had anything other than a powerful sense of ownership over Larry and Francey. The twins were part of her estate. She seemed to equate them with the Byrne homestead, in Oldtown. They were part and parcel of her desire to reclaim the glory she believed was once hers. In reality, this sense of importance was utterly misplaced: the Byrne family which Vera had married into was once financially and politically powerful in the city, but had long since fallen on hard times. Vera's biological family, so far as I knew, were from a rural background, with little or no claim to any fame or high status. It seemed that Vera relished the heightened gravitas she felt she had attained on becoming Malachi's wife, and was not going to give it up without a fight.

I arranged a meeting with Ethel Merriman, the Health Service Executive social worker attached to Larry and Francey's case. The office Ethel worked out of was situated in a low, prefabricated building in the grounds of the hospital where Johnny Curran had spent his convalescence, right next to the mortuary. Ms Merriman was probably fifty-five or -six, but looked like she would prefer to be estimated as much younger. Her suit was cut loosely, and I guessed it had probably cost her most of a week's wages. She had ash blonde hair and a grave demeanour: everything she said was invested with deep seriousness and the weight of great authority. I doubted there was much laughter in Ethel Merriman's life. The job can do that to you, if you let it.

The room I was shown into was cramped, with just enough space for a desk and two chairs. The walls were adorned with posters advertising various support services for the sexually abused, or people in financial difficulty, or those addicted to alcohol. Casting my eyes about, I could see nothing that spoke of Ms Merriman's personality.

'I'd like to speak to you about Vera Byrne,' I said, after we had sat down. I was not offered tea or coffee, and my host pointedly checked her watch as I began speaking.

'Yes, Vera. A remarkable woman, wouldn't you say?'

'She is certainly unique,' I acknowledged.

'No, not unique. I have met many women who have recovered after enslavement at the hands of a barbaric partner. Each was remarkable in her own way.'

'I don't doubt it. Would you say that Vera has fully recovered?'

Ethel blinked, as if I had leaned over and tweaked her nose as I asked the question.

'She has transformed herself physically. Her home is a model of cleanliness and good taste. She is attending classes in women's studies and personal development. She arrives at her access visits with the children punctually, and interacts with them in a healthy, respectful manner. She visits her husband sporadically, to carry out specific exercises in emotional detachment, so that she can successfully exorcise his influence from her psyche.' She took a deep breath. 'I would most certainly say she is on the road to a full and well-deserved recovery. What she has already achieved is a testimony to her strength of character.'

'Have you read the case file?'

'I should be insulted by that question.'

'I mean no insult by it.'

'Of course I have read it. Many times, thoroughly.'

'Then you know that the twins have indicated, as has Malachi, in his way, that Vera was actually the instigator of the abuse. A brief meeting with Vera's husband will prove to anyone that he is quite incapable of the depth of premeditated cruelty the twins' disclosures contain.'

'I am aware of the allegations you have made, Mr Dunphy. Your reports are quite creative. Have you ever considered a career in writing?'

'I'll keep it in mind. You see no grain of truth in what you've read?'

'I see only the age-old story of a brave woman being blamed for the faults of a loutish man. Vera had no choice but to act out Malachi Byrne's lurid fantasies, and she fully accepts the damage she was forced to inflict upon her children. She is doing her utmost to mitigate that harm, and I feel strongly the best manner in which the healing could be facilitated would be to return Larry and Francey to her care. I have made a recommendation to the senior social worker that we begin preparing the children for the move.'

I felt all the strength drain from my body. It was what I had feared. I had to struggle to form the next sentence. Haltingly, I said: 'I have been supervising access. The children are regularly hysterical afterwards, and I do not believe that Vera has their best interests at heart. I, frankly, cannot believe you are even contemplating reunification.'

Ethel Merriman leaned forward slightly. Her perfume was heavy in the small room. It smelt expensive, and oddly flirtatious.

'Mr Dunphy, you were asked to consult on this case by residential services. To be honest, I think they were a little premature in calling in an "expert"' — she made inverted commas in the air with her fingers. 'I understand the children were quite challenging at that time, so we'll permit the staff at Rivendell their little indulgence. However, the twins are quite well behaved now, so I really don't see why you need to remain involved. Let me also leave you in no doubt —' she stood up, indicating that our conversation was over, '— I do not care what you think about my decisions. You seem to have chosen your side, and, surprise surprise, you've allied yourself with the husband.'

I remained sitting. I wasn't finished, and Ethel Merriman was not going to bully me, regardless of how tall she made herself. 'I'm on the children's side, Ms Merriman. They're the only ones who count.'

'And yet I know you are visiting that thug of a man in prison for cosy little chats. I've heard you bring him gifts, and have even been seen holding his hand. Are you perhaps a little infatuated?'

I laughed. There was nothing else to do. 'My God, Ethel. You've got me. I'm having a jailhouse romance with Malachi Byrne. I've been baking cakes with files hidden inside, and going home to watch DVDs of "Prisoner Cell Block H" while I cry myself to sleep.'

'You may mock me, but I have my sources. Do you deny you've been seeing him?'

I stood, then, so we were eye-to-eye. I wasn't intimidated, but I was certainly angry, now. 'Think, for a second, about the Byrnes. There are still so many questions unanswered: whole swathes of the children's lives, their family heritage, the pathology that led to their parents behaving in the way they did. Also, Ethel, I've been afraid that some short-sighted pen-pusher will come along and decide to give Vera back custody of the twins, and the only one who can say for definite that she was the brains behind the abuse is Malachi. So, yes, I've been visiting the Shaker, even though it near kills me to do it. I bring him fruit, and comic books, and some clothes, and I've been trying to gain his trust, so that perhaps he'll admit to what actually happened. Unfortunately I've not really been getting any-where, because Vera's "exercises in emotional detachment"' — it was my turn to make inverted commas in the air — 'scare him half to death. He's still under her influence, and as long as he is, I don't think he'll ever talk.'

'A fact that is inconsequential, as he has nothing to say.'

I sighed deeply and shook my head. 'I'll say this final thing, Ethel, then I'm going. Larry and Francey will not survive a reunion with their mother. I have not one single doubt in my mind that she will kill them. Not today or tomorrow. She'll do it slowly, cruelly and sadistically. She's a sick, dangerous woman, and she's taken you in hook, line and sinker.'

I opened the flimsy plastic door of the office, and then looked back at her, sadly. 'I'm going to fight you on this. It pisses me off, if I'm honest, because we should be working together, but I can see that is never going to happen. I'll see you around.'

I walked back to my car through the icy rain and then found that my hands were shaking too much to drive. I sat with the engine running and the heater on, and smoked three cigarettes before I was able to pull out of the car park.

———

I made some pasta, drizzled it with extra virgin olive oil, tossed wild mushrooms, garlic, blue cambozola cheese and roquette through it, and ate in front of the evening news. The world was going to shit, but I didn't need the television to tell me that. So I got my coat, scarf and gloves again, and went to catch the last boat to Salt Island.

Malachi met me with the kind of smile an errant child might give an indulgent uncle. He had some bruising about his right eye, and a partially healed cut on his thinly stubbled head.

'Have you come to visit me Mister?' he asked. 'Oh yeah, you said I could call you Shane.'

'Have you been fighting again, Malachi?' I asked, frowning.

'Yeah. Yeah, I had to hit some fellas that was tryin' to take stuff from my room. I think I hurt one of 'em pretty bad. He fell down and he din' get up again. The men in the hats had to come and carry him away.'

The phrase 'honour among thieves' is an overused one. In prison, small luxuries like books, chocolate or cigarettes are guarded jealously, and pilfered at the earliest opportunity. I could only guess the thieves had made a mistake and gone into the wrong cell, or that they were new inmates, and did not know who they were messing with.

'Did you get put in the hole?' I was referring to solitary confinement, often utilised as a punishment.

'Yeah, they sent me down to that dark room alrigh', but I got real scairt an' I screamed an' screamed 'till they let me out. I din' like it down there so much.'

I shuddered at the very thought. 'I don't blame you. I don't suppose it's a nice place to be at all. Here, I brought you these.'

I handed him the customary plastic bag of colourful comics. I had added a punnet of plums this time. He ripped the net covering without looking, and put one into his mouth whole. He was flicking through the pages of the latest *Beano*, smiling contentedly.

'What age is Dennis the Menace meant to be?' he asked.

'I don't really know. Around nine or ten, I guess.'

He looked up at me, with a huge smile on his porcine face. 'Same as my Larry!'

'That's right. Just like Larry.'

Malachi suddenly spat out the stone from the now devoured plum with such force, it ricocheted off the wall, some ten yards away. Luckily, no one was in the pip's trajectory, because being hit by the projectile would have been tantamount to getting shot.

The giant man took another plum. He seemed to have overcome his distaste of fruit, but I couldn't see any weight loss to speak of. Vera was probably bringing him in a mountain of chocolate on her visits. I made a mental note to ask the warders.

'Malachi, I was talking to the children's social worker today.'

'Were you? Vera says she's a real nice lady.'

'Mmm. Well, she's thinking of placing Larry and Francey back with Vera. She wants the children to go back home.'

Malachi was still engrossed in Dennis and his illustrated hijinx. He nodded as I spoke.

'Do you think that's a good idea, Malachi? Do you think Vera will be nice to the twins if she gets them back?'

Malachi slowly raised his eyes.

'She says … she says she's mad at them for tellin' you 'bout what we done. She tole me she's goin' to teach them how to keep their mouthses shut.'

'And how would she do that? How does Vera teach lessons?'

'Dunno.' A shrug, his voice very small, now.

'Well, would she sit them down and have a little chat? Use a black-board like in class at school?'

'Or how Mr Buttle teaches me my letters!'

'Yeah, like that. D'you think Vera would teach the twins like that?'

Malachi shook his head, and expelled the pip from his mouth. It clattered off the stone wall with a crack.

'How would she do it, Malachi?'

Another shrug, this time accompanied by a grunt. I desperately did not want to put words in the man's mouth — I needed him to say it, to tell me that the lessons Vera yearned to mete out on the children would be nightmarish tortures, agonies she had been concocting during the long, lonely nights she had spent walking the corridors of the Byrne homestead in Oldtown, tracing her old king-dom, checking to see if the work she had ordered was being done to her specifications. I tried again.

'Might she give them presents? And if they do what she wants, she might give them more nice things — maybe a new bike for Larry, rollerblades for Francey; a Playstation ...'

'No, she wouldn' do that.'

'Has she taught them lessons before? Have you seen it?'

A nod. Tears were brimming in his tiny eyes. His lower lip had developed a tremble. I felt like a total bastard for putting him through this, but I had no choice. 'How'd she do it?'

'She ... she hurted them.'

'Badly?'

'She hit them and kept on hittin'. She done bad things on them. Done sex with them, or made me do it. Hard. Till they screamed ...' he had to stop, tears rolling down his jowls, splashing onto the pages of the comics, smearing their garish landscapes.

'Malachi, we can stop this, right now. We can make sure she doesn't get them back.'

'Can we?'

'Yes. I'm going to ask you to do something, and I know it's a hard thing. I'd like to bring a friend of mine here, my boss. I think that if you tell him what you've just told me, we might be able to stop Vera getting the children.'

'That's all? I wouldn' have to tell no one else?'

'You might … remember when you had to go to the courthouse, with the judge?'

'I din' like that so much.'

'I know. But you might have to.'

'And Vera wouldn't know I tole anyone?'

I took a breath.

'She'd have to know, Malachi. I'm sorry . . .'

The table, spilling comics and fruit, hit me broadside and knocked me flat on my back. For a moment I didn't know what had happened, but then I felt rather than saw the table being swept aside, and knew he was coming for me.

Shane, you fucking asshole, I thought to myself. *You pushed too hard.*

I tried to scramble into an upright position, but I wasn't fast enough, and a kick lifted me into the air, knocking all the breath out of me. I landed on my side, hitting my hip painfully on another table as I fell. I tried to bellow for assistance, but I couldn't take enough air in to shout, and I just had to roll into a foetal position and pray someone had noticed. I could hear footsteps as the few other visitors scampered out of the way, and, above that, the whistling of Malachi sucking breath in and out of his misshapen nose. I readied myself for another blow, but it never came. Shouts and thuds added themselves to the ruckus, and, peering carefully up, I saw that three prison officers were attempting to subdue my attacker. Another grabbed me and pulled me bodily through the wreckage to the safety of the waiting room.

'You are one lucky little fucker,' the man said, in a broad Navan accent. 'I've seen him virtually kill lads in a matter of seconds. He obviously didn't want to hurt you, going so gentle.'

I rolled over onto my back, every inch aching. 'Yeah, I'm blessed,' I croaked. 'Someone must be looking down on me.'

'Damn straight.'

The man, who, I noticed, was probably no more than five foot two or three, held out a hand, and pulled me up. Through the reinforced glass, I watched as Malachi, still crying as he fought, was finally brought to his knees with a tazer. I looked away.

'What set him off, hey?' the little prison guard asked.

'I guess I just pushed the wrong buttons,' I said, tapping a cigarette from its pack.

'I'd steer clear of any buttons at all if I were you, lad,' my rescuer said. ''Cause that is one villain you just don't want to get on the wrong side of. He's as thick as a plank of wood, and he just hasn't a clue of the harm he can do. Most kiddie-fiddlers get a divil of a time in here, but he's so scary, the bad boys leave him alone, in the main. An' you know what, if he's left to his own devices, he's not so bad, really. Kind of like a big baby. Hard to believe he done what they say he done, know what I mean?'

'I do,' I said. 'The problem is, I need something that's locked up inside his head. He's the only one that can save some kids from a pretty awful fate.'

The diminutive man slapped me on the back, causing my stomach to scream with such pain, I thought I would vomit. 'Let me give you some advice, lad, free, gratis and for nothing,' he said. 'If you need some info to save these kids, look for it elsewhere. He's got nothin' to give you. You continue tryin' to get into his skull, he'll do for you, sooner or later. He was only toyin' with you this evenin'. Next time 'round, he'll rip your head clean off.'

In the visiting room, Malachi's hands and legs were being fastened with plastic cuffs.

'What if there is no other way?' I asked.

'Then I'd say your kids are rightly screwed,' the warder said brightly, and went in to start righting the furniture.

Chapter 10 ∿

I looked at myself in the bathroom mirror the next morning. I still bore the fading signs of my physical therapy with Katie Rhodes — claw marks etched their message across my forehead. Now I had a patchwork of bruises about my abdomen, and a black, bloodied splotch on my hip. There was also a raised lump on the back of my head, where I had landed on the floor when Malachi pitched the table at me. I felt like I had been chewed up and spat out, and looked about as good.

I showered and drove to the office. I had no meetings scheduled for the morning, and needed some time to get my thoughts together. The prison officer had been right — approaching the Byrne problem through Malachi was as useful as tapping a dry well. There had to be another way.

I poured myself a cup of coffee, took a banana someone had left in the fridge, and went to my desk. I am not particularly well organised at the best of times, and a bundle of files sat precariously on the corner of my workstation. I sat down painfully and pulled them over, opening the filing cabinet behind me with my other hand, immediately regretting having stretched that way. On top of the heap was Katie's case file. I flipped it open, and an hour later was still poring over it, and jotting down notes on a piece of paper. Katie was an enigma, and where I had drawn a blank with Larry and Francey, perhaps I could make some headway with the fierce, dark-haired elf.

The main problem I faced was that Katie presented me with a litany of abuse, both at the hands of her family and others, none of which showed up on her files. This in itself would not normally be problematic, as children often disclose abuse years after the fact. Katie, however, had chalked up years of social work intervention before I had come in contact with her, and made a disclosure of sexual abuse, where she had pointed the finger of blame at Una, the female babysitter. There was no mention of 'Jumbo', and while Katie's parents were recorded as being neglectful, there was no reference to either sexual or physical abuse. It seemed odd, although not impossible, that Katie would name one abuser, while never mentioning the others.

There was also a severe lack of physical evidence. All children are given a medical examination on being placed in care, and the results of Katie's exams (she had been institutionalised three times before her parents died) were all on file. There was nothing out of the ordinary on any of them, although the final medical showed her hymen had been broken, which was certainly indicative of sexual abuse. Yet young girls can sometimes rupture the hymen through strenuous physical activity, so even that was hardly conclusive. There was no bruising that might be the result of beatings, and, while thin, she was not underweight.

Yet Katie presented with unspeakable physical aggression and a deep-rooted abandonment complex. While she no longer played out the 'drunken parent' game every time we met, it still surfaced regularly. She refused to return to the beach when I suggested it, but I had written up the results of her previous visit and they made for grim reading.

The questions I was left with were fairly simple, and echoed Clive Plummer's predicament eerily: was Katie recounting real events, or were these games depictions of disturbed fantasies? The staff at the unit seemed to believe the latter. Dorothy had proposed to me that the onset of adolescence might be the catalyst. Katie, who had spent the bulk of her life in care, had never had the usual male/female role models, and, combined with sexual abuse at the tender age of three, was simply not equipped to deal with such extreme physical and emotional changes. Her confusion and fear had manifested themselves in aggression and dark mental fictions.

Yet I was not convinced by this hypothesis. The stories were too detailed, too urgent. I had enough experience to know that when a story keeps on recurring, it is because the child is trying to tell you something. It should never be written off as a fantasy without first being thoroughly investigated. I had a feeling that these stories may, in fact, be linked to things that had actually happened to her, events buried so deep in her subconscious they could only be disseminated through the veiled medium of play.

I started at the beginning again, and went through each piece of correspondence in the file, each report, and made a note of the names. Finally, I had a list of six different social workers and a couple of childcare workers who had had contact with Katie during her short life. I pulled over the phone, and dialled the first number.

'Can I speak to a social worker called — um — Wanda Holden, please?'

'Wanda doesn't work here any more. She's based in Dublin now, I think.'

'D'you know which office?'

'No, sorry. I heard she'd moved to disability, though.'

And so it went. I spent the rest of the morning tracking down each worker, and asking them if there was anything unusual they could remember about Katie, something that might shed some light on her intense, frightening games. Three social workers were out of the office, but I left messages, asking them to call me back. Of the others, none had anything to add to my existing knowledge, but they all said they'd check back over their records, and if anything occurred to them, they'd get back to me. I was placing the file, and the others in the pile, back in their cabinet, when my telephone rang. Thinking it was one of the voice messages being responded to, I snatched the receiver from its cradle.

'Shane Dunphy, Dunleavy Trust.'

'Shane, it's Gertrude Bassett. I've had enough, the boy is impossible. I'm sorry, but I want him gone.'

I sat back down. 'I don't follow you, Gertrude. Start again.'

'It's simple enough, what I'm saying, Shane. I want you to come out here, and take Patrick away. I'll not have him under my roof for one more day. He's at school now, but when he gets home, I'd like him to be taken someplace else to live.'

I scratched my head. This was a bolt out of the blue. I had never expected that Gertrude would actually end the placement. She'd had Patrick for so long, I assumed she'd ride out the difficulties.

'Why don't I come out and we can talk about this. Let's not be hasty. You're upset. I can organise some respite care, perhaps. You'll regret losing him the moment he's gone.'

'I'm not being hasty. I've thought about it carefully. His clothes and odds and ends are packed, he'll be home at four o'clock.'

The line went dead. She had hung up on me.

'Shit,' I said to the empty office. Everything I attempted seemed to be coming to naught these past couple of weeks. I reached for the phone and dialled a number. 'Marian?'

'How's it goin', Shane?'

'Get your arse back to the office. The Bassett placement has broken down, and you are not leaving this one sitting in my lap.'

'I'm on my way,' she said.

While I waited for Marian to arrive I rang the fostering section of the city's HSE, and found that Gertrude had already called them. An emergency placement had been established for Patrick, and I requested that Marian and I be permitted to be the ones to take him there, and make sure he settled in.

I was furious with Gertrude, but even more so with myself. I had failed the Bassett family, and there was no other way to look at it. Their problems were relatively simple, and I had not given them my full attention, seduced by the more exciting and volatile features of my other cases. It was a weakness I had recognised in myself before, and here it was rearing its head again. This time, however, the results of my complacency were grim indeed. Patrick did not deserve to be cast aside again, and I worried about how he would react to the rejection.

Bethany was another victim. She and Patrick obviously shared a close relationship, relying on one another to keep the history of their existence before fostering alive. I didn't know what this forced separation would do to them.

I couldn't face lunch, so I got some more coffee, and sat in the kitchen smoking until I heard Marian chatting with Mrs Munro, the receptionist.

'Okay,' she said, plonking herself down opposite me and unwrapping a sandwich. 'Tell me all about it.'

I did. She ate and listened, getting up only to get herself some water from the cooler.

'Well, it's a fine mess, at any rate,' she said when I'd finished. 'There's no hope of talking the old dear down, then?'

'Well, I'm sure as hell going to try, and you're going to help me, but I don't rate our chances.'

'Right. There's no point in hanging about. Let's see if we can't save the day.'

As we were going out the door, she stopped. 'I thought I'd left a banana here this morning.'

'Some bollix obviously pinched it,' I said, and, smiling to myself, led her out to the Austin.

———

Gertrude must have been watching from the window, because she had the door open before we were even through the gate.

'I know ye've come out early to try and talk me out of my decision, but I can tell you both, it's a waste of all our time,' she said.

'Gertrude, this is my colleague, Marian Brodbin,' I said. 'She's come to help me move Patrick.'

'I wish we could have met under more pleasant circumstances,' Gertrude said, taking Marian's hand.

'Let's go inside and have a chat, shall we, before Patrick gets here?' Marian said, and Gertrude stepped aside.

Marian sat beside me in the room where I had attempted mediation, gazing out at the bizarre rock garden while Gertrude fussed about, getting tea and Battenberg cake. Finally, we were all seated.

'Would you like to tell us what has happened since the last time I spoke to you?' I asked.

'He got violent with me again,' Gertrude said, actually smiling. 'That's the straw that has broken the camel's back, and I always knew it was going to be. I will not be terrorised in my own house. And he's getting so big now. What if he was to attack little Bethany? I don't think I could protect her. And poor old Percy isn't the man he used to be.'

'Where did he hit you?' I asked.

'I was struck about the chest,' Gertrude said, demurely.

'He punched you in the chest?'

'No, he used a missile.'

'Oh. He threw a rock?'

Head shake.

'A shoe?'

'No.'

'A heavy book?'

'Is it important?'

'I think so.'

'Well, if you must know, he threw an item of clothing.'

'A hurling helmet?'

'Oh, it was a jersey,' Gertrude finally snapped. 'He threw a dirty football jersey at me.'

I had suspected as much.

'And what brought on this outburst?' I asked, feeling my colour starting to rise.

'We were fighting.'

'Over what?'

'It was the usual stuff. I barely remember.'

'Gertrude, I'd like to be able to go over this with Patrick, so he can understand why you are sending him away — you whom he has called "mother" for the past seven years. I think the details are important.'

She paused, searching for a tone of condemnation in my voice. Finding only concern, she decided to continue. 'I was gathering clothes for a wash.'

'Gertrude, can I try to get this straight,' Marian interjected. 'The two of ye were gathering dirty clothes for a wash, and began to argue?'

'Yes.'

'And, in the heat of the moment, Patrick tossed a dirty football jersey at you — was it going into the wash anyway?'

'Yes, I had just asked him for it.'

Marian and I both looked at the woman.

'So you *asked* him to give it to you?' I said, this time the condemnation sticking out like a sore thumb.

'It was the way he threw it.' Gertrude folded her arms and sniffed. 'I know him. It was an act of violence and defiance.'

'Gertrude, what you are proposing to do is a very severe response to what, I have to tell you, is a fairly mundane act of teenage rebellion,' Marian said. 'He might have thrown the jumper with a little too much force, and of course you have more experience with him than we do, but do you think that warrants chucking him out of the house? You call this boy your son, Gertrude. You're his Mum, in every way that counts.'

'I don't know you,' Gertrude retorted. Everything Marian had just said had obviously gone over her head. 'Why did you bring her here, Shane?'

'I thought a fresh eye would be useful,' I answered, honestly. 'At times you and I have become so combative, I thought a new perspective might help. And, if you're dead set on sending Patrick away, it's policy to have two workers on a major move.'

'Well, I can tell you both, I am immovable on this,' Gertrude said. 'I am very firm on this issue. I want him gone. Today.'

Despite the fact that Patrick had lived with Gertrude for seven years, his belongings fitted into one bin liner. My heart sank even further when I saw it.

'Couldn't you loan him a suitcase?' I asked. 'At least let him salvage some pride.'

'I don't have one to spare, at the moment.' Gertrude said sharply. 'Now, he'll be home in a minute, and I want you to meet him at the door to tell him the news.'

I turned and stared at the portly, purple-haired woman. She was a good head shorter than me, and stood, gazing up at me, a look of merriment on her chubby, wrinkled face. The desire to scream and run out of the house was almost overwhelming. 'Are you trying to tell me that Patrick has no idea he is moving this evening?' I asked slowly.

'Well now, I was hardly going to tell him yesterday, and drive him to even worse displays of thuggery, was I?' Gertrude said, looking at Marian as if to say: *he just doesn't get it, does he?*

'Which means Bethany doesn't know either,' I said.

'She'll be as relieved as me and her father,' Gertrude smiled. 'It will be like a weight has been lifted from us all.'

Marian put her hand on my shoulder and squeezed — *keep it together, Shane* — and said, as slowly and clearly as she could: 'Gertrude, this has been Patrick's home — his world, really — since he was seven years old. You are proposing to turn his life upside down, to take him away from everything he has known, and you aren't giving him even a day or two to prepare himself to do it. Can't you see you're being a bit harsh?'

'Harsh?' Gertrude laughed at her. 'He's been harsh with me every day for the past twelve months, so he has. I've lived in fear for my life. No, I don't think I'm being unreasonable. Anyone will tell you I've done my best for that lad. My health has suffered.'

I took a series of deep breaths, and heard a bus pull up outside.

'That'll be them,' Gertrude said, gaily, and pushed me towards the front door.

I heard the children approaching: Bethany's musical laugh and Patrick's voice, its timbre off-kilter — a symptom of the embarrassing process of breaking. I heard their shoes clattering on the doorstep, then the *ding-dong* of the old-fashioned doorbell. I turned the handle, feeling sick to the pit of my stomach.

'We knew you were here, we knew you were here,' Bethany sang as she skipped past me. 'We saw your old car parked up the street, and I said to Patrick: "Shane's come to visit us." Can we go for ice-cream again?'

'No, sweetheart, not today. I'm sorry,' I said as her brother, grinning, shoved past, nearly knocking me aside with his heavy schoolbag.

'Who's this?' Patrick asked, looking at Marian.

'This is my friend, Marian Brodbin. She works with me.'

'Am I getting a girl worker?' Bethany asked.

'You don't need a worker, precious,' Gertrude piped up. 'You're absolutely perfect just the way you are. Shane and this other lady have come to tell Patrick something. You come with me for a moment while they have a talk.'

'But I want to hear what it is. Is it a surprise?'

Still protesting, Bethany was ushered upstairs, leaving the three of us standing in the hallway. Patrick had already spotted the bin liner, and was eyeing it with a clouded look.

'Why is Bunny in that bag?'

I looked, and saw the ears of a stuffed rabbit sticking out the opening of the plastic sack. It seemed so incongruous to me — I had never pictured Patrick with a cuddly toy.

'If she's trying to throw all my stuff out, she can forget about it — Bunny was given to me by my real mother, and I'm keeping it! What else is in there?'

He made to grab the bag, but I got in his way. 'Hold on for a sec, Patrick. She's not putting your things in the bin. Come on, let's sit and talk for a minute.'

I led the boy through to the sitting room, and we sat together on the couch.

'There's no nice way to say this, Patrick, so I'm just going to come right out with it. Gertrude doesn't want you living here any more. Another foster home has been organised, and Marian and I have come over to bring you there.'

Patrick, at first, made no show of emotion at this news. He sat, looking coldly at me, his jaw tight. I was reminded of his body language during the mediation sessions. I got the feeling he was locking down all his systems. If he closed off, he couldn't be hurt.

Marian seemed to be thinking the same thing. 'That's a pretty big bit of news, Patrick. Do you have any questions for us?'

He blinked three times in quick succession. 'Is Bethany staying here?'

'Yes, she is,' I said. 'I promise you, I'll make sure you see her as often as you want.'

'I'm glad she's staying,' he said quietly. 'She loves it, here, and they love her. They couldn't ever really get to like me.'

'That's not true,' I said. 'I think Gertrude loves you very much. She just doesn't know how to handle a teenaged boy, that's all.'

'So where am I going?'

'Just outside the city for a few nights, until we find somewhere else. It's what's called a short-term placement.'

'Will there be other children?'

'No,' Marian answered. 'Just you and an old lady named Prudence. She's been fostering for a long time, and she's had lots of boys your age.'

'We'll make our way there now,' I said. 'Let you get settled in, and then I'll be out tomorrow to see how you're getting on. This'll work, Patrick. I know it seems bleak now, but we'll get through it.'

He nodded.

'Go and get Gertrude and Bethany, will you Marian?'

She nodded and left us.

As she went out the door, Patrick squeezed his eyes tight shut, and tears began to run down his cheeks. He made no sound, his body did not shake. He cried silently and with heartbreaking dignity.

I reached out and gripped his arm. 'That's okay,' I said. 'It's alright to feel bad.'

As soon as the tears came they were gone, and by the time Gertrude and a very subdued Bethany came into the room, he was standing, his pathetic bag of clothes and toys in his hand, ready to go.

'Don't leave,' Bethany said, as soon as she saw him. 'Tell her you'll be good. Say you won't fight with her any more.'

'It wouldn't make any difference, Bethany,' Gertrude said. 'My mind's made up.'

'But … we were supposed to go and see Santa together this week-end,' Bethany said, panic descending on her now, her voice catching. 'We always go and see him, you, me and Patrick. Who'll take him now?'

'He should have thought of that when he was throwing things at me, shouldn't he?' Gertrude said, patting the sobbing child on the head in a useless attempt to comfort her. I suddenly realised I had never seen Gertrude hug either of the children.

Bethany, on the other hand, rushed over to Patrick, and grabbed him tightly. 'Tell her you didn't mean it! You're my brother. You're not supposed to go away. Stay here with me. I don't want you to go.'

'See what you've done, Patrick,' Gertrude said, watching this drama unfold with a wry smile. 'See how you've hurt your sister?'

'That's enough, Gertrude,' I said, my rage barely contained, now. 'Can't you just let them say goodbye?'

'Come along, sweetie.' Gertrude, as she had been doing since the first day we met, pretended I had not said a word. 'Patrick has to go now.'

'Don't cry, little Bethany,' Patrick said, holding his sister fiercely and kissing her forehead. 'I'll see you soon. Shane will look after me, and he'll make sure we see one another. We'll have that ice-cream together.'

Marian had turned away, she was crying too. I knelt down beside Bethany. 'I'll take you to see him, I really will. I promise he'll be safe and looked after, and I'll take him to see Santa too, if he wants to go.'

'He does, don't you Patrick?' Bethany said, looking up at her brother.

'Maybe I'm getting a little bit old for Santa now,' Patrick smiled, wiping tears from her face with his sleeve.

'That's okay,' Bethany said. 'He doesn't mind if you're a bit old. You wrote him a letter, didn't you?'

'I did. We wrote to him together.'

'How will he know where you are to bring you your presents if you don't go and tell him?'

'Maybe I will. Or I could write to him again, couldn't I? It's not too late to get a letter to the North Pole.'

'Yes!' Bethany held onto that hope urgently. 'Write to him as soon as you know where you'll be staying. Promise me. Cross your heart and hope to die.'

'I promise.'

'Cross your heart!'

Patrick pushed her gently away, and made a cross shape across his chest.

'It's time to get going now,' Gertrude could contain herself no longer. I stood up and hugged both children, pressing them together, then gently separated them. Bethany sat down on the couch and continued to cry forlornly. I took the bin liner from Patrick, and with my arm still around him, walked out to the car. Marian followed. Gertrude remained where she was. She never said goodbye.

———

It took us a good hour to reach Hay Cottage, which was situated in a small village north of the city. I put a Top 40 station on the radio, and, to my surprise, Patrick sang along with gusto to the various hits of the day as the houses grew further and further apart, and fields opened on either side of us. I hadn't known at that time that he had any interest in music. But then, I had known him such a short period — there was bound to be a lot I didn't know. Marian seemed to be familiar with most of the songs too, and she joined in with him on the choruses. I was glad she was there — I would have found the drive very difficult had she not been.

Hay Cottage was a long, low building made of red brick with a green slate roof, bedecked with rather sad-looking ivy. A long drive led up to it, and as the Austin wound its way along the tree-lined avenue, I watched in the rear-view mirror as Patrick took in his surroundings. The garden was large and not particularly well-kept, an ancient weeping willow in the centre giving a sense of doom to the place. The whole scene only added to my depression, and I doubted that Patrick felt much better about it.

I parked outside the bungalow, and rang the bell, which was, literally, a bell attached to a piece of rope. Marian and Patrick followed behind me, neither enamoured by the overall atmosphere.

'Well, I hope someone's home,' Marian said, watching the wind blow the dragging, tentacle-like branches of the willow in a kind of zombie-like lurch. I shivered, and rang again.

Slow, shuffling footsteps approached, and the door finally creaked open. A bright-eyed, hunched old woman peered out at us. 'Yes? How can I help you?'

I introduced us all. 'We're here to drop Patrick off with you for a few nights. The HSE has been in touch, haven't they?'

'Oh yes,' the old lady said, smiling up at the three of us. 'He's coming tomorrow.'

I looked at Marian with worry. 'No, he's here now.'

'He can't come now. I have visitors. There's nowhere for him to sleep.'

The wind howled behind us, whistling and screeching across the expanse of garden, and rushing on to the open pastures behind the house. 'Prudence, can we come in please, it's freezing out here,' Marian beseeched, and the old lady nodded, opening the door wide and admitting us.

It became clear to me within minutes of being shown in to Prudence's ornate, lace-bedecked parlour, that this was a placement doomed to almost immediate failure, even if our host had been expecting us. All around were antiques, porcelain dolls of indeterminate age, paintings that looked as if they might have been loaned from a gallery in Venice, and furniture I felt bad sitting on. If Prudence had, indeed, fostered teenaged boys before, I wondered what kind of youngsters they were, and how they had managed to co-exist in any kind of harmony with all this very delicate-looking bric-a-brac.

The entire place smelt of pot-pourri and boiled cabbage. We were given tea and rock buns ('I baked them just this morning'), and while Marian sat and made small-talk, I excused myself and went out to call Ben. I had to wander around the garden for five minutes before I finally found a bar of coverage.

'Ben,' I shouted over the wind and static. 'We've got a problem.'

He didn't waste time, but told me to stay exactly where I was, and that he'd ring back in five minutes. I squatted underneath a rhododendron bush, and smoked a cigarette that I had to keep cupped in my hands to prevent from being blown out. What seemed like an hour later, the phone rang.

'There is only one bed available in the city this evening,' he told me. 'It's in residential.'

'Beggars can't be choosers. Give me the address.'

'Do you know St Callow's Home?'

I froze. This was the residential unit I had been speaking to Devereux about on the boat from Salt Island. They were having a problem with peer abuse.

'I don't think I can send him there, Ben. It's not safe.'

'It's all I've got. There's no choice.'

'I'll ring you back. I need to make another call.'

I dialled Devereux's number.

'Speak.'

'D'you remember St Callow's? We talked about it a couple of weeks ago.'

'Yes.'

'Is that problem still an issue?'

'Why do you want to know?'

'I have a kid who's about to be placed there.'

'I'd advise against it at present, Shane.'

'That's all I need to know.'

'Right.'

He hung up.

I dialled Ben again. 'I can't send him there, Ben. I know there's no place else, but I just can't. He'll be abused. It just isn't an option.'

Silence came down the line, interspersed with bursts of white noise. Then: 'So what are you going to do?'

'There's only one thing to do.'

'What?'

'He'll have to come home with me.'

'Are you serious?'

'I don't see that there's much choice. Gertrude won't have him. Prudence won't have him. St Callow's is a mess, and I will not, in good conscience, send him somewhere I know he'll be raped. I have a spare room. I'm a qualified childcare worker, and I have garda clearance. It seems the most sensible thing, under the circumstances.'

Ben cleared his throat. I could sense the conflict he was going through. 'I'm not asking you to do this, Shane. If you do, it's your own choice. I might agree with you, but we both know it's above and beyond the call of duty. I am telling you there is a bed in res, if you wish to use it.'

'I do not wish to avail of that bed, Ben. Patrick Bassett is coming home with me this evening. I will not be taking him back to Hay Cottage tomorrow. Would you please call Fostering Services, and inform them to start looking for a new placement?'

'Okay. If you need anything at all, call me. Can Marian stay at yours tonight? Safety procedures and all that.'

'I'll ask her.'

'Okay. I'll talk to you later.'

I hung up and walked slowly back to the house.

Marian looked at me, aghast. Patrick was still listening politely to Prudence regaling him with stories of the various children she'd cared for. We stood outside the door to the parlour, speaking quietly.

'Jesus, Shane. It's kind of crossing a line, isn't it? I mean, it's something you just don't do.'

'I bet you've considered taking a client home before, on more than one occasion.'

'Of course I have — we all do, from time to time, but you just deal with the feeling and get on with the job. It's called keeping a professional distance.'

I took Marian's hand. 'I won't place this boy somewhere I have no doubt he'll be molested. I've messed this case up, and he and his sister are the ones suffering for it. I'm not going to aggravate that misery any further by throwing peer abuse into the mix. Do I really have a choice?'

Marian smiled. 'Come on. Let's rescue him from Prudence.'

'Can you crash at my gaffe this evening?'

'I kind of knew that was coming. Yeah. Run me by my flat, and I'll pick up an overnight bag.'

'Thanks.'

'Well, I got you into this. It's the least I can do.'

'It is, really.'

'Shane, don't rub my nose in it.'

'Okay. But in fairness, it is. You said this was an open-and-shut case. Have it wrapped up in no time, you said.'

'Shut up, Shane.'

———

I put Patrick in the spare bedroom. Despite the fact that it was barely 7.30 when we got back to my apartment, he was exhausted by the emotional upheaval. I was shattered too, so I ordered a Chinese takeaway, and when we'd eaten, Patrick said he'd like to go to bed.

I checked in on him fifteen minutes later, and he was almost dozing off, Bunny nestled in beside him.

'You alright, champ?'

He nodded, his eyes half shut.

'This is a nice place,' he said, his voice thick with sleep.

'It keeps the rain off.'

'How long am I staying here?'

'Until we can find somewhere decent for you. A few days, anyway.'

'Can we call Bethany tomorrow?'

'Of course.'

'Night.'

'Night, Patrick.'

Marian was sprawled out on my couch. I got her a beer from the fridge, and put *The Inkspots* on the stereo: *If I didn't care more than words can say; if I didn't care would I feel this way?* I sank into an armchair opposite her.

'I like that music,' she said. 'How's our boy?'

'He's fine.'

'And what's the plan for tomorrow?'

'I'll drop him to school in the morning. Ben's checked, and they have an afterschools programme, so I can pick him up when I'm finished work.'

'You'll catch hell for this from the rest of the team. You know that, don't you?'

'I'll cross that bridge when I come to it.'

'And I'm aware this has all been an elaborate ploy to get me into your lair, but I can't stay here forever. I'll give you tonight, maybe tomorrow, but after that, I'm going home.'

'I know.'

We were quiet for a while, listening to Hoppy and his crew croon.

'I really had no idea this case was going to be such a difficult one,' Marian said, sounding sleepy herself, now.

'I know you didn't. It's okay.'

'If I had, I wouldn't have given it to you.'

'Really?'

'Of course not.' Pause. 'I'd have passed it on to Loretta.'

Chapter 11 ～

Johnny Curran was trying to tell me something. His face was screwed up, and his entire small frame was straining to get the word out. I waited patiently, knowing that trying to second-guess him would only cause the boy to stop trying altogether, but I had to admit, it was painful to watch. Eventually, in frustration, Johnny shook his head, and, in the odd, rolling manner he had come to use, limped over to a cupboard in the trailer, and pulled out a plastic base with a steering wheel and various coloured buttons embedded in it. He lurched back over to me, holding up the toy triumphantly.

'You'd like to play with this?' I asked him.

He nodded vigorously. 'Well, okay then. Where will we go for our drive?'

Johnny dragged himself up onto the seat beside me. His bandages were gone, and while the bone structure in his face was slightly misshapen, the scar-tissue had receded. He placed the steering wheel on his lap, and pantomimed a serious, thinking expression that almost made me guffaw with laughter.

'So, where are we off to?' I asked again. 'I'm not going unless you tell me where.'

'D … d … Dublin,' Johnny managed to say at last.

'Great. Let's go then!'

The little boy turned the big, orange plastic ignition key, and the tinny, electronic sound of a car engine emitted from the toy.

'Hey, don't drive so fast,' I warned, causing him to squeal in mirth.

Johnny laughed a lot. It seemed that, despite his injuries, regardless of the fact that he was physically disabled and was having to grapple with a severe speech impediment, life was just a wonderful thing to him. He approached every moment of each day with unfettered joy.

And it was infectious.

When I was with him, I found myself forgetting the worries and stresses of other cases and simply enjoying his company. I was not alone in this, either. I had noticed a change in the whole Curran family. Of course, their release from the tyranny of domestic violence had been positive for their dynamic, but it was more than that. It was like they were learning to be a unit again, and Johnny was the nucleus about which they were growing and developing.

Tilly spent several hours each day helping him with his walking. The physio had outlined a series of exercises that Johnny needed to go through daily, and his mother never failed to see that he did. I loved to watch this process, as each step was an accomplishment of which Johnny was delightedly proud, each inch of floor space a major battle won. We spent a lot of time cheering and congratulating him, and ourselves. His brothers and sisters treated him with gentle respect, and never failed to reward him with praise at every small victory the days presented them with.

'I think I can see Dublin in the distance, driver,' I said. Johnny was steering with a very serious expression, concentrating for all he was worth on the imaginary motorway we were travelling down. He glanced at me and nodded.

'So, where will we go when we get into Dublin? We're coming to some junctions and flyovers, now, so we should start to think about that.'

'Z … z …zoo.'

'You want to go to the zoo? Well, we need to go around by the park, then.'

Tilly was preparing dinner at the other end of the room, and must have been listening to our game, because suddenly, in a clear, strong voice, she began to sing: 'Mamma's takin' us to the zoo, tomorrow, zoo tomorrow, zoo tomorrow; Mamma's takin' us to the zoo, tomorrow, we're gonna stay all day …'

Johnny and I stopped to listen. Tilly, not noticing we'd gone quiet, continued her song. She sang in the old traveller style, with a clear lilt to her voice and the notes drawn out in a melancholic manner.

On the final chorus, I scooped Johnny up, and danced over to her, singing as we went, and encouraging the child to join in also — he tried his best, emitting a rhythmic chugging sound: 'We're goin' to the zoo, zoo, zoo; how about you, you, you? You can come too, too, too. We're goin' to the zoo, zoo, zoo.'

Johnny howled with laughter at Tilly's obvious embarrassment. She flushed and turned abruptly back to peeling her potatoes. 'I didn't know ye were listening to me,' she said. 'You have me scarlet now.'

'You're really good, Tilly. I didn't know you could sing.'

I put Johnny on my shoulders, and jogged him up and down.

'Oh, we always had music about when I was growing up. Me Mammy is a well-known singer among our people. She plays the banjo, too, you know. I used to love to hear her when I was a lackin. I'd sit on the floor in the evenin's, when the men had gone out lampin', and she'd sing all the old songs. That banjo, with its long neck — I always thought it looked like a part of her. She's got the longest fingers I've ever seen.'

'I'd love to hear her.'

'She's very old now. She doesn't get out much, any more, but she enjoys a session when she gets the chance. My brothers both play the pipes, too.'

'Do they? God, I love the pipes. I'm from Wexford, and we've great pipers there.'

'Didn't Felix and Johnny Doran come from Wexford?'

'Well, they were from Wicklow, I think, but their grandfather, John Cash, was a Wexford man, and he was the first of the really celebrated travelling pipers.'

Tilly stopped peeling for moment, and turned to look at me. 'You know an awful lot about travellers for a settled fella.'

I laughed. It was strange that this conversation had never happened before. I was reminded of the gulf that still existed between Tilly and me.

'I grew up on a big, corporation housing estate. There were lots of travelling families living around and about us — some in houses and some who came and went seasonally in trailers. It was probably the last time that a lot of travellers still moved around the country in that way. It hadn't been made as difficult, back then.'

'It was hard, even when I was young. No one was ever glad to see us coming,' Tilly said.

'Well, the travellers were always a part of my community. I won't say that it was all plain sailing between them and us, but I learned that they were people, just like anyone else. I also picked up on the fact that they had a culture and history that kind of ran parallel to the settled community's, and that they'd been marginalised and given a tough time, over the years. When I started playing music, I always paid attention when I came across travelling musicians. They had a style like no one else I'd heard.'

'You play?'

'A bit.'

'What do you play?'

'This and that. I like traditional stuff.'

She picked up a potato, and continued peeling. Johnny kicked his legs against my chest, to remind me he was there, and I jogged off around the trailer again, singing Tom Paxton's old song: 'Mama's takin' us to the zoo, tomorrow …'

An hour later, I was putting on my coat to leave, when Tilly approached me shyly. The caravan was dense with the smell of cooking, and steam from the potatoes, now boiling on the hob, trickled down the windowpanes.

'Shane, I'd like to ask you something.'

'Shoot.'

'We're having a kind of a party, tonight — sorta to bless the trailer and sorta for Christmas, and sorta 'cause Johnny's doin' so well, now. Me Mammy'll be here, and me brothers, and there'll be some playin'. I was wonderin' if you'd like to come?'

To my great surprise, I was embarrassed. I believed that Tilly, while by no means resenting me in the way she had done before, still only put up with me because she had to. I was so caught up in what was going on for Patrick, that I hadn't noticed her tentative steps towards friendship.

'I'd really love to come, Tilly. But I've got a kid staying with me for a few days, and I wouldn't like to leave him with anyone else, just now.'

'Sure there'll be all my wains here. He'd be very welcome.'

I grinned. 'Well, in that case, I'd be delighted. What time?'

Tilly laughed. 'If you really know anythin' about travellers, you know that there is no time. Come later on, when you feel like it.'

Patrick seemed a bit anxious at the news we'd be going out. I thought it would do him good, though. A party and music session, held in a trailer parked in a layby beside the River Torc, was so alien to any experience he had ever had while living with Gertrude, I figured it would take his mind off his problems, for a few hours at least. In my innocence, I totally forgot about the kind of prejudices he was likely to have picked up, not just living with the Bassetts, but through attending a mainstream Irish school. It was not until we were unloading my instruments from the boot that he finally aired his views.

'Shane, I'm really not sure about this,' he said, eyeing the missile-shaped trailer with genuine distaste.

'Why not? It'll be fun, trust me.'

'But Shane, these people …'

'What about them?'

'They're … well, they're knackers.'

I stopped dead. There it was. I could have kicked myself for not expecting such sentiments, but I had somehow believed, as a child in care from a poor background, that he would be more open-minded. I had to make an effort to stop myself from snapping at him for using that word: *knacker* is like an Irish form of *nigger*. It is a hate word, used to deride members of the travelling community, many of whom make their living trading in horses.

'Patrick, these people are my friends. Please don't use that word around me. And, frankly, show some respect, for others as much as yourself, and don't ever use it again.'

He lowered his eyes, knowing he'd annoyed me. 'I'm sorry, but these are not good friends to have. We shouldn't be here.'

'Why not? What makes them bad people?'

'Jesus, Shane. They're dirty and they rob things and they don't live in houses. You can't trust them.'

I hefted my heavy banjo case from the boot, and put it on the frozen ground. 'All the things you've said are true of many people I have known in the settled community. Now,' I passed my mandocello over to him. 'We have been kindly invited to a party here, and I'm looking forward to it. These people don't even know you, but they're prepared to open their doors to you, too. If you get in there, and still feel this way, we won't stay long. But at least try to enjoy yourself, eh?'

Patrick, looking suitably chastised, nodded, and carrying the cases, we ascended the steps, and I knocked.

The night that followed will be forever etched in my memory as one of those magical evenings that we are granted all too rarely. My arrival seemed to signal the beginning of the music, and before I was even introduced, Tilly's two brothers, who I eventually worked out were called Bill and Tom, began to play a hornpipe, which I knew was called *The Golden Eagle*. The trailer was very hot and crowded, as the six Curran children, Tom's wife and five kids (Bill was fifteen, and not yet married), and Maggie, Tilly's mother, were all present. Bottles of Guinness and cans of cider were available for consumption, but as I was driving I stuck with tea. Crisps, sweets and soft drinks were there for the children. Patrick was very reticent at first, but the sheer exuberance of the gathered youngsters soon won him over, and they chatted, played *Yu-Gi-Oh* and sang along with great gusto.

Maggie Connors was undoubtedly the matriarch of the clan. She was the only one who was formally introduced to me, and she immediately asked me to play her a song. She was a haggard-looking woman, with a huge beak of a nose and a mop of dishwater-coloured hair, her face weather-beaten and lined like a walnut. She had a massive bosom, and her ancient five-string banjo sat perched on her knees precariously, fighting for room.

As a member of the settled community, and a care-worker to boot, I was expected to prove myself. Tilly may have vouched for me, but her mother and brothers would want to make up their own minds.

I took the mandocello from its case, and, once sure I was in tune, played a song I hoped would win their favour, the great traveller love ballad, *One Starry Night:*

> *One starry night, as I lay dreaming*
> *One starry night, as I lay in bed*
> *I dreamed I heard wagon wheels a-turning*
> *When I awoke, my own true love had fled*

Maggie sat and listened respectfully, as did Bill and Tom (the children showed no such grace, and continued to laugh and talk raucously throughout). The song probably dates back to the medieval period, and is a simple tale of lost love, told to the backdrop of the restless travelling lifestyle. I always find it deeply evocative, and can see the protagonist in my mind's eye, a young man, barely out of his teens, desperately searching for his missing sweetheart, roaming the length and breadth of Ireland on a horse-drawn cart, sleeping at night in an old, patched tent, never giving up hope:

> *I've searched the highways, likewise the byways.*
> *I've searched the bo'reens; the camping places too.*
> *I have enquired of all our people*
> *Have they tithe or tidings, or any sign of you?*

Maggie joined in with me on the final verse, her voice deeper and richer than her daughter's. Her fingers when they hit the banjo strings, gnarled and dexterous, reminded me of the branches of the willow in the garden of Prudence's house.

> *I bid farewell, love, to you forever*
> *I may ne'er see you, in this world again*
> *I thought I had your love to cherish*
> *But cailín bán a stóirín, it was only lent.*

We played the last sequence of chords, and the song finished. Maggie looked at me fully for the first time, and nodded.

'You played that well, sir.'

'Thank you. You play very well, too.'

She nodded her assent. 'Let's see how you fare with a few reels.'

Using a thimble, which she had on her thumb, as a plectrum, she began to pick a fast tune, *The Tarbolton*. I put down the mandocello, picked up my guitar, and fell in with a driving, rhythmic backing. Bill joined in with a countermelody on the pipes, and Tom produced a tin whistle.

Traditional tunes are usually played in sets, and *The Tarbolton* is often joined to two other tunes: *The Longford Collector* and *The Sailor's Bonnet*. These three are referred to as 'The Sligo Tunes' by many musicians, after the great fiddle player, Sligoman Michael Coleman, who initially recorded them in America in the early years of the twentieth century. Therefore I was expecting the changes when they came and was able to move from tune to tune easily enough, slipping from the Key of E minor to D and then to G as the reels required it. Maggie noticed my familiarity with the material, and seemed pleased. I had passed another test.

We had just started the second part of *The Longford Collector* when I looked up, and to my surprise saw that Johnny was standing in the centre of the floor dancing. I almost lost my place in the tune, so surprised was I. Bill saw it too, and whooped joyously. 'Go on there, Johnny boy! Show us what you can do.'

Johnny's movements were hardly graceful. They were not by any means the standard steps used by Irish dancers when attempting to express the reel in physical form. In fact, I was more reminded of the young Forrest Gump, from the eponymous movie, dancing to Elvis's *Hound Dog*, than to anything choreographed by Michael Flatley. Yet neither I, nor any of the other witnesses to the strange gyrations, felt moved to laugh. In fact, I can scarcely recall ever seeing anything so marvellous.

The children, delighted at Johnny's decision to get up on the floor, joined in. Some of the girls knew how to step dance, but none of the boys did, and before long we had bodies flying this way and that in a kind of spectacular, chaotic celebration. Maggie led us into *The Sailor's Bonnet* for a fourth run (Irish tunes are played three times, as a rule), to keep the momentum going for the dancing, and then we finished with the customary reel ending of three descending notes, and the children collapsed in a sweaty, exhausted, laughing heap.

'Tilly, sing us a sad one,' Bill called.

Tilly declined, but I guessed that this was expected, because both brothers continued to heckle her until Maggie spoke up decisively: 'Sing about the poor collier.'

Tilly nodded, and a hush fell over the room — even the children remained silent.

Goin' to the Zoo had not done Tilly justice. She sang unaccompanied — sweet and clear and pure, like mountain water. Her shyness was not an act, for she kept her eyes closed throughout, and occasionally I picked up a gentle tremble in her delivery, but it only added to the delicacy of her performance. She took my breath away.

The song Tilly sang seemed oddly appropriate, telling as it did the story of a girl whose husband is taken from her by the violence and brutality of war, and returns changed terribly. The song follows the course of the psychologically and physically ruined man's relationship with his partner: even when he is there, he is not really present. I have a recording of the song by the transcendent Anne Briggs, but had, until that evening, never truly been hit by the emotional resonance of it. I realised, as I listened to Tilly sing, that I had not even considered how much she might miss Gerry, her husband. I had only ever looked at her situation from my own perspective — that she would be glad to see the back of him because of his abusive nature. Yet she had certainly loved him. It would not be so unusual for her to be lonely, to miss his company. I heard the loss, and the longing, in her song, and realised how near-sighted I had been.

As I walked o'er the stubble field, below it runs the seam
I thought of Jimmy hewing there, but it was all a dream.
He hewed the very coals we burn and when the fires lies leeting
To think the lumps was in his hands — it sets my heart a-beating.
So break my heart and then it's o'er; so break my heart my dearie.
Then I'll lie in the cold green ground, for of single life I'm weary.

More jigs and reels followed, and Maggie sang a gorgeous version of *Peggy Gordon*. By a kind of mutual consent, we finished there, as it was late, and the children had school in the morning.

'How 'bout a cup of tea for the road?' Maggie said.

'Yes, Mammy,' Tilly said, and put water on to boil.

'I'm just going out for a smoke,' I said.

I walked a little distance away from the trailer, watching the black, roiling mass of the River Torc rush and tumble past. To my left, cars and trucks thundered to their destinations on the dual carriageway. Above me, stars winked and twinkled.

'Shane!'

'Over here,' I said, and turned to find Tilly wrapping her coat about her. 'What's up?'

'Nothing. I just thought I'd take the air with you for a bit.'

She came over beside me. 'Cold night,' she said, her breath coming out in clouds.

'Beautiful, though,' I added.

The awkward silence I expected to come never descended. Neither of us felt the need to speak. Finally I flicked the butt of my smoke over the railing into the water below.

'Thanks for inviting me and Patrick here tonight,' I said. 'It was a fantastic evening.'

'You're very welcome,' Tilly smiled. 'Thank you for … for staying with us. You've given me and the little ones a chance to start our lives again. I know I made it hard for you, but you never gave up on us.'

A hundred niceties came to mind, but I ignored them.

'It was my pleasure,' I said.

She nodded, and we both watched the Torc stream away into the darkness for a time, comfortable in one another's company at last.

———

The presbytery was a large stone building in the grounds of the city cathedral, within shouting distance of the main shopping area. A skinny secretary showed me into a surprisingly threadbare waiting room, and I sat and waited for almost ten minutes, flicking through back issues of *The Irish Catholic*, and some magazines about the work of missionaries in Africa. Just as I was about to go out to the reception room to make my presence felt again, I heard muffled steps, and a tall, thin, grey-haired man with a priest's collar came in, beaming.

'I'm Eddie Downey,' he said, shaking my hand. 'How can I help you?'

The priest had deep, intelligent eyes, and smelled of pipe-smoke and brandy. He was in his late sixties, possibly older. There were tufts of hair on his cheekbones, where he had not shaved high enough, and the shoulders and collar of his black shirt were dusted with dandruff.

'I'm from the Dunleavy Trust, Father. I've been working with Clive Plummer.'

'Ah yes, young Clive,' Father Downey shook his head, and motioned for me to sit. 'Tragic. A young life ruined.'

'Father, Clive became severely upset after a visit from a priest last Monday morning. No one at the hospital seems to know who the priest was, as he neglected to sign the visitor's book. Clive's father suggested it might have been you — you're a friend of the family, and he thought you might go out and see Clive.'

Father Downey studied me for a time, his bushy brows knitted.

'Yes indeed, I did visit Clive. Was it last Monday …' he considered for a moment. 'Yes, I believe that must have been me. I'm sorry he was upset afterwards. I suppose I reminded him of his poor mother's passing. I was with the family a lot, before the Lord took her. She and I were close. I tried to bring as much comfort as I could.'

'I'd be grateful if you could try and remember anything you and Clive talked about during your visit,' I said. 'He's lapsed into a very confused state, and I'm grasping at straws as to how to bring him back. Did he express any fears to you, anything that sticks in your mind?'

The priest shifted on the sagging couch, his long legs crossed. 'To be honest, I thought him to be in quite a jovial mood.'

'Did you mention his mother?'

'Of course. She and I were close friends. We said a prayer for her, before I left.'

'But he was happy to participate in that?'

'He asked me to pray with him.'

'I'm sorry to have bothered you,' I said. 'I'm exploring every option, you understand. I'm scared we might lose him.'

Father Downey showed me to the door. 'He's bad then?' he asked, as we stood on the step.

'Clive is locked deep inside himself. He's trapped in some kind of nightmare, where all about him are demons and devils, all this horrible imagery. I can't reach him, Father, and I'm out of ideas.'

My companion tutted, gently. 'Yes, he was beginning to become fascinated by the occult, before his dear mother was taken.'

This was something I had not heard before. 'Really?'

'Oh yes. Tarot cards and Viking runes, paganism, crystals … it was a hobby of hers, you see, all that New Age nonsense, and Clive, who was very dedicated to her, became fixated upon it.'

'Roberta never mentioned that to me.'

'Yes, well I imagine it's quite a sensitive subject. I believe Cynthia and her husband felt that these rituals might be able to effect a cure for her cancer where medical science had failed. I tried to warn them that dabbling in such things could have a negative influence, but they were too wrapped up in it all to hear me.'

I thanked him for his time, and went to my car. This was certainly an important discovery, and answered a lot of outstanding questions. There was a logic to what Father Downey had said.

I dialled Roberta's number on my mobile phone.

She admitted that she had no knowledge of Clive having any interest in magic, spiritualism or any other aspect of the occult. But then, she said, she hadn't been around, and teenaged boys did often dabble in that kind of thing for a time. It wouldn't be unusual.

I agreed with her, and drove back to the office. All afternoon, something was niggling at me, and it was almost dinnertime before I worked out what it was. I drove to the Plummer house, and asked

Roberta to let me into Clive's room again. I spent an hour and a half going through his clothes, books and belongings, until I was absolutely certain. The search proved my suspicions to be correct.

Roberta had assured me — and I'd asked her again, to be sure — that not a single thing had been removed from her brother's room since his incarceration. I had now looked in every drawer, on every shelf, between each page of every book, and nowhere did I find one shred of evidence to suggest that Clive had even a passing interest in the occult. There were no Stephen King or James Herbert novels. There was not even so much as an Iron Maiden CD, a DVD of *Buffy the Vampire Slayer* or a poster of the girls from *Charmed*.

Either Clive had a stash of magical paraphernalia hidden somewhere, or Father Edward Downey was lying.

PART THREE

Closing Time

Oh, all the comrades that ever I had, I'm sorry for
their going away.
And all the sweethearts that ever I had, I would wish
them one more day to stay.
But since it falls unto my lot, that I should rise and
you should not —
I'll gently rise, and softly call: 'Good night and joy be
with you all.'

'THE PARTING GLASS', TRADITIONAL IRISH DRINKING
SONG, FROM THE SINGING OF TOMMY MAKEM

Chapter 12 ⌣

I was in a café, having a smoked turkey sandwich with Dijon mustard and a cup of coffee when my phone rang. It was a number I didn't know.

'Hello, is this Shane Dunphy?'

'It is.'

'My name is Thelma Rice. I'm a social worker, based in the Dublin city centre offices.'

'How can I help you, Thelma?'

'Well, it's more how I can help you, actually. I was contacted by a colleague who told me you've been asking about a young girl named Katie Rhodes?'

'Yes. I'm working with her at the moment.'

'She must be in her teens now.'

'She's fourteen. How do you know Katie?'

'Well, it's an odd story, actually, but I think it tallies with these games you told my friend about. You mentioned abandonment scenarios coming out in play.'

'That's right.'

I motioned to a waitress for another cup of coffee.

'I was working on a child protection team some, gosh, it must have been ten years ago now. I was on the duty roster one particular morning — I don't have the files any more, I moved from that post a long time ago, but this story sticks in my memory, so you needn't worry about my getting the details mixed up — and a call came in from a concerned woman in the Dolphin's Barn area.'

In Ireland, the duty social worker is the person who sits at the end of the phone to take calls as they come into the community care office. The duty team, usually two or more staff, will then carry out an initial investigation into these cases to see if they warrant any further intervention, and, if they do, will pass them on to the relevant departments.

'According to the caller,' Thelma continued, 'an elderly man she knew had a very small child living with him, who seemed to have appeared from nowhere, and who was being severely neglected. This woman lived two doors down from the old guy, and maintained that he was a bachelor, with no relatives she was aware of. She regularly saw the child sitting at the window, though she was rarely seen outside the house, and was certainly not being sent to school. The little girl seemed to be wearing the same clothes every day, and was generally being maltreated, she believed.

'Well, I went out to the address at the first opportunity. His name was Alphonso Drake. He was in his early seventies — he refused to tell me *exactly* what age, so he might actually have been older — and he was, he insisted, living alone. The place was pretty dishevelled — old, rickety furniture, window-panes so grubby you could barely see out of them, a kitchen with so much mould it was starting to develop a personality — you've seen it all yourself, I'm sure. I sat and talked for a while, and was actually on the verge of leaving — I was in the hallway, when I spotted it: a child's doll, sitting under a chair. I had him, then, and he called her downstairs.'

'Katie?'

'She was just four years old, a tiny bundle of black hair and attitude. She wouldn't say a word to me, just turned her face into his leg. I asked 'Phonso where he'd got her, and he said she just turned up on his doorstep one day. She'd been living with him for three months at that stage, apparently. She didn't look badly cared for, I must admit. Her clothes were a bit worn, but he said he washed them by hand, and put her in one of his old shirts while they dried, and I can vouch that they weren't hugely dirty. She had to stay in the house when he went to buy food, but he only ever used a little newsagents at the top of the road they lived on, which was also a post office, where he drew his pension, so she was never alone for more than a few minutes.

'I asked him why he'd never called anyone, and he said because he knew they'd take her away. He was lonely, and liked having her around. He seemed to think she was his niece. He was in some way related to the Rhodes', through the mother's side, I think. She called him Uncle, at any rate.'

'My God. What did you do?'

'I couldn't leave her with him, could I? I checked missing persons reports, but she wasn't on any of them. We didn't know where her parents were, and the old geezer couldn't even remember their first names. We put her in res.'

'Did she open up any more when she was there?'

'A little. She finally said her Daddy had thrown her out of the car onto the side of the road, and that she had walked to her uncle's house.'

'At four years old?'

'That's what she said. When she was asked how far she'd walked, all she could say was "a long way". How she even found his house, I'll never know.'

'So, did her parents come looking for her, or what?'

'Nope. We finally tracked them down. They were living in Meath, and when I got hold of the mother and told her we had her daughter in care, she seemed genuinely surprised. Of course, she and the husband completely denied the abandonment allegation. They maintained they'd made an arrangement with 'Phonso to look after Katie for a while. They needed a break, they said, and he liked the company.'

'And she ended up back with them, I suppose?'

'Beds were short, as they always are, and here were a Mum and Dad who seemed to want their child. They attended some parenting classes — what can I say?'

'Any idea why this never showed up in her files?'

'Her parents never lived in Dublin, as far as I know. I'd guess no one ever thought to ask us for any paperwork on Katie.'

'Thelma, you've helped a lot.'

'How's the kid doing? She was an angry little girl, the short time I knew her.'

'Well, nothing much has changed, then.'

'That's what I figured.'

———

Katie was nowhere near as happy as I was to discover this little nugget of information from her past.

'Never happened,' she declared, when I recounted the story.

'You don't remember, huh?'

'No, you're not listening to me: *it never fucking happened.* I would definitely remember somethin' like that.'

We were sitting on beanbags in the playroom. I had the guitar slung across my lap, and was strumming it absently. 'Well, actually, with such an upsetting event, you might well forget it. I've worked with lots of children who had bad things happen in their lives, and their memories sort of walled up those things, so they couldn't hurt them.'

'That's stupid.'

'It's the way our minds work.'

'*I'm* not like that. If somethin' happens to me, I remember it. I can tell you anythin' about my life you want to know. Go on, ask me anythin' y'like.'

'Okay, tell me about your Uncle Alphonso.'

'I just told you, I don't have a motherfuckin' Uncle Alphonso!'

'See, you actually do. So, you can't remember everything.'

'You're a titwanker.'

I didn't respond, just strummed a diminished ninth chord. Katie sulked for a while, pretending not to look at me, but keeping watch out of the corner of her eye.

'What if this Rice Krispie woman is wrong? What if it wasn't me? That could have been some other kid, right?'

'I've asked them to send me copies of all the reports that were made about the little girl and the old man. I think it's unlikely Thelma was wrong, but I suppose she might be mixed up about it. We'll see.'

'I don't want her to be right,' Katie said, after several more minutes of silent sulking.

'I know.'

———

Darth Vader glowered over the prone shape of Luke Skywalker, who was cowering on an outcrop above a dizzying drop, the pastel world of Cloud City falling away beneath him, giving way to oblivion. Luke was nursing the stump of his severed hand, determined to kill himself rather than let this embodiment of evil finish him off. The young man's face was a mask of pain, fear and anger, Vader's helmet and visor, as always, impassive as the apparatus within sucked air in and out of his body.

'Luke,' the voice of James Earl Jones intoned, 'I am your father.'

'Nooo!' Luke screamed, every fibre in his body willing it not to be true.

'No!' Patrick gasped beside me, as one of the greatest cinematic shocks in history cast its spell upon him.

'Didn't see that one coming, did you?' I asked, unable to suppress a smile.

'He can't be. I mean, it's just too twisted.' Patrick, like Luke, was not going to go down without a fight.

'I'm afraid he is, in fact, Luke's dad.'

The remainder of the movie played out, Patrick now in awed silence.

Ben informed me that it looked very like the boy would be with me for a week, and I had made the decision early on that I would not fall into the trap of going into therapeutic overkill. Our time together would be as easygoing and fun as I could make it. Marian had agreed to come over most evenings to help maintain safety, for both of us, but obviously there were times, such as this, when we were alone together.

These occasions I filled with activities I thought Patrick might enjoy, and that I guessed he may not have experienced with

Gertrude and Percy. So, we watched some of my favourite movies (besides the original *Star Wars* trilogy, we managed to take in the *Indiana Jones* films, *The Lost Boys*, *The Goonies*, *Back to the Future* and *Gremlins*), none of which Patrick had encountered before, and all of which he enjoyed unreservedly. I taught him some chords on the guitar, and let him explore my CD and vinyl collection, which was nothing if not eclectic.

The thing that Patrick seemed to enjoy most, however, was a highly mundane activity. Yet he relished every moment, and it became an evening ritual: we cooked together. Initially, the idea of his actually preparing his own food proved a difficult one to get his head around.

It was Patrick's second night with me and, after we had all gotten in and removed our coats, I began to cut vegetables to roast with a chicken. He wandered into the kitchen, looking perplexed.

'What are you doing?'

'Making supper.'

'Oh.'

He watched for a while, apparently confused by the whole process. 'What's that?' he asked, pushing aside carrots, peppers, onions and parsnips to point to a greyish, knobbly-looking root.

'It's called a celeriac,' I said. 'People used them before the potato was brought over from America.'

'Does it taste like a spud?'

'Not really.'

Patrick picked up a piece of this strange new vegetable. 'Can I have a bit?'

'It isn't really good to eat raw. But go ahead, if you want to.'

'No, it's okay.'

I finished cutting all the vegetables into bite-sized chunks, and then put them in a marinade of balsamic vinegar, olive oil, honey and whole-grain mustard.

'What does that stuff do?'

'It partly cooks the veg, so that they take a shorter time when I put them in the oven, but it also tastes good. Think of it as a sauce.'

I made some lemon butter, and began to rub it into the skin of a free-range chicken.

'How long will the food be?' Marian called in from the sitting room, where she was watching *EastEnders*.

'A good hour yet,' I shouted back.

'I'm starving!'

'Have some fruit.'

Muttering something about being in dire need of carbohydrates, Marian stomped past and grabbed an apple from the fruit basket. 'I might not last an hour,' she said testily, and went back to the denizens of Albert Square.

'Why doesn't she cook dinner?' Patrick asked.

'Because I'm a better cook.'

'But she's a girl.'

'So what? The best cooks in the world are men.'

'No they're not!'

'Yes they are. Anyway, I like to cook. What's the problem?'

'It's just … well it's …'

'Sissyish? Girly? Not a very tough, manly thing to do?'

'Yeah.'

I laughed, and put the buttered chicken on a rack in a baking tray, and arranged the vegetables around and under it. I ground some salt and pepper over the whole thing, and scattered some chopped parsley over that, then put it all in the oven.

'I live alone most of the time, right?'

'Okay.'

'I can't eat out all the time — I'm too bushed most evenings when I get in, and I couldn't afford to even if I wanted to.'

'I know.'

'But I like to eat, and I like what I eat to taste good. Now, the best way to ensure that I'm properly fed is to learn to do it for myself. The same goes for other jobs about the apartment. If the dishwasher needs unstacking, or the floor needs to be vacuumed, I don't wait for some girl I know to come in and do it — I just get on with it.'

'Did your Dad cook? Did he teach you?'

'Well, my Dad could kind of cook. One pot stuff. Stews, mostly. We always used to say that, when my Dad cooked, it was always a 50/50 thing. It would either be absolutely one of the best things you ever ate, or completely disgusting. He had a go though, I'll give him that. He wasn't afraid to try.'

'Percy never cooked. Or cleaned the house. I can't remember if my real Dad did or not.'

I put the vegetable peelings in the bin and began to wipe down the worktop. 'D'you want to lay the table?'

Patrick pulled open the cutlery drawer. 'What about your mother? Did she teach you?'

'Oh, she taught me a lot. Not much about cooking, though.'

'No?'

'She was fairly traditional, in that way. I think she probably thought I'd find a wife to do it for me, if I'm honest.'

Patrick began to set places on my small dining table. 'But she didn't mind you working with kids.'

'No. She encouraged me to do that.'

Patrick seemed to ponder that for a while. 'My real Mum and Dad were great.'

'Were they?' I asked, cutting slices from a loaf of white soda bread.

'Oh, yeah. We lived in this beautiful little house, out in the country. There were flowers in the garden, and my Mum kept chickens. We could have an egg for breakfast every day, if we wanted to. My Dad would come home at night, after the show at the circus, where he did motorbike stunts, and sometimes, Mum would let me stay up to wait for him. He'd always bring me home something — a bag of candyfloss, or some popcorn. At the weekends, he'd sit me in front of him on the bike, and take me for drives around the country lanes. Everyone knew him, and people would wave when we went past.'

'That sounds really cool, Patrick. It must have been tough when you were taken into care.'

'My Daddy had an accident, and had to go into hospital. Even the best stuntmen have accidents,' Patrick said. 'Mum couldn't take care of Beth and me, and him at the same time. So they sent us to someone who could look after us, just for a while. That's what fostering means — that they'll be coming to take you back.'

'Yes, sometimes it does.'

'They'd have come too, only Gertrude stopped them.'

I put the bread in the centre of the table, and got a bottle of water from the fridge. 'I'm not sure that's true, Patrick. Foster parents can't stop birth parents taking back their children. It's not the way it works.'

'Well, that's what Gertrude said.'

I didn't labour the point. He wasn't ready to have the fantasy killed just yet.

'You mentioned before that you had another sister.'

'Yeah.'

'I never heard Gertrude mention her, and she doesn't seem to be on your file either.'

'She was only a little baby when we were taken away.'

'And you can't recall her name?'

'No.'

I thought this extremely odd, but decided to change the subject. 'Want to get the guitars, and we'll have a strum before we eat? Annoy the hell out of Marian?'

A grin spread across Patrick's face, and he went out to the cupboard in the hallway where I stored the instruments.

'You're not playin' those things while I'm watchin' my soaps!' Marian shouted as he went past her carrying the two cases.

That was, by and large, how the week passed by. We did the ordinary stuff of living, got to know one another a little bit better, and most of all, we talked.

———

Two days after we'd watched *The Empire Strikes Back*, Patrick and I were jogging along the Torc in the early morning. My gym wouldn't permit children under sixteen into the exercise room, so I had been forced to alter my routine slightly. Patrick was not overweight, but I felt the exercise wouldn't do him any harm, so I managed to persuade him to join me on these early morning runs.

We had reached the halfway point, where we usually turned around to head homewards, when he stopped.

'Stitch?' I asked, opening a bottle of water and handing it to him.

'No. I want to ask you something.'

'Okay. What's up?'

He gulped down some of the water, and leaned his butt against the railings. 'Do you think it would it be easy to find my real Mum and Dad?'

I took the bottle back from him and had some. 'Well, I'd say it'd be easy enough. I mean, they're not hiding, or anything.'

'How would you begin looking for them?'

'You'd begin with whichever social work office dealt with you being fostered to the Bassetts. They'd have your folks' address, for back then at least. From there, you just follow the trail.'

'Will you help me?'

I screwed the lid back on the bottle and leaned against the railing beside him. 'You really want to do this?'

'You know I do.'

'Patrick, have you thought about what it'll be like if you find them, and discover you don't really like them?'

'Don't be stupid. I know what they're like. I remember them, Shane.'

'My brother lives in the house I grew up in. He bought it off my Dad. I'm always amazed, every time I go back there, how small the place looks. When I was a kid, I thought it was a big, big house. My bedroom seemed a huge room. Now, when I see it, I wonder how we all weren't falling over one another. Do you understand what I'm trying to say?

'What you remember is a version of what your life seemed like when you were very young. You're fourteen now, a young man. You've lived a different life, known some tough times since then. You've been through all this crap over the last few days. That's changed you, I've seen it. Your Mum and Dad will be new to you, and you will be to them.'

'I don't care about that. Who have I got, Shane? Who is there left for me?'

I nodded and turned to look at the river. 'What if your Dad never recovered from the accident? Suppose he's paralysed, or brain damaged?'

'Then he'll need me all the more.'

'What about your needs? You're fourteen. You should be trying to dodge your homework, having girlfriends, getting a part-time job so you can buy that snazzy pair of runners you've had your eye on. This is heavy, heavy stuff.'

'I've been dreaming about them for as long as I remember, Shane. I want to see my sister. I want to know what it feels like to be hugged by my mother again, before I go to bed. I want to smell my Dad's aftershave in the mornings, and hear him singing in the bathroom. I want my family back.'

I put my arm around his shoulder. 'Patrick, there are two reasons why your Mum and Dad never came to get you from Gertrude's. Neither one is her fault. Either they didn't want to, or they couldn't. Now, the couldn't might be because your Dad was just too ill, or because Social Services wouldn't let them have you. None of those is good news. Not a one of them.'

'I have to know. Will you help me? I don't have anyone else to ask.'

I squeezed him, and stood up. 'I'll help. Come on, the day's getting old, and I ain't getting any younger.'

Patrick whooped, and took off at a sprint. I had trouble catching up with him.

Chapter 13

The dishes had been cleared away and a fire was burning pleasantly in the hearth. Marian was dozing in one of the armchairs, snoring gently. Patrick was sitting in the other, awake, but with his eyes closed. He was listening to Eric Clapton's original, electric version of *Layla* at full volume through earphones. My young friend had become slightly obsessed with Clapton, and with that song in particular. He had encountered it purely by accident, but had spent every available moment since then listening to, or reading about, his new hero.

We'd been in a music shop in town, getting plectrums and some strings for the old guitar Patrick was learning on (I'd noticed that the ones on it had virtually no resonance left and were hampering his progress) when the famous opening salvo of Slowhand's magnum opus came over the shop's speaker system. I was putting the packet of strings and picks into my bag when I noticed Patrick standing with his mouth hanging open and a blissful expression on his face.

'What is *that*?' he asked, mesmerised.

'The song? It's *Layla*, by Derek and the Dominoes.'

'Derek who?'

'Derek and … it's Eric Clapton with a backing band, basically. He's an English guitarist.'

'He's the man, compadres,' the ponytailed, middle-aged guy behind the counter said, overhearing our conversation. 'You'd want to hear some of his blues stuff, little dude, or his work with The Cream. *Sunshine of Your Love*'ll rock your fucking socks off, man, pardon my French.'

'Come on, Patrick. I want to get to the butcher's before it closes.'

'Can I listen to the rest of this?'

'It's a long song,' I said, checking my watch. 'There's a lengthy solo at the end.'

'Let the kid hang,' ponytail said, playing air guitar earnestly. 'He's in the zone. Listen to the guitar sound, Short Round. Original, American 1956 Fender Stratocaster through Tweed amps; little bit of distortion combined with natural overdrive. Sweet.'

We stood as the first part of the song played out, and the chords of the piano-driven coda resounded around the store. Patrick seemed confused for a moment. 'Is it still the same song?' he asked.

'Yep. This is the solo I was telling you about.'

He listened in further wonder. 'It's — it's not like anything you'd ever hear on the radio.'

'Kid's right,' our companion said. 'No one would have the god-damn guts to release a track like that today.'

'Tom Waits does some pretty left-of-centre stuff,' I said.

'Well,' ponytail conceded, 'yeah, Waits is pretty out there.'

'Leonard Cohen is still coming out with good material.'

'Hey, man, Cohen is a righteous dude, no argument from me.'

'And, of course, Clapton *is* still recording ...'

'Can I please listen to this?' Patrick interrupted.

From then on, Patrick was hooked. I had a few greatest hit collections, as well as *Layla and Other Assorted Love Songs*, and Cream's *Disreali Gears* at home, and dug out some articles in back issues of *Mojo* and *Rolling Stone*. I could understand why someone like Patrick would identify with Clapton's story: the man had been born in a working class area to an unmarried mother, when such a thing was a huge taboo. At nine years of age he found out the woman he thought of as his mother was in fact his grandmother — he had grown up believing his real mother was his sister. His meteoric rise to prominence in the crucible of the blues explosion in London during the 1960s, and his subsequent tortured lurching from one addiction to another as he strove to find some kind of peace, are well documented, as is his impossible, doomed relationship with Patti Boyd Harrison. His fabled guitar duel with her then husband, Beatle George Harrison, is probably an urban myth, but makes for a great story — Patrick insisted on reading it aloud to me, relishing every detail. The tragic, accidental death of Clapton's young son, Conor, and his courageous channelling of that grief into his now legendary *Unplugged* album marked a new phase for the now elder statesman of rock — it all must have seemed so romantic, so exotic, and in many ways, so familiar to Patrick. For a young man who was desperately trying to find his place in the world, there were so many parallels: Eric's quest to find out who he was; his sense that no matter what he achieved, it was never enough; his dependence on drugs, alcohol and women to try and numb the pain that could never go away; his love of the blues, the music that is, more than anything else, the purest expression of hurt and suffering — and of course, for a teenager, the various images of the ultimate guitar hero, looking mean and moody, usually in a sharp suit, a smouldering cigarette stuck into the strings on the neck of his guitar, were irresistible.

I like Clapton, so I didn't mind him playing each of the CDs over and over ('Shane, that guy in the shop was right — *Sunshine of Your Love* really did rock my fucking socks off!' '*Patrick!*'), but eventually, even I lost patience, and handed him a set of earphones so he could enjoy his newfound passion without having to inflict it on the rest of us.

On the night everything fell apart, Patrick was engrossed in his continued study of all things Eric. I was sitting on the couch with my feet up reading John Connolly's *Bad Men* when my mobile phone rang piercingly through the silence. Marian shot awake with a start, swearing loudly, then saw what had disturbed her, and lay back down, muttering darkly about dismantling all my communication technology.

'Yeah,' I said.

'Shane, it's Tilly.' I could hear she was crying, and stood up, going into the kitchen.

'What's wrong? Where are you?'

'I'm at the hospital. There's — there's been an accident, Shane.'

'Who? What happened?'

'It's Johnny. He's in a bad way …'

I heard scuffling, and then Ben was on the line. 'Shane, can you come over here, please?'

'What the fuck happened, Ben? Was it one of Gerry's family?'

'Just come. I'll tell you when you get here.'

'Is Johnny going to be okay?'

'It doesn't look good, Shane. I'll see you shortly.'

I shook Marian awake, and told her there was an emergency, and that I'd have to go out for a bit. I said the same to Patrick, and drove as quickly as was safe to the hospital.

Ben met me at reception. He got us both coffee from a vending machine, and brought me out to a smoking area, which was deserted in the bitterly cold night.

'Johnny, Milly and Benjy were playing outside the caravan, earlier today,' Ben explained. 'Something inane, tig or whatever. As you know, Johnny's gross motor skills have come along in leaps and bounds, so he could run almost as fast as the other children. From what I can gather, they were all having a jolly old time.'

'And?'

'You've seen the railing that is supposed to prevent passersby from falling into the river?'

I felt a pool of ice begin to spread through my guts. 'Yes.'

'As I said,' Ben went on, dragging deeply on his cigarette. 'Johnny can run as fast as the others. His main problem is—'

'—stopping,' I said.

'Yes. Benjy was "it". Johnny was putting up a brave attempt not to get caught, and he apparently managed a really impressive burst of speed. The children say he hit the lower bar on the railing, tried to anchor himself on it, but went head first over. He fell the ten feet into the Torc below.'

'Jesus Christ.'

'My sentiments exactly.'

'How … how did they get him out?'

'Benjy would have jumped in, but Milly had the good sense to run up to the motorway. She managed to flag down a passing motorcyclist. Johnny was nowhere to be seen when they got to the spot, but this man, by an amazing stroke of luck, is a lifeguard, home from Australia for Christmas. He went into the water and eventually managed to find the child and get him to safety. He administered mouth-to-mouth, and Johnny did revive for a time. Sadly, he lapsed back into unconsiousness.'

I had a moment when I felt dizzy, totally disoriented. I held onto the wooden table we were sitting at, and felt Ben's hand on my arm. 'How is he now?' I forced out through the mounting vertigo.

'He's in a coma. The injuries he sustained from Gerry have already weakened him, and the stress caused by this was just too much. He was underwater for around five minutes — the lack of oxygen, you understand. If it hadn't been so cold, he'd be dead, according to the doctors.'

'Where is he?'

Ben told me, and, in a daze, I went to find Johnny. Tilly was sitting beside his bed. She didn't acknowledge me when I came in, and I simply pulled up a chair beside her. Johnny Curran looked impossibly pale. He was attached to more machines and a drip, and I wondered if it might have been better had he been left in hospital altogether. What good had taking him home done?

'He's dyin',' Tilly suddenly said. I had been lost in my own thoughts, and had to ask her to repeat herself. 'He's slippin' away.'

'No,' I said. 'He's sick. But he's a strong kid. He got through the last time. He'll fight this too.'

'He's only a baby,' Tilly said, her voice so quiet I had to strain to hear her. She was in shock, and I wondered if she really knew what she was saying. 'This is too much. I'm his mother. I know. He's far away, now. He doesn't want to come back. He's tired of fighting.'

'Don't say that,' I said, fighting to keep the tears from my voice. 'He'll be out playing again, soon. I just know he will.'

She didn't speak again. We sat and watched the machines whirr and beep, and prayed silently to our own Gods.

———

I left them two hours later. The doctor had told us it was unlikely that there would be any change that night, and that we should go home and get some rest. Tilly simply shook her head, no. I, on the other hand, took the doctor's advice, and told her I'd be back in the morning. I needed to get out of there — I felt bad about it, but the crushing sense of déjà vu was just too much for me. How many hospital beds had I sat beside? How many lives had I watched ebb away?

I couldn't go home yet. My mood was too dark, and I wasn't going to inflict myself on Patrick and Marian, so I put a Seán Tyrrell tape on the car stereo and simply drove. The Austin hummed comfortingly beneath me, the Clareman's rich tenor voice and beautiful mandocello playing soothed my mood, and the mechanical act of steering, changing gears, and braking worked as an anaesthetic.

I drove nowhere in particular. The city streets scrolled past meaninglessly. I simply needed to be in motion. If I kept moving, the sense of dread that I felt hovering just above me would remain where it was, and leave me be.

It was close to eleven when I found myself at the gates of St Vitus's Psychiatric Hospital. I knew that Clive would have been in bed for a couple of hours, but I wanted to walk. The grounds of the hospital were beautiful and would be deserted at this time of night. The gates were always open, to permit the various night staff access at the odd hours they came and went. I went on up the drive and parked in my usual spot.

'Evenin', Mister.'

I must have jumped about ten feet into the air. I spun around from where I was locking the car door, to see an old woman in a cleaner's uniform leaning against the wall, near the front door, stubbing out an unfiltered cigarette. It was the woman I'd seen in the canteen and passed in the corridor a couple of times.

'G'night,' I said, suddenly feeling very embarrassed at even being there.

'It's a late hour for you to be callin'. They're all abed now. Your young fella's out cold. They gives him medicine to help him off to dreamland every night. You won't raise him now.'

'I didn't come to see Clive,' I admitted, going over to the woman and tapping a cigarette out of the pack. I offered one to her, which she accepted with a smile, immediately ripping the filter off in a swift, single movement.

She was probably in her sixties, with a face that had once been very beautiful, and had softened into gentle lines that were perhaps even more attractive. She was still slim, and her arms were corded with visible muscle. This was someone who had done physical labour all her life.

'I'll be honest with you,' I said, lighting both of the smokes with my Zippo. 'I wanted to walk around the grounds for a bit. I like it out here. It's peaceful.'

'Can't sleep, eh?'

'No. I doubt that I'll see much rest tonight.'

'Yeah. I don't sleep too good myself — never have done. That's why I likes the night shift. Oh, I do some day work too — 's how I seen you comin' and goin' — but I likes the nights best.'

'I'm Shane, by the way.'

'Mildred.'

We smoked quietly for a bit.

'It's awful sad about your lad.'

'He's not my son. He's a friend.'

'No matter. It's still sad. It's a bad thing to have a young soul like him in a dark place like this. You'd think after all the scandals and tribunals and whatall that they'd know not to do that no more.'

'Not enough beds, Mildred, or so they tell me.'

'It's a disgrace, is what it is.'

'You've got that right.'

'I seen you talk to the doctors, and they listens to you. How does that be?' she asked me. 'You a doc too?'

'No. I'm kind of like a social worker.'

She looked at me harder than she had before. 'Kind of?'

'Yeah. I'm a childcare worker. Most people don't really understand what that is, so I usually explain it as being like a social worker.'

'I don't have much time for social workers, I has to say.'

'No?'

'I've known a few — nuns most of 'em was, and they had very little likin' for the kids they worked with.'

'It's changed some, but you still get a few who don't like kids much. In general though, most social workers are pretty decent people.'

'Well, Shane, we'll agree to disagree on that one.'

'Okay.'

She stubbed out her cigarette on the wall. I offered her another. 'I should be gettin' back — floors to wax — but sure, I'll not leave you smokin' by yourself.'

'You working here long?' I sparked the flint for her.

'Ten years next month.'

'You must have seen a lot of people come and go.'

'Doctors, nurses, patients, admin staff — oh yes, I sees them all.' She paused for a second. 'And I sees the priests comin' and goin' too.'

I looked at her curiously. 'The priests?'

'Yeah. I know your boy was fierce upset after Father Downey came to see him.'

'You know Eddie Downey?'

'Oh, I knows him alright. I knows him of old.'

I flicked the butt of my cigarette away. It made an orange arc through the dark night air. 'How do you know him?'

Mildred looked all about her, to see if we were alone. Even though there was nobody else around, she seemed unhappy. 'Let's take a biteen of a walk, shall we?'

'Okay.'

We followed the narrow pathway that led to the farmland. 'Do you know what a Magdalene is?' she asked, after we'd covered a hundred yards.

'You mean the women who were in the Magdalene Laundries?'

'Yes. I am — I mean I *was* — a Magdalene.'

Magdalene Asylums were institutions for so-called 'fallen' women — initially prostitutes — but, as their popularity grew, they began to cater for those unfortunate females who had the misfortune to become pregnant outside of wedlock, who were intellectually disabled, or who were simply too attractive for their own good and were in danger of attracting the attentions of the opposite sex.

Once a woman was interned in one of the asylums, she could not leave until a member of her family, or a priest, signed her out. These veritable prisons were operated by different orders of the Roman Catholic Church, most famously the Sisters of Mercy and the Good Shepherd Sisters. The inmates were required to undertake hard, manual labour, most often laundry work, with the result that in Ireland such asylums became known as Magdalene Laundries. It has been estimated that 30,000 women were admitted during the 150-year history of these institutions, the vast majority against their will. The last of these shameful gulags in Ireland closed in September 1996.

'I'm sorry,' I said, unsure what kind of response to give. I had never met a Magdalene before.

'Thank you, my dear. I worked like a mongrel dog for the Sisters of Mercy in the laundry in the city here for twenty-five years. My Daddy used have his way with me, see, if my Mammy said no to him. I told her, and she couldn't bear to look at me no more. The Sisters came and took me, and that was that. I was with them till the laundry closed in ninety-four.'

'Mildred, I can't imagine what you must have been through. I'm struggling to even know what to say.'

She tutted away my consolation. 'I know, Shane. It's awful nice of you to be so upset for me. Don't you be concernin' yourself 'bout it, now. I'm an old woman, and I've not got long left to go. But see, I reckon God owes me a debt. All that was done to me by them old witches was done in his name, so when I goes upstairs, he'd better have the penthouse suite ready for me, or I'll have somethin' to say about it.'

'Well I reckon that's fair enough.'

'I think so. Now, while I was in that laundry, we used get visits from a few priests to hear our confessions and say Mass and such. I has to say, the most of them was not cruel to us. They wasn't really nice either, but they came in, said their prayers and left again. A couple, though, were bad 'uns.'

Branches rustled overhead. There wasn't much of a wind, just a cold breeze, but it was enough to make the trees whisper to us. The stars twinkled through gaps in the foliage like distant eyes.

'Bad how?'

'Shane, I haven't told a living soul what happened in there, and I'm not liable to begin now. I'll take that to my grave. Just accept that these men was devils, and that's all I'm goin' to say about the subject.'

Devils. There was that word again. I wondered if she had used it purposely.

'Father Edward Downey was one of them priests,' Mildred said. 'He was a mean, sly-minded creature then, and I don't believe he's a whole lot different now. When I saw how poor Clive was after he came to see him, I knew.'

'What did you know?'

'That if there's somethin' hauntin' that poor child, Father Downey is somewhere behind it.'

She stopped and turned away from me. I could barely see her through the darkness — could just make out her slender shape in the gloom. I knew that she was reliving her time in the laundry, that discussing it must have brought memories gushing back. I wondered if there was ever a time when it wasn't on her mind, if she experienced any moments of peace. I doubted that she did.

'Believe me, Shane. You must keep that monster away from the child. He'll use him until there's nothing left but a shell full of hurt.' She sighed deeply. 'I have to go back to work now.'

———

My mind was awhirr. I drove more on instinct than anything else. It took me an hour to reach the house, a one-bedroomed cottage set in a small, well-tended garden south of St Vitus's. Ringing the bell roused no response, so I pummelled the door with my fist until a light came on. When it was opened, I rammed hard against the wood with my shoulder, wrenching the chain that prevented my access out of the wall.

'You can't come in here,' the man inside shouted. 'I've already called the police!'

'No you haven't,' I said, eyeing him with distaste. 'You know they won't exactly come rushing to your assistance, and trust me, you don't want to involve them in what I'm here to discuss with you.'

Father Ishmael Green stood in his pyjamas in the hallway, shaking with what could have been anger, but was probably fear. I knew that a man like him must live in constant dread that someone would break in his door in the middle of the night, with a heart full of hate, and revenge. He was lucky that, this time, it was only me. There were plenty of others who would have wanted to do more than talk.

I had known Green most of my life. He was posted in Wexford while I was growing up, and even as a child, long before the sexual abuse scandals in the church had become public knowledge, there were stories about his conduct with altar boys and school children. I had been fortunate enough to never have attracted his attentions, but I discovered later that several boys I knew had fallen into his clutches.

I was not surprised when, while I was still at college, a successful case was brought against him and he served five years for sexually abusing pre-adolescent boys in the school where he was chaplain. On his release from prison I was asked to interview him about his association with a number of other clerics, known associates of his who were suspected of similar misconduct. The authorities hoped, seeing as he'd known me when I was a kid, he'd be more likely to talk. They were wrong.

During the interview he cagily fed me odd titbits of information, nothing substantive enough to have any of the predators conclusively prosecuted, but just the right amount to convince me he did, indeed, possess a wealth of knowledge about the movements of these dangerous men. In fact, I got the strong sense he wanted me to know that he knew, that he had the ability to bring the whole, torrid mess down if he so wished.

Two years after I spoke with him, he left Wexford for good, com-ing to the city in the hopes of losing himself. He had informed the police of his move, as he was on the Sex Offender's Register, and it was a stipulation of his release that he let them know of any change of address. Hence, I had heard of his presence in my locality.

'What do you want, Dunphy?' he asked, as I closed the door.

'The first thing I want is a decent cup of coffee.' I said. 'Do you have the heating on? I'm fucking frozen.'

He pushed open a door to my left. The embers were still glowing in a small fireplace. I fumbled about on the wall inside the door until I found the light switch. 'Go and make the coffee. None of that instant shit, either,' I said. He shuffled off, and while he was busy in the kitchen I built back up the fire. He came in minutes later, carry-ing a tray with a small cafetière on it, some biscuits and a cup of what looked like warm milk.

'So,' he said, sitting down opposite me. I could see he had regained some of his composure. He was satisfied that I wasn't going to give him a hiding, and seemed to have decided to engage in whatever form of psychological games were to follow. 'To what do I owe this rather unpleasant surprise?'

I pushed down the plunger and poured myself a cup. The room was tiny, but decorated with an artistic eye. The carpet was a rich scarlet deep-pile, and a flat-screen TV and home entertainment system dominated one wall, while each of the others had a picture that was certainly not a print in pride of place.

'You haven't poisoned this, by any chance, Ishmael?'

'You do me no credit. I am not a violent man.'

'Violence takes many forms.'

'Have you hauled me from my beauty sleep after midnight to dis-cuss philosophy?'

I cut to the chase. 'Do you know Edward Downey?'

Green smiled. 'We're back to this. I'm disappointed in you.'

'Don't fuck with me, Ishmael. I'm really not in the mood. How much child pornography do you have stashed away in your nice little cottage here? Do you think I couldn't have a very large gang of uniformed cops over here tomorrow, going through all your private stuff? How would you cope with going back inside?'

The smile left his face instantly. 'It's like that, is it?'

'It's very much like that.'

He sipped his milk, and picked up a shortbread biscuit. 'Have one. They're home-made. I'm eating them, so you know they're safe.'

I took one. It was actually very good, as was the coffee. 'Mmm,' I said. 'So — Edward Downey.'

'Yes, I know Eddie.'

'And?'

'What do you want to know?'

'I think you can guess.'

Green laughed heartily. 'Come, now. You didn't think it would be as easy as that, did you? You can call your friends to look for all my toys, have me locked up with beasts and low men again. But will that help you?'

'It'll make me feel a whole lot better.'

'Tsk, tsk. You're a more complex person than that. It might amuse you, but it certainly wouldn't benefit whichever innocent — probably not so innocent any more, I'd guess — you're trying to rescue. So let's not continue to joust. I'm a lonely man, with little to divert me. Tell me the story.'

I skirted the details of Clive's case. I was not going to be drawn into titillating this deviant with graphic details, so I left out the self-injuring, the dead mother and my difficult relationship with Roberta. But I told him of the boy's nightmare visions, of his relapse after Downey's visit, and of my conversation with Mildred. Green listened intently. He was an intensely intelligent man, and his attention was like a physical thing. I felt his focus on me like a foul mist. When I was finished he put his cup on the walnut coffee table that stood between us, and took a wooden humidor from the mantelpiece behind him.

'Can I tempt you with a cigar?'

'No, thank you.'

'Well, this is certainly an interesting little quandary you've got, isn't it?' he asked as he clipped the end off the Havana, and moistened it carefully. 'A thorny set of circumstances, for sure.'

'I don't need you to tell me that. Is Downey a sex offender, Ishmael? Is he likely to have abused my client?'

'It's impossible to say, really, isn't it?'

'I'd bet you can make an educated guess.'

He laughed again, clearly enjoying himself, now. 'An educated guess. That's a good phrase. How far did you go in college, in the end?'

'What's that got to do with anything?'

'Indulge me.'

'I have a Masters degree.'

'In what?'

'Sociology.'

'Karl Marx, Emile Durkheim, that kind of thing?'

'Yes.'

'See? Education. I took a course in sociology while I was in prison. Of course, I don't have a Masters, but I daresay I could hold my own in a discussion.'

'I'm sure you could. Now, back to Downey,'

'He came to visit me, while I was inside. During the period I was studying the social sciences, actually.'

'Were you friends back then?'

'No. I had met him, once or twice, through shared acquaintances. But we weren't close, no.'

'So why the visit?'

'Your little nugget about the Magdalene whores is, I'm afraid, old news. Eddie was being investigated, and that was why he came to talk to me. I think he wanted to look me in the eye, see what prison had done to me. He was, to his credit, exonerated. It's all on record. You won't catch him on that.'

'Shit,' I said. 'You're still not answering my question, though. Do you think this man has sexually abused the boy I'm working with?'

Green puffed on the cigar, blowing a cloud of blue smoke in my direction. 'You say the hallucinations are all rooted in occult imagery — demons, devils and the like?'

'Yes. Downey told me my client was obsessed with the occult, but I can find no evidence to back that up. I think he's lying.'

'I'm going to tell you something, and you can make what you will of it. It means nothing, and of itself is neither illegal nor incriminating.' His eye had a sparkle in it, and I knew he was congratulating himself on how clever he was.

'Go on.'

'Occultism — the kabbalah, the gospels that were not included in the published bible, Celtic spiritualism, pagan rites — these are all fetishes of the good Father Downey. He developed an interest in such things while he was in the seminary, and has continued to pursue studies and research into arcana throughout his ministry. He's been warned against it several times by the bishop, but has defended his activities in the name of ecumenism. He just loves all those fallen idols, you see: Mary Magdalene, the Whore of Babylon — all those sex rites and acts of incest and sodomy in the old testament — he can't get enough of them.'

'What are you saying?'

'I'm just thinking aloud, that's all,' Green smiled, blowing a row of smoke rings toward the ceiling. 'You're coming at the problem from the wrong angle. You see, your boy isn't obsessed with the occult — but Edward Downey is.'

Chapter 14 ～

It was three before I got home, and, despite my fears, I fell onto the couch (Marian had my bed, Patrick the one in the spare room) and knew nothing until my alarm went off at seven.

It was Marian's turn to drop Patrick to school, so I got my gym bag and went to the leisure centre. I spent an hour in the pool and twenty minutes between the sauna and steam room. Feeling considerably better, I picked up some wholemeal muffins and a large coffee and went to the office. Ben was standing chatting to Mrs Munro when I arrived, and grinned at me. 'How're you doing?'

'I'm alright.'

'Good. You ready for our meeting this morning?'

'Meeting?'

'The case review for the Byrnes? You asked me to call it?'

'Oh, that meeting,' I lied sheepishly.

'I'm going to pretend I believe you remembered, and remind you that people will be arriving at eleven o'clock. That gives you two hours to get your shit together.'

'Any change with Johnny Curran?'

'No. They've managed to persuade Tilly to go home, but it wasn't easy. You can head over after lunch, if you've nothing else on. For the moment though, I have to ask you to focus on Larry and Francey. Can you do that?'

'I'm on it.'

'Good.'

'When we've both got some time, remind me to tell you about some other news I picked up last night.'

'We'll chat later. For now, you need to prepare a report that will persuade the gathered professionals that the twins should not, as yet, be handed over to their mother. Who will, of course, be attending the meeting.'

'No pressure, then,' I said, and went into my office.

———

At eleven o'clock, I joined a group of ten people, including Larry and Francey's teacher, workers from Rivendell, the centre where they lived, a child psychologist, and several social workers and psychologists in the conference room. Sitting across from me, glowering, was Ethel Merriman. I smiled sweetly at her. She turned away, pretending to be engrossed in a conversation about guardian *ad litem* arrangements that Ben was having with the senior social worker from our district.

Vera was outside, and would be called in after the professionals met, to be given a jargon-free account of what had been said. She would then be given the opportunity to participate in the decision-making process.

Ben opened the meeting by giving a chronological account of the Byrne case, pointing out, step-by-step, the events that had brought us to this point. This is not usual in a review, but he and I wanted to make sure the details of the twins' story were not glossed over.

He then went to each person in turn, and invited them to give their reports. It was much as I had expected. Larry and Francey were both coming on in leaps and bounds — they were still way behind in school, but were catching up rapidly, and their behaviour in the residential unit was, in the main, exemplary.

'We still see occasional relapses,' Bríd, the manager of Rivendell, stated, 'But they're few and far between.'

I was interested that she made no reference to the fact that such regressions all occurred immediately after access visits with Vera, but I made no comment on it.

The social workers went next, one speaking about the children, one commenting on Malachi, and finally Ethel, who sang Vera's praises.

'Vera Byrne is a woman who deserves our respect and congratu-lations,' she said. 'She has suffered much, but displays a zest for life, and a commitment to learn, grow and develop, both for herself and the good of her children. I believe that Larry and Francey will benefit greatly from being returned to her full-time care at the earliest convenience, and that proper monitoring will show them to be, not only totally safe, but also very happy in this arrangement.'

It was then my turn. I focused on what I knew about Vera from personal experience, how she had told me that her goal was to get the children back because they 'belonged to her' and about what I had seen at access visits. I told the group about the work that was being done on the Byrne homestead in Oldtown, especially the shed where the children had been imprisoned, which had not only been repaired, but reinforced. I ended my presentation with a detailed breakdown of disclosures given by the children, in their own words.

'I submit that this is not only the wrong thing to do,' I said, look-ing at each person around the table in turn, 'but is, in actuality, a reck-less and irresponsible act from a gathering of people whose job it is to protect these children. We have, as a community, failed Larry and Francey from the moment they were born. They were forgotten, left to languish in the most appalling of circumstances, abandoned to endure the most sadistic, premeditated abuse I have encountered in a career spanning more than a decade. The twins have told us, categor-ically, that their mother was not the begrudging, bullied participant in the abuse she has tried to persuade us she was, but that she, in fact, was the real driving force behind their torture. I implore you to give the children's testimony due consideration, and not to be blinded by Vera's performance. Because I assure you, a performance is all it is.'

Meg Utley, the senior social worker, had listened intently to my report. 'That's a very bleak reading of the situation, Shane. What you've said is certainly interesting, and worrying, but can you see that you're asking us to base our decision on conversations you've had with Vera that no one else was privy to, on gut feelings about her intent which you can't substantiate, and disclosures that could be interpreted in any number of ways?'

'I understand your reservations, Meg,' I said, choosing my words carefully. 'But, with respect, I've been the worker on this case with the greatest number of contact hours, with the children and both parents. Surely that puts me in a better position to see what's happening than anyone else.'

'I agree with you, Shane. But we need really solid grounds to deny Vera custody of her children. You've been doing this work for long enough to know, as well as any of us, that our intention, in any child protection case, is to keep the family together if at all possible. Since Malachi was imprisoned, Vera has, from what I can see, behaved in a very reasonable manner. Her husband, on the other hand, has continued his campaign of violence, even though he's behind bars. You've been on the receiving end of it yourself, for God's sake!'

'Malachi is like a two-year-old child in every way other than his size,' I said. 'You cannot hold him responsible for his conduct. As it happens, he has actually expressed remorse for what he did to the twins, which is something I have never heard Vera do in any meaningful way.'

'I take grave exception to that!' Ethel Merriman piped up, her face a deep puce colour. 'I have had many discussions with Vera about the acts she was forced to perpetrate upon her children. She has a sincere sense of regret about the effect these abuses have had on Laurence and Frances. She has articulated her sorrow about this to me many times.'

'Yeah, I think that falls under the category of "conversations that no one else was privy to",' I said. 'The only emotion I've ever encountered from Vera in relation to her role in the children's brutalisation was pure, unadulterated glee, and her only regret is that she was interrupted when the kids were taken into care.'

'I will not stand by while this wonderful woman's character is dragged through the mud in this manner,' Ethel Merriman said, negating what she had just said by standing up.

'Ethel, please sit down,' Ben said gently. 'This is a particularly difficult case, and one where it is natural that feelings will run high. I suggest we all take a short break, and then call Vera in to speak.

Before we have a breather, however, I think we need to seriously consider the evidence on all sides. The fact is, we have a kind of polarised picture of this woman, and that makes me, for one, uncomfortable. Can we really send the children back into her full-time care if there is a shadow of doubt as to her competence?'

'The only doubt is coming from him,' Ethel Merriman spat.

'I have some doubts,' Bríd said.

'I suppose, if I'm honest, so do I,' Meg said.

'As do I,' Ben said. His eyes met mine. I nodded. It was time to play our trump card. 'But,' Ben continued, 'Shane and I have a suggestion.'

———

Vera Byrne was dressed in a dark blue suit, with a skirt cut just above the knee. Her hair had been freshly styled and dyed, and her perfume as she sat next to me was much more expensive, and more subtle, than Ethel Merriman's. I was struck, as I often was, by the force of her personality. There was no sense of the worry and trepidation most people would have experienced had they been in Vera's position. All she radiated was confidence. She believed she was preaching to the converted — it appeared she genuinely thought she'd be walking out of the room when the meeting was over with a pledge that her children would shortly be returned to her tender mercies.

'Thank you for coming today, Mrs Byrne,' Ben said, peering at her over the top of his round, wire-framed glasses.

'You're welcome,' Vera said, her expression neutral, her tone measured. It wasn't the answer any of us were expecting. Vera was, it seemed, playing her cards close to her chest.

'We've all had a chance to share our thoughts on how you, Malachi and the children are doing, and I'd like to just sum that all up for you, now,' Ben continued. 'Then, you can tell me what you think of our conclusions, and maybe give us a sense of your plans for the future, how you feel you're coping on your own, and anything else you'd like to share with us.'

'I've only really got one thing I'd like to share, and it's a question,' Vera said, still deadpan.

'Certainly,' Ben smiled.

'When can I bring my children home?'

Ben's smile never wavered. 'All in good time, Mrs Byrne. Now, Larry and Francey have been performing wonderfully well at school. Larry is reading at the level of a six-year-old, which is a huge improvement ...'

Vera sat impassively through Ben's talk. She never interjected, or asked for anything to be clarified or repeated. It took close to ten minutes, during which Ben's voice was the only thing heard in the room. He didn't try to cushion the negative comments, but asserted clearly the doubts that I had voiced, and that he, Bríd and Meg had echoed. When he was finished, he sat back, removing his glasses. He took a sip of water, and held up a hand, signalling that Vera could now respond. When she didn't, he tried to draw her out.

'Some of that must have been quite difficult to hear.'

Vera shrugged. 'I know what a few of you think of me. It's not news.'

'Well, here is your opportunity to explain to any of us who still harbour some fears for the twins how we are wrong. Would you like to avail of this forum?'

Vera looked about the room, her eyes falling on me last of all. I looked back at her, holding her gaze. 'I've made every effort,' she said, 'to show you all that I am a different woman now. I don't see what else I can do.'

'Could you explain why you've been having work done on your old home, when it has been stipulated that it is no longer fit for habitation?' Meg asked her.

'That is one of the only things I have to leave my children when I'm gone,' Vera answered. 'I have no money, no fancy jewellery or fine books. All I have to pass on is that house. I don't plan to live in it, but I thought, as I saved a few euro here and there, I could begin to have it fixed up.'

'And the shed at the back, where they were locked up — you thought it would be proper to have that repaired?' Meg pressed.

'I'd have imagined having it demolished would have been more appropriate.'

Vera said nothing for a moment. She stared at Meg with a look that was impenetrable. I wondered if she was trying to buy time to make up an answer, or if she was too angry to speak and needed a moment to gather herself.

'I've been reading a lot of books on healing, at the moment,' Vera finally said, and her voice was level and without emotion. Damn, she was good. 'One of the things I have learned is that pretending a bad thing didn't happen is a surefire way of turning it into something huge, and terrible. Hurt breeds and grows in the silence, that's what I've read. You have to face up to it. Have you heard that said before?'

Meg nodded, seemingly fascinated. 'Yes, Vera. I have, indeed.'

'I locked Larry and Francey up there, for days and nights on end, without food or clothes. I beat them and I performed unspeakable carnal acts upon them both. Knocking down that shed will not erase what I, or my husband, did. But it might serve to give those memories even more power.'

Meg nodded. 'Very well,' she said.

'So, when can I have the twins?' Vera said again, turning her focus back on Ben.

'We've gone over that, and I think we all agree that you are making a concerted effort to improve yourself,' Ben said. 'However, as I've said, some of us retain doubts.'

'I —' Vera started to argue, but Ben hushed her immediately.

'—with that in mind, what we have decided is that, before the twins are returned to your care, we would like you to see a therapist. Just for a short series of sessions. I imagine the terrible — er — abuse you experienced at Malachi's hands has left some emotional scars. This will give you the opportunity to explore that. Look on it as some "you" time.'

I was looking directly at Vera when Ben told her this. From where I sat, I could see her in profile. The only sign of the inner rage she must have been feeling was a barely visible tightening of the jaw.

'How short?' Vera asked, through clenched teeth.

'Oh, well I suppose that'll be up to the therapist to decide, but I think it'll be no more than ten sessions or so.'

Vera nodded, slowly. 'I don't have any choice, do I?'

'You always have a choice,' Ben said briskly. 'You can do this, enter into it whole-heartedly, and be reunited with your children having gained some understanding and insight into what happened to you, and what led you there. Or you can refuse to participate, and the children will remain in care until we're satisfied there is no risk in sending them home to you.'

I thought I saw a twitch in Vera's eye, a nervous tic. Sitting so close to her, I could feel the rage boiling inside her, coiling like a wild animal. The unspent energy of it almost had the hair on my arms standing on end. We waited for Vera to answer.

'Of course I'll see your therapist,' she said at last. 'Let me know when you'd like me to start.'

'Ethel will get back to you with dates, the address, that sort of thing,' Ben said, making a note in his diary. 'Well, I think we're finished here.'

———

When the last person had gone, Ben and I sat, looking across at one another.

'That was a fine idea of yours,' Ben said. 'Very crafty, but a damn good plan.'

'Thank a very short, rather cynical prison officer,' I said, balancing my chair on its back legs.

'I don't think we can stretch the therapy out indefinitely. Ten, maybe twelve sittings will be as much as she'll tolerate.'

'I'm banking on her not getting anywhere near that amount,' I said. 'She's too proud. She'll snap. Can you imagine her lying on the couch and allowing some upstart shrink to ask prying, personal questions about her childhood? She'll flip. I give her three weeks. Maybe less.'

'You know,' Ben said, 'it's possible we've just done her the biggest favour of her life. She might just benefit hugely. Could put her on the road to recovery.'

'Ben, I wish I could say I'd like that to happen.'

'Just pray we haven't underestimated her,' Ben said, standing up and gathering his notes. 'She could just run rings around the poor therapist and come out crazier than she went in.'

Chapter 15 ༕

If Katie's family were living in Meath when she had been found in
Dolphin's Barn with Alphonso Drake, then there were only a
couple of routes they could have taken on the way into Dublin. I
figured it would be unlikely they'd use only back roads, so I spent a
few days, with Katie beside me, travelling the highways and byways
in an attempt to see if any of the landscapes might jog the girl's
memory: could we find the spot where she had been abandoned?

The idea came to me during the case review with Vera, actually.
Her speech about hurt 'breeding in the silence' had impressed me, in
a perverse kind of way. Katie seemed to have very effectively
repressed all memories of any time with her uncle. I reasoned that,
by confronting it head on, we might find the key to her anger and
resentment.

The problem, however, was that nothing seemed to ring any bells.
We approached Ireland's capital city using the obvious route, past
the Blanchardstown Shopping Centre and via the Red Cow roundabout. Katie simply seemed bored. 'Can we get something to eat?'
she asked as I surreptitiously watched her in my peripheral vision,
waiting for her to break down, or at the very least shout 'Eureka'.

I then tried a more circuitous path, coming through Athboy and
taking the winding country roads through Sallins, coming out onto
the Naas dual carriageway. Katie sat back in the comfortable seat of
my Austin, listening to Gerry Ryan discuss the hygiene conditions of
some of his callers' automobiles.

'You keep this car really clean, actually,' Katie commented. 'Even
if it is an old piece of shite.'

'Thanks. I appreciate the vote of confidence,' I said.

'You're welcome,' Katie said, rolling down the window. 'I just
farted, by the way.'

It was three days later that I identified the gaping hole in my plan. I was sitting in the kitchen, with Dorothy and a new member of staff at the unit, Tina. Tina had just returned from a holiday in Turkey. Regardless of the fact that she had been on the job for less than a week, the lady seemed to think it pertinent to bring in the vast collection of photographs she had taken while on vacation. Dorothy and I spent an hour and a half, which felt much longer, viewing various snaps of Tina and her middle-aged friends reclining on the beach, drinking vulgar-looking cocktails in a variety of (mostly Irish) bars, and draped around a selection of swarthily handsome, and considerably younger, men. We 'ooed' and 'aahed' in all the right places, and were reaching the blissful end of the process when Katie wandered into the room.

'Watcha doin'?' she asked, sitting on the edge of the table.

'We're looking at some pictures of Tina's holidays,' Dorothy said, trying to hide the pain in her voice and the look of abject boredom that was fighting to erupt on her face.

Seeing an opportunity to escape, I piped up: 'Have you ever been on holiday, Katie?'

'Ah yeah, with some of the other units I was in. We went to Courtown a few times.'

A thought suddenly occurred to me. 'Did you go away when you were at home?'

She thought for a moment, then nodded. 'Yeah. We went to Courtown as well, actually. Popular holiday destination, Courtown.'

That was it. I excused myself, and rang Thelma Rice.

'Thelma, I need you to think — what time of year was it when you got that call to go out to Dolphin's Barn?'

'It was the summer,' Thelma said, immediately. 'Either late July or early August.'

Of course. It made perfect sense. How many parents, on long drives with small children in the back seat, have imagined stopping the car and dumping their noisy, whining brats on the roadside, then pulling away from the kerb, immersed in blissful silence? It's a common fantasy, and one that, usually, remains just that — in the realms of make-believe. Had Katie's father acted upon his cruel impulse, actually ejecting his four-year-old daughter from the car, leaving her miles from home?

The problem was that the Dublin-to-Wexford road had changed dramatically in the ten years since Katie's alleged abandonment. There was now a motorway, which had not existed back then, a series of flyovers and several roundabouts that would make the approach to Dublin much less familiar than I would have liked. I decided to give it a go anyway.

I made a mix-tape of songs and pieces of music I knew Katie liked, and told her we were taking a trip. The approaches from Meath had taken less time — none more than an hour, and I had sneaked them in by taking her to see the Hill of Tara, or going to Bettystown, then home through Dublin. The N11 was off the beaten track. The dark-haired girl shrugged, however, and took her coat. 'It's not like I'm doin' much else,' she said.

During our extended drives, I had come up with a game to keep us from getting too bored. It was based on something my sister used to play on long journeys when we were kids, and was all about observation. The game had three different levels: the first stage involved each person looking for red cars. You had to shout out 'red car' before your competitor did when you spotted one, and, if you got in first, you were given a point. The goal at this juncture was to reach a score of twenty red cars. You then went on to phase two. In this part of the contest, you had to spot red cars with yellow registration plates, the cry here being 'red car yellow reg'. These were, of course, much less common, so you only had to observe five of them. The final section involved spotting one yellow car — which is harder than you think. The game could easily take more than an hour to complete, and I was amazed to find that Katie quite readily stuck with it, and became extremely proficient. In fact, her devotion far outstripped mine, and there were many occasions when I wished I had never conceived of the diversion.

The N11 dual carriageway segues onto the M50 motorway just after the Bray flyover. I didn't think there was much chance Katie had been left on the roadside anywhere before this point — she would simply never have been able to make it into the city from anywhere further away than that.

A decade earlier the road would have run past the Cornelscourt shopping centre, and then on past Donnybrook. Katie's father would have had to go into the city centre, and then go on through Phibsboro to link onto the M50 and from there take the road to Meath. Now, there are three routes a driver can take: one that goes to Montrose and from there into the city; one onto the M50 and then to Belfast; and one which goes to Dun Laoghaire and the coast. I took the first exit to the left, and then the second off the roundabout, which led towards the city.

'Red car yellow reg!' Katie bellowed.

'Where?' I had been concentrating on navigating, and hadn't really been looking out for our targets.

'There — quick, or you'll miss it!'

I saw the rear end of a red Fiesta, which did indeed have a yellow registration. 'Okay, that puts you on two in this round.'

'Yeah, and you don't even have twenty red cars yet.'

'You're the champ, Katie.'

'I know. I'm so great.'

'Right then, I'm back in the game now, and I bet you a bar of chocolate at the next petrol station that I'll be even with you within the next ten minutes.'

'No way! You're on. And I'd like a Mint Aero, please.'

'You can buy me a Yorkie, when I win.'

'I don't have any money.'

'Yes you do!'

'No I … hang on a minute — I know this place.'

Cornelscourt shopping centre loomed on our left. 'Stop the car,' Katie said suddenly. I signalled and pulled over. The child flung open the door and was out on the roadside, running, almost before the car came to a stop. I switched on my hazard lights, and went after her. She stopped a hundred yards from where I parked, her head lowered, her breathing harsh.

'What is it, Katie? Tell me what's wrong?' I remained well back, giving her space.

'Why did you bring me here?' she asked, her back to me. There was no anger in her voice, just resignation.

'You asked me to stop.'

She squatted down, resting her hands on the grass verge. 'Here,' she said in a rasp. 'It was right here.'

'What? What happened here?'

'I was only small. Just a little girl.' She stood up again, and paced up and down. 'I'd been bold on the trip up from Wexford. I wanted to go to the toilet and he wouldn't stop, so I wet myself. He got real mad, 'cause I'd pissed all over the seat of the car. He shouted at me, and I started to cry. He said to me: "If you don't stop roarin', I'm goin' t' come in back and give you somethin' to really cry about." So I stopped. Only, it was hard not to cry, 'cause I felt rotten. I was embarrassed I'd pissed myself, and I was all wet and it smelt bad. I began to feel sick.'

She sat down all of a sudden, as if her legs would not hold her up any more.

'I told him. I said: "Daddy, I'm gonna be sick." Her voice took on the timbre of the four-year-old. It was eerie to hear. "Fuckin' hell," he said, and he stopped the car, right over there.' She pointed to a spot a little behind where the Austin stood idle. 'I opened the door, and sort of fell out onto the grass. I scratched my knee, and it hurt, but I crawled, right to here, and I puked. I remember I'd had cornflakes for breakfast, and they were in it, and some spaghetti hoops I had for dinner the night before. Isn't it funny that I remember that?'

I nodded.

'While I was pukin' I heard the car revving. I couldn't look up, or move, because I didn't want to get sick all over myself. I was already stinkin' of wee. I think I heard him shoutin' at me, but I'm not certain about that. Then, when I was sure that I wasn't goin' to get sick again, I looked up. But the car wasn't where it had been. It was far away, off up the road. I — I didn't understand what had happened. I thought he was playin' a trick on me, and I remember that I stood up, and I

ran after him —' she struggled to stand, and began to lope awkwardly in the direction of the city, an almost exact approximation of
a clumsy, four-year-old's run. 'Daddy! Daddy! I'm okay now, I feel
better. I'm sorry ...' She stopped. 'Don't leave me here, Daddy. Please
come back.' Then the tears came. I had only ever seen her cry noise-
lessly before. This, however, was not quiet. The abandoned child had
returned, had possessed her, and all the panic, the anguish and loss
fell upon her with savage ferocity. She screamed, beat the earth and
turned around in frantic circles. I remained where I was, not
wanting to crowd her or confuse her with my presence, until I sensed
she was about to lose any last vestige of control. Her eyes had
become wide and staring, and I was worried she would turn the
mania upon herself. I stood up and went to her swiftly, wrapping my
arms around her slim frame. She fought against me at first, then
looked up, her thin face tear-streaked and twisted in misery. 'Help
me,' she whispered. 'Oh God, help me, Shane.'

　'I'm right here,' I said, holding her tightly. 'I won't leave you, Katie.
I won't leave you alone.'

———

Cornelscourt is slightly more than eight miles from Dolphin's Barn.
The following day I parked in the shopping centre and hiked the
route that, ten years earlier, a terrified little girl had been forced to
traverse. I was thirty years old, and exercised regularly, but when I
finally arrived in that fine old area of Dublin, I knew I'd been for a
long walk.

　How Katie did it, how long it took her, and how she remembered
that she had a relative in the city, not to mention managed to find
his house, I never discovered. Dorothy suggested that she must have
got it wrong, that her father had to have left her nearer to Alphonso's
home. Ben wondered if the Rhodes family might actually have been
regular visitors to the old man in those days, and that it was the
obvious place for Katie to go. 'Children are remarkably resilient,' he

reminded me. 'Her subconscious would have kicked in, acted kind of like a homing instinct.'

I decided it wasn't important. The truth was she had been forsaken by her father. Katie had good reason to be as incensed at the world as she was. It had treated her with callous disregard.

I can only imagine the torment that child went through during that lonely march, the road stretching before her like an endless track to nowhere, cars zooming past full of uncaring faces, the sense of disorientation a constant companion. I have thought of it often, tried to put myself in her place, but I can't. It is just too far beyond my own formative experiences to comprehend. Katie chose, in the peculiar, common-sense way children have, not to dwell on the awful memory. While she made reference to it in subsequent conversations, she never directly discussed it ever again. It was as if that part of her life had been unearthed, examined and could now be reinterred, to rest in peace.

————

An ideal placement was found for Patrick, and a week and two days after he had come to stay with me he moved to an experienced foster family, who were happy to have him over the long term, if necessary. I continued to see the boy as often as I could, and, to my chagrin, the subject of his birth family was a regular topic of conversation.

I hedged around the subject, trying to buy myself some time. The truth was, Patrick's family had proved ridiculously easy to find. Like so many poor families, they never strayed far from where they had always lived, in a block of local authority flats near the Haroldstown area of the city. I knew this part of town well — it was gangland, an urban wasteland beset with drugs, prostitution and hopelessness. Patrick's description of living 'out in the country' must have stemmed from the number of horses that could be found in proliferation about the flats and estates, and from the huge amount of disused waste and scrubland. Even in this era of the Celtic Tiger, places like

Haroldstown languished in a state of torpor. No one, not even the government, wanted to invest in them. Houses and flats sat for years in states of neglect, windows boarded up, with squatters and homeless people using them as toilets and places to shoot up heroin or drink flagons of cheap cider.

Patrick had, during his time with Gertrude and Percy, become so far removed from this type of life, was so alien to it, I wondered if anything positive could come from bringing him back there.

One evening he was over at my apartment. Christmas being just around the corner, we were baking mince pies, while listening to Phil Spector. I had made short-crust pastry, and Patrick was rolling it out.

'Why do they call that stuff mince-meat?' Patrick asked, motioning at the jar of fruit, spices and liquor.

I was mixing an egg wash. 'They actually used to put minced beef into it. I have a recipe for pies that includes real meat, but I'm afraid I'm not a brave enough gourmet to try it.'

'It might be interesting,' Patrick said, setting aside the rolling pin and beginning to grease the pie tin without having to be asked.

'I'll tell you what, I'll dig out the book, and we can give it a shot. But *you're* trying one of the pies first — deal?'

'Hold on, now,' Patrick said, laughing. 'I might have to think about that one.'

We worked on in companionable silence.

'I've found your folks,' I said, at last.

He walked over to the table and ripped off some kitchen towel to wipe the butter from his fingers. 'Where are they?'

'In the city. About a twenty-minute drive from here.'

'You're joking.'

'No. They were never anywhere else, from what I can gather. They're still in the same place as when you lived with them.'

'That cottage?'

I cleared my throat. 'No. They live in a block of flats, Patrick.'

'Are you sure?'

'Yes. I'm certain.'

The boy came back over to the counter and began to use a pastry cutter to make bases for the pies. 'When can I go and meet them?'

'I can take you tomorrow.'

'Excellent! Thanks a million, Shane. This is like the best Christmas present ever!'

'Don't thank me yet, Patrick. I want you to think about the reality of what you're proposing to do. We could find that they are exactly as you recall, and you and them will begin to rebuild your relationship, and it'll be great. On the other hand, it might be very different from what you expect. You have some lovely memories of your home, of your Mum and Dad, and your baby sister. Do you want to risk losing all of those wonderful recollections? You could just keep on living with them, and be content.'

Patrick finished putting the round pieces of pastry into their individual cases, and pulled over the jar of mincemeat. 'I've thought about very little else since we decided to find them, Shane. I really want to do it.'

'Okay. Then you need to understand something, and it's not an easy thing to accept.'

'I can take it.'

'I know you can. But it's not a pleasant thing to hear. Your father and mother signed what's called a Voluntary Care Order, which means they made a decision to put you and Bethany in the care of the state. That Order is still good, Patrick. It's on your file — I checked. That means that they could have come and taken you at any time, and, for whatever reason, didn't.'

Patrick nodded, still adjusting the filling in the pies. I took a second ball of pastry from the fridge, unwrapped the clingfilm it was in, and began to roll it out, to make the lids for the pies.

'Now, I'd like you to understand that, no matter what, signing an Order like that is never easy for parents. Sometimes, it's the greatest gift they can give their children, but it always, *always* hurts them to do it.'

'You mean me and Bethany weren't just tossed aside by them, don't you?'

'Yes. That's what I'm trying to say.'

'I have to ask my Mum and Dad why they didn't come and get me. I'd like to know why they kept the baby and not me and Bethany. Why didn't they even visit us? It's been seven years, for God's sake.'

'You'll get your chance to ask, Patrick,' I said. 'You might not like the answers you're given, you might not get any answers at all — but you can ask.'

———

I could see the gradual decline in the quality and cleanliness of the buildings about us mirrored in Patrick's face as we drove into Haroldstown.

'They live here?' he asked, looking at the tiny, crumbling houses, the track-suited, shaven-headed men walking pitbull terriers and Dobermann pinschers, and the dressing-gown clad women carrying bags of groceries back from corner shops.

'I hate to tell you, Patrick — but they live in the rougher area.'

'This isn't the rough area?' Patrick said, as we passed a crowd of overweight, cackling girls dressed in belly-tops that caused their bulging midriffs to spill out over the broad belts of their hipsters.

'I'm afraid not.'

As we travelled south, the flats could be seen, gradually rearing up out of the decaying concrete like termite mounds. Patrick couldn't keep his eyes off them. They seemed to be calling to him in a language I could neither hear nor understand. 'That's where they live, isn't it?' he asked. 'I come from those towers.'

'It's nothing to be ashamed of,' I said gently. 'This is not a whole lot different to where I grew up. There are good people here. They might not have a lot of money, but you don't have to be well off to be a decent human being.'

'But it's so *horrible*,' he said. 'It's ugly. Everything seems so dirty and broken down.'

I didn't say anything to that, because there wasn't a positive response. He was right.

I had been unable to find a contact number for Patrick's parents. They had no landline, and if they had mobile phones, which they probably did, they weren't registered. I had asked a community worker in the area to try and make contact, but he had also failed. This meant we were calling unannounced.

The elevator in the flats was broken, so we climbed up the concrete stairs, taking in shallow breaths against the urine reek. Patrick was stern-faced as we went upwards, and I knew he was doing his best to prepare for what lay ahead.

We passed an old woman, who sat on a step between the second and third floors, muttering to herself and nursing a naggin of cheap whiskey. She made no effort to move as we approached, so we climbed over her and kept going.

Patrick's parents lived on the fifth level, in number 37. It looked no different to any other door we had passed — the paintwork was cracked, some moss grew on the small glass panel, and the number 'three' hung drunkenly upside down. I pushed the bell, but no sound emitted, so I knocked. We waited. No one came.

'I don't think anyone's home,' Patrick said. 'Maybe we should go.'

'Not yet,' I said, years of calling to places like this telling me that there was, in all likelihood, someone inside. I knocked again, even louder, and for much longer. This time, we both heard movement inside, and someone complaining.

The door was opened by a painfully thin, acned man.

'What?' he asked. He was wearing a filthy white T-shirt and oversized boxer shorts. I could see the pock-marks of mainline heroin use on his emaciated arms. He was so skinny, and so strung out from the drugs, it was impossible to tell his age. He could have been anything from twenty to forty. I had the sense he was young, but it was no more than a feeling.

'I'm looking for Freda and Paddy Keany,' I said. 'Are they at home?'

'Who wants to know?' he asked, his voice querulous.

'I'm a care worker from the Dunleavy Trust. This is Patrick, Freda's and Paddy's eldest son.'

The thin man looked from the boy to me, and then back again. 'Their son?'

'This is Patrick,' I said.

'Fuck,' the man said, chewing his scabrous lower lip. 'We … we don't got nothin' for him here. No cash, if that's what you're lookin' for.'

I sighed, and took a step forward, so I was very close to his face. He smelled of sweat and rancid breath. I could tell that he'd been chasing the dragon for years. He was dying from the inside, the heroin killing him. 'Are Freda or Paddy at home right now? If they are, we'd like to see them. If not, maybe we'll wait.'

He began to shake, as if he was experiencing a seizure. 'Look, fella, Paddy's long gone. He's hasn't been back here for years. Freda's inside, though. Yeah, come on in. Why not? She'll be glad to see her boy, I reckon.'

He stepped aside, and we went in.

There was a short hallway, which looked like it had not seen a lick of paint for several decades. There were holes in the plaster, and waterstains that ran down the walls from the ceiling had been left unrepaired. The entire place smelt of unemptied rubbish bins and there was an underlying stench of human waste, as if a sewer pipe had burst. I glanced down at Patrick, who looked pale and frightened. I felt a deep sense of pity for the boy. There was no going back, now.

The main living area was a higgledy-piggledy mess of unwashed clothes, food cartons and abandoned syringes. Beneath the detritus there was a faded, grease-clogged floral carpet that was threadbare in many places. The walls were devoid of any adornment other than dirt, and an ancient black and white portable television, with a wire clothes hanger as an aerial, was tuned between two stations in the corner.

The thin man collapsed immediately onto a sofa that appeared to only have three legs — it teetered over to one side drunkenly. A huge, ancient armchair sat slightly off centre in the room, and in it slumped a hugely obese woman, smoking a cigarette, a blissed-out expression on her sweaty, round face.

'Freda, this here's — sorry, I didn't get your name, fella,' the skinny addict said. 'But look, he's brought your boy!'

The fat woman was dressed in leggings and a cavernous, off-white sweatshirt. Her hair was the same colour as Patrick's, and, beneath the rolls of fat, I could just make out a familial likeness. My companion was staring at her in disbelief. She shifted with some difficulty in her seat, and peered at him.

'Patrick,' she said in a high-pitched, girlish voice that sounded ridiculous coming out of such a huge woman. 'Is that my little boy?'

Patrick took a step towards her, and knelt down. She took his hands, and leaned forward a little. 'Yes, it's you. I'd know that face anywhere. You always had your Daddy's eyes, so you did.'

'Mum,' Patrick said, and then said nothing for several minutes. This creature was so far removed from the image of his mother he had painted for me and Bethany as to be almost from a different species. I could only guess as to the myriad thoughts and emotions that were coursing through him, in that period of silence. Finally, in a shaking voice, he said: 'Where's Dad gone?'

'Oh, he left us, love. He went away with some skank whore who said she'd give him half her takings if he watched out for her. We're better off without him, lovey.'

Patrick swallowed, and turning his mother's arms over, saw the track marks. 'Do you take drugs, Mum?'

She tittered. 'Oh, just a little bit. Martin there brings me some, now and again, to pay for his rent. He stays here with me now that bastard Paddy's gone. It's alright. I'm not hooked or anything.'

'Daddy — he was a stuntman. In the circus. He had a motorbike ...'

Freda shook her head. 'No, you silly. He had a Honda 50, a little scooter, for a while. But he had to sell it to get us some stuff when we'd nothing. Oh, he used to love that bike, alright. Always dreamed of joining one of those biker gangs. But he was all talk, your Dad. He was a loser.'

'Do you know where he went, when he left?' Patrick asked, his voice trembling.

'I don't know and I don't care,' Freda said, rubbing his cheek.

'Good riddance to bad rubbish, that's what your Granny used to say.'

The thin man, Martin, was rooting in the drawer of a small table which sat beside the subsided couch where he was lounging. As I watched, he took out a blackened spoon, a bag of powder and a hypodermic needle. I leaned over, and said quietly: 'Either do that somewhere else, or wait for the boy to finish visiting with his mother. Okay, fella?'

The junkie said nothing, but put his equipment back in its hiding place.

'My sister,' Patrick, still on his knees before the fat woman, was saying. 'I had a little sister.'

'Yes, Bethany,' Freda said, glancing at the television. I sensed she was getting bored, or needed another fix. Our visit was drawing to a close, either way.

'No, we had another sister. She was just a baby when you sent us away. Where is she?'

Freda's brow creased. 'Oh,' she said, suddenly. 'You must mean Winnie.'

'Yes!' Patrick said, looking over his shoulder at me in triumph. 'That was her name: Winnie. Did you put her in care too?'

'Oh, no, love. Winnie died.'

Patrick seemed to visibly collapse at this news, and I was worried he might have actually passed out. It was only when he continued talking that I knew he was still functioning.

'What happened to her?' he asked. 'Was she sick?'

'Yes, darling. She was ill, alright. The doctors told us she was born hooked on the stuff. I don't know why, I mean, I only had a few snorts of it while I was pregnant, but sure, there you go. She just kept crying, and she got sicker and sicker and then, one night, she didn't cry any more. It was for the best, really. She was suffering, the poor mite.'

'Do you have any photos of her?' Patrick asked, his voice coming from somewhere deep within himself, a place he had walled off from the waking nightmare he found himself in. 'I can barely remember what she looked like.'

'Of course we don't,' his mother laughed. 'She was only three months old when she died. Sure, who takes pictures of sprogs when they're that small? She wasn't really a *person*.'

Patrick almost had his head on his mother's knees, he had sunk so low onto the grubby floor. 'I'd like to go now, Shane,' he said.

I took his shoulder and helped him up.

'Wasn't it nice of them to call, Martin?' Freda squeaked. 'You'll come again, won't you Patrick?'

Patrick, trembling slightly as he leaned against me, nodded almost imperceptibly.

'We'll be seeing you, Mrs Keany,' I said, and pushed the boy towards the door.

'Oh, Mister, before you go,' Freda said. 'You couldn't spare us a few quid, could you? It's just, the rent's due, and we're a bit behind.'

'Sorry,' I said, starting to move with a greater sense of urgency.

'I'll tell you what,' Freda continued. 'How 'bout a blow job? I'll blow you for thirty euro. Now you won't get a better offer than that today.'

Patrick said nothing, but was leaning hard against me. We were at the front door now, and I struggled with the handle. Mercilessly, Freda kept talking.

'Okay, well, if you don't want me to do it, Martin would be happy to oblige you, wouldn't you Martin?'

'Oh, yeah —'

The door swung slowly open, and I shoved Patrick out, closing it behind me. Half-carrying him, I somehow got us down the stairs and to my car. Without a word, I drove as fast as I could away from the flats. Glancing over at him, I saw that he was crying bitterly, the waves of grief crashing over him with such force he struggled to catch his breath. His whole body was racked with sobs. I reached over and took his hand, and when we were safely outside Haroldstown, I pulled over and hugged him. There were no words that could make better or even lessen what he had just experienced.

'I'm sorry, Patrick,' I said, rocking him gently. 'I am so, so, sorry.'

It is painful, but it is a fact, nonetheless: the truth does not, always, set you free.

Chapter 16 ⌒

Johnny Curran died at five o'clock in the morning on Tuesday, the twenty-third of December. He never regained consciousness, and his tiny body just gave up struggling. The doctors told me it was a peaceful, painfree way to go. 'He just drifted from one dream to another,' the young medic said, when I finally got to the hospital. 'If there's a good way to die, he found it.'

I usually sleep with my phone switched on, because I use the alarm clock on it to wake myself up in the morning. For some obscure reason, probably because I was very tired and didn't want to be disturbed, I'd switched the mobile off, and didn't get the message until close to eight. I listened to the dry, emotionless voice informing me that Johnny was gone, then sat on my bed and cried.

I work with many children, and while I care about each and every one, I am loath to use the word 'love' to express how I feel about them. Love is too serious a thing to be bandied about, and I would never wish to diminish the relationships I form with the kids or their families by overstating what I do or patronising them. Somehow, though, Johnny, with his beautiful open face, his deep, knowing eyes and his dogged determination to rise above his circumstances and be the best he could be, had found a chink in my armour. I realised, as I sat alone in the dark morning, that I loved him, and that the thought he was gone was almost unbearable.

I went to the caravan, but no one was home. I paid a quick visit to the hospital and spoke to a doctor, who told me Tilly had already taken the body, but that he didn't know where she and her brothers had gone.

At eleven o'clock, I arrived at the office. I hadn't been sitting at my desk for ten minutes before Ben came in.

'What are you doing here?' he asked.

I looked up at him, then turned my attention back to the wild garden. 'Sitting,' I said obtusely.

'I'm giving you the rest of the day off. You've had a tough few weeks, and this morning's news has been a shock, to us all. Go on home, now.'

'I should never have let them park the trailer there,' I said. 'I knew it was dangerous.'

'You pointed that out to Tilly, as I recall,' Ben said. 'She is an adult and decided that was where she wanted to be.'

'He's gone, Ben. How can he be gone, just like that?'

'I don't know, Shane. Life is bitter, sometimes.'

'I didn't even get over to see him last night. I got home late, I was tired, I switched off the phone and went to bed. I could have given him an hour, for fuck sake.'

Ben put his hand on my shoulder. 'You've been putting in eighteen-hour days this past while. I am ordering you, as your boss, and telling you, as a friend, to go home now, and get some rest. There's nothing you can do here. I'll chase down Tilly, and find out about the funeral arrangements.'

I nodded and stood up. Ben hugged me, told me to take care of myself, and then I took his advice and went home.

———

That night I was at the bar of my local, nursing a pint and a hot whiskey, and feeling abjectly miserable. The pub was largely empty, and the barman, with the wisdom and insight only years of dealing with the morose can provide, was giving me a wide berth. I was drunk, and planned on getting a lot drunker before the night was out. I was watching a pint of Guinness settle when a voice spoke at my shoulder.

'Self-pity doesn't suit you, Shane.'

'Fuck off, Devereux,' I said, recognising his accentless tones.

'I'm afraid I'm not about to do that. I need your assistance.'

He pulled up a barstool beside me, but shook his head when the barman came over.

'You might as well have a drink, because I ain't movin',' I said.

'I heard about the Curran boy. It's very sad, but there are others who are still in the land of the living — just — who require your assistance. Sitting here crying into a glass of whiskey is indulgent and pointless.'

'Maybe I feel like being a little self-centred tonight. Have you thought about that? Am I not entitled, every once in a while?'

'You seem to have been doing it quite a bit of late.'

I looked at him in disbelief. 'What in the name of fuck are you goin' on about?'

'I'd say kicking in Ishmael Green's door, and putting him wise to your investigations into Edward Downey qualifies. What did you think you were doing? You might as well have put an ad in *The Irish Times*.'

'Get out of my face before I get annoyed,' I hissed.

'Oh don't be ridiculous,' Devereux said. 'Do they serve coffee here?'

'Dunno.'

They did, and five minutes later, Devereux had moved me to a table in the corner, with a large mug steaming in front of me.

'It has come to my attention, as it has probably come to the attention of many, after your recent antics, that you are interested in the conduct of Father Edward Downey.'

'And this affects you how?'

'I've been keeping an eye on him myself for a while, now.'

'Why?'

'Does the name Garry Michaels mean anything to you?'

'Wasn't he a kid who committed suicide some time back? I heard he'd been in and out of care, sleeping on the streets —'

'All true, except for one point the newspapers neglected to mention: in the three months before he took his own life, Garry and his mother were involved in a "prayer group" run by Edward Downey.'

'So?'

'This was no ordinary Roman Catholic gathering. From what Garry's mother told me, they performed séances, nature rituals, and table-tipping ceremonies. Garry was asked to attend private counselling sessions, to discuss issues of his spirituality.'

'Yeah, all perfectly run-of-the-mill, new-age nonsense. I agree, it looks like Downey is a bad guy, but what have we got to go on? It's all guesswork.'

'He dresses it up as paganism and alternative lifestyle, but children are always on the periphery of it,' Devereux said. 'More than one of the kids involved have ended up very messed up. Downey preys on the sick, on those whose lives are out of control, on the mentally disturbed. He targets them, and draws them in, offering them community and a cure for all physical and spiritual sickness. It's a cult, and probably a front for something even darker. What I'm certain of is that children are the currency they're trading in.'

'If you know all this, why are you here ruining my night?'

'Clive Plummer.'

'What about him?'

'Have you spoken to his father?'

'Not really. It's his sister I have most contact with.'

'Mr Plummer and his wife were close, weren't they?'

'From what I've been told.'

'Look at all the damning evidence you've collated. Perhaps it's time to present it to him, see what comes out.'

'Jesus, Devereux. I've been doing a lot of confronting, lately. I'm kind of sick of it, to tell you the truth.'

'Drink up your coffee. We've got work to do.'

———

I wasn't fit to drive, so we took Devereux's plain black Volvo.

Roberta answered the door.

'I need to see your Dad,' I told her.

'He's in his study,' she said. 'Who's this?'

'He's a colleague,' I said. My head was starting to ache, and I didn't want to get into a lengthy conversation with her. I wanted to get this over with, crawl into bed and sleep for a long time.

Jensen Plummer was sitting in his shirtsleeves at a large wooden desk when Roberta showed us in. He stood and offered his hand. He was a tall, well-built man, with a thin crop of white hair. He had a friendly face, but dark rings showed under his eyes.

'It's a little late to call, Shane,' he said. 'I hope you'll be brief.'

'We'll be as quick as possible,' I said. 'I want to talk to you about Clive and Cynthia's relationship with Father Downey.'

'Can I ask what the significance of this line of questioning is?'

I told him. He listened carefully, and when I had finished, he reached for a crystal glass that sat near his elbow and took a long drink. 'Edward came to visit us shortly after we got married. I'd known him for a while, through the local historical society, but I had no idea of his interest in the occult. Cynthia had always dabbled in spiritualism, but I saw it as a harmless interest — angel cards and auras — it seemed a sweet kind of thing, really. I left her to it.'

'Edward Downey found out about her interests?' Devereux asked.

'Almost at that first visit. Cynthia used to like to read the cards for guests, a kind of party trick, I suppose. I remember she was particularly excited about reading Father Downey's. He is a priest, and I suppose that added a frisson to the whole thing.'

'When did Clive become involved?' I asked.

'When Cynthia became ill, Father Downey asked her to attend some prayer evenings at the presbytery. I didn't realise until she'd been to a couple that they were actually more a kind of pagan gathering, but as long as it made her happy, I didn't give a damn. I think it was after the third or fourth one she asked me if she could take him. She told me that Father Downey had told her that, because Clive was her son, he'd amplify her natural energies, accelerate her healing. Clive said he'd be glad to go — he was completely devoted to his mother — and I thought no more about it.'

'When did you begin to realise something was wrong?' Devereux asked.

'I wish I could say it was an immediate thing, but it wasn't. Clive was a bit reserved after some of the meetings, but he's a teenager, I passed it off as adolescence. I talked to Cynthia, and she admitted to me that there was a sexual element to some of the ceremonies they performed, and that perhaps this was stirring up some hormonal issues for Clive.

I told her I didn't want him witnessing anything inappropriate, but she laughed and told me it was more imagery and suggestion than anything else. So I said no more about it. I never thought for a moment she'd allow anything harmful to happen to our son.'

'But she did, didn't she?' Devereux said.

'I didn't find out what they'd done to him until it was too late,' Plummer said. He took another hit of his drink. 'Cynthia was in hospital, and knew she was going to die. She wanted me to get Clive help. My wife realised what she had done was wrong, but she was desperate for a cure. I can't be angry with her. Wouldn't it have been better for him to have a mother? She thought that was what she was doing, you see. She was trying to live.'

My head thumped dully. Acid welled in my throat, and I longed for a cigarette. 'Mr Plummer, in her effort to live, your wife almost killed her son. *Your* son,' I said.

He looked at Devereux and me with rheumy eyes. I realised, as we sat in the darkened room, with its shelves of books and dusty oil paintings, that he was an old man, who probably didn't have much time left himself. This whole business had just about killed him, too.

'I loved her,' he said, simply. 'I still love her.'

Devereux stood up, tying the belt of his leather trenchcoat. 'She's dead, old man,' he said. 'Look to your son, before he joins her.'

We passed Roberta on the way out. She was standing by the door, tears glistening on her cheeks. She had obviously been listening to what had passed in the study.

'I'm sorry,' I said.

'So am I,' she replied.

———

Father Downey smiled when he saw us.

'Let's go to my room,' he said. 'It's more comfortable, and on a cold night like this, I think a snifter of something with a bit of a kick to it is called for, don't you agree?'

His room was more an apartment: a large living space led onto a small, neat kitchen, and a doorway connected to what I assumed was a bathroom and sleeping area. The entire place was opulently adorned: the vow of poverty seemed to weigh little on our host. Devereux ran his eyes along a selection of leather-bound volumes on one of the many shelves, while I looked at an unusual painting on the wall, which I thought I recognised. Downey returned with a tray on which sat three lowball glasses, a decanter of something amber and a jug of water. 'Will Black and White be alright for you?' he asked.

'Is this a mandala?' I said, pointing at the picture.

'Well spotted. It is indeed. Painted by Carl Gustav Jung himself. A vision from the world of the spirit, he called it. He produced thousands of them, during his life.'

'How did you come by it?'

'An auction.'

We sat. Devereux did not beat around the bush.

'We know about the children,' he said.

'Now, what, pray tell, do you know about "the children"?'

'Enough.'

Downey laughed, and sipped his drink. He took a Peterson pipe from the pocket of his cardigan, and tamped the contents of the bowl with his thumb. I took the cue and lit a cigarette, feeling my headache ease immediately. The whiskey wasn't hurting it, either.

'Gentlemen,' he said, when he had the pipe drawing satisfactorily. 'Conversations like this have become an occupational hazard, part and parcel of being a priest, particularly a priest who refuses to conform, and who believes that ministry is the most important part of the job.'

'Do you call it "ministry" what you did to Clive Plummer?' I asked.

'I've already told you, I tried to dissuade Cynthia from her fascination with the darker aspects of spirituality.'

'Her husband has just told us a different story,' Devereux said. 'She confessed on her deathbed, told him what you coerced her into doing.'

'It sounds to me like you have been duped by the ramblings of a dying woman and the ravings of a psychiatrically disturbed child,' Downey smirked.

'We'll see what your bishop thinks, and how the police view the evidence,' Devereux said. 'Occult paintings by acknowledged experts in the field hang on your walls. Your bookshelves are laden with tomes on everything from the Book of Enoch to the works of Aleister Crowley. I don't believe it would be too difficult to make a case against you.'

'They've tried to put me away before, Mr Devereux,' Downey crowed. 'It didn't work then, and I don't think it'll work now. But feel free to try.'

'You are a predator, Father,' Devereux said, every word ringing with focused, righteous anger. 'You have spent decades living in a society where you and your kind could hunt with impunity, but heed this, and mark my words well: *those days are over*. If I ever hear that you have approached Clive Plummer, or his family, again, I will see to it that you spend a very, very long time in prison. And don't think you'll be safe in a nice, secluded wing with your fellow sex offenders. I'll ensure someone with a monumental axe to grind finds you. I have many contacts on the inside.'

'Is that a threat, Mr Devereux?'

'No, Father. A polite warning. Take it or leave it, as you see fit. But I advise you to heed me.'

The priest sipped his whiskey and regarded us both: Devereux, his glass before him on the table, untouched; me, nursing mine, looking decidedly the worse for wear.

'And I suppose,' he said, 'I should watch my back, as you'll be lurking behind every corner, waiting for me to slip up, to do something stupid.'

'Count on it,' Devereux said.

'Do you think you're the first person to come here with the express purpose of frightening me? Can you really think no one has ever sat where you are and told me to watch my step, to keep away from this person, or that person? I am above all such recriminations.

I serve a higher power, and my conscience is clear. As, incidentally, is my police record.'

'I'll be seeing you,' Devereux said, and we left.

He dropped me off outside my apartment building. 'Tell the staff at St Vitus's what we know. I think it might alter how they approach the boy's treatment,' he said.

'I will. Is there any hope of Downey being prosecuted?'

'Every piece of information there is against him brings it closer. If Clive were to recover his faculties and disclose … I think that would be a major blow against him.'

'I wouldn't hold out for that.'

Devereux nodded. 'Get some sleep,' he said, and drove away.

Chapter 17 ～

Katie stared at the ceiling of the playroom. She spent a lot of her time doing that now. It was as if the frenetic energy, the bottomless pit of anger, had been drained, replaced by a colossal sadness.

'How about we go and see a movie?' I asked, lying on a beanbag beside her. 'There's a few decent ones on at the Multiplex at the moment. When was the last time you saw a film?'

'I don't feel like it.'

'Why not?'

'Just don't.'

'We could go and get a pizza.'

'Don't like pizza.'

'Yes you do!'

'Not any more.'

'Since when?'

'I just don't want to, okay?'

We lay for a while, saying nothing.

'What's wrong, Katie?'

'Nothin'.'

'Yes there is. You've been like this for days. I think it's time we talked about it.'

'There's ain't anythin' to talk about.'

'I think there is, and I'm not leaving until you tell me. So we can lay here, staring at the paintwork until tomorrow if you like, because I, as you might have noticed, can be very determined when the mood takes me.'

'That's fine by me.'

'Good.'

'Great.'

'Brilliant.'

We lay some more. Finally:

'It's just that I'm all alone. I don't got no one.'

I pushed myself up on one elbow. 'How'd you mean?'

'Me Mam and Dad are dead, and they never wanted me anyway. Me Da left me by the side of the road, for fuck sake — I mean, you can't get much more not givin' a shit about your kids than that, can you?'

'Your Dad probably had his own problems, Katie.'

'Will you give it a rest? When he wasn't dumpin' me out of cars he was molestin' me. He couldn't've cared less if I lived or died. I'm too mad to be in a house with other children, and I'm too stupid to go to school. You're the best friend I've got, and you're only here because the staff in the house used be scared of me.'

'They're not any more.'

'That's not the shaggin' point, Shane. I'm a disaster. No one has ever given a fuck about me. They might as well lock me up, 'cause I just don't see the point of goin' on no more.'

'I give a fuck, Katie. Doesn't that stand for anything? Dorothy and the team here all care a great deal about you. And I bet, if you think really hard, you'll find that lots of people have cared about you.'

She sighed and rolled over, so her back was to me. I had come to understand that it was a defence mechanism of hers. It meant she was afraid she'd start to cry, and didn't want me to see. She muttered something.

'What was that, Katie?'

'My uncle — he liked me.'

'Which uncle?' I asked.

'Uncle 'Phonso. The oul' fella. I remember, he cried when they took me away. I was cryin' too, and holdin' on to him. He was always really nice to me. I never saw him again.'

———

The old house in Dolphin's Barn had a new coat of paint on it, which worried me when we got there. Katie looked exceptionally nervous.

'What if he doesn't know me?'

'Thelma — the Rice Krispie woman, as you call her — spoke to him just this morning. He's looking forward to seeing you. He remembers you very well.'

'He must be about a hundred years old, now.'

'He's eighty-one, but bright as a button, I'm told.'

Her voice softened. 'My Uncle 'Phonso. I like the sound of that.'

The door opened, and there he was. He wasn't much taller than the child, dressed in a thick woollen cardigan, grey trousers that came halfway to his chest, and a purple tie that was askew. He had long wisps of white hair that hung about his shoulders, and little black eyes that showed a vivid mind. When he saw Katie, he smiled, showing more gums than teeth.

'Is that my Princess?' he asked. 'I can't believe you've come back.'

'Princess,' Katie said, her voice catching. 'You used to call me that. I remember.'

And then they were holding each other, and I felt a little bit like an intruder. Katie was no longer alone.

———

The city streets were full of rabidly focused Christmas shoppers. Patrick and I gazed in a toyshop window, looking for something appropriate for Bethany, for whom, it appeared, the phrase 'the child who has everything' was coined.

'What about that one?' I asked, indicating a disturbingly lifelike blonde doll.

'She might not have that one, but she's definitely got one like it.'

'I'll tell you what, here's an idea. It looks like she's got every doll ever made. How about you get a load of doll accessories?'

'Doll what?'

'Accessories — clothes and shoes and … um … handbags and … uh … stuff of that nature.'

'That's a good idea. Let's go.'

To my utter amazement, there appeared to be as many accessories for dolls as there are for real people, and it proved a difficult undertaking. However, we finally left the shop with a good selection. 'She'll like that,' said Patrick, grinning.

'Okay, who next?'

'I want to get something for Gertrude, and for my real Mum.'

'For Freda?'

'Yes.'

I stopped and looked at him. 'You want to go back there?'

'Will you come with me?'

'I'm sure as hell not letting you go on your own.'

'I have to see her again.'

I shook my head. 'Shit, Patrick. Come on, let's get a cup of coffee and you can explain it to me.'

'The people I'm with now,' Patrick said, when we were settled in a café bedecked with seasonal decorations, 'they're really good people — a strong family. The other kids there, they've all got stories like mine. They treat me really well. It's nice. Kind of weird, because I'm not used to it, having such a big family, but it's a good feeling. And I know you're here for me, too. I feel safe, knowing that.'

'I am.'

'What it's taught me, Shane, what I've learned from all this, is that you can't give up. There were times — when it fell apart with Gertrude, and when I saw where I'm really from — when I thought about just giving in. I even considered killing myself. But then something would happen, something I didn't expect — you'd take me home and treat me so well, I'd hear a wonderful piece of music, I'd meet my new family — there are so many good things in the world.'

I looked at Patrick over the rim of my coffee cup and thought how much he had grown in the past few weeks. He had always been a solemn child, perhaps too old for his years, but this short speech was remarkable, even by his standards.

'Freda gave up on me,' he continued. 'Gertrude gave up on me. But I won't give up on them. I can be better than that.'

'Gertrude has her problems, Patrick,' I said, trying to speak as plainly as I could without being devastating. 'She probably had a tough upbringing herself, and that made her like she is. But I think, deep down, she knows she made a mistake throwing you out. Freda, on the other hand … I can try to put her in touch with some support services, but I don't think she particularly wants any help. You could be setting yourself up for a lot of hurt.'

'You can't choose your family, Shane. She's my mother. I'm going to try to be there for her.'

I finished my coffee, and grinned at him. 'Okay. I'll see what I can do.'

He smiled his wistful, sad smile at me. 'I know you will,' he said.

———

Clive Plummer, scarred and hollow-eyed, the old anorak even looser-fitting on him now, walked slowly and with tentative purpose, along the little pathway behind St Vitus's. Roberta was beside him, I a little behind them both.

'I don't remember any of that,' Clive said. The sedatives they were pumping him full of had been reduced, but he was still a bit groggy. 'All I can see when I try to is the monsters. It's dark and they're all around me, hurting me. Mum isn't there.'

'I think your mind created those nightmares, as strange as it might seem, to protect you,' Roberta said. 'What happened was really, really awful. I suppose being attacked by demons seemed better than … than what really did occur.'

We walked on in silence. Every now and then, Clive would stop, to identify a particular piece of birdsong. 'She thought it would make her get better, didn't she?' he said. 'That by doing those things, the cancer would go away.'

'Cynthia had a form of vascular cancer that affects less than one per cent of all cancer sufferers. There is no known cure for it, and it almost always results in death,' Roberta said. 'She was grasping at straws, trying everything she could think of to try and beat it. I think her mind was affected by the cancer itself, and by the drugs. If she'd been well, she never would have agreed to involving you.'

'I wish she was here,' Clive said.

'I know,' Roberta said, putting her arm around her brother. 'She owes you answers, and an apology. She owes us both that.'

'No,' Clive said. 'I wish she was here so I could tell her I understand. That I forgive her.'

And we walked on, a blackbird celebrating the new day in a nearby tree.

Chapter 18

I could hear Ben talking on the telephone from my own office. 'Well, I'm sorry to hear that. Got quite aggressive, did she? Accused you of entrapment? Well, I suppose all her reading mustn't have quite prepared her for the therapeutic process, eh? She admitted to that? Really? And would you be prepared to give testimony to that effect? Of course I understand client confidentiality, but I believe child protection concerns outweigh that as an ethical consideration. Oh, she says she's leaving? Immediately? Okay, thanks for the call. Talk to you soon.'

I heard him hang up, and footsteps as he made his way down the hallway to my room.

'That was Vera Byrne's therapist.'

'Oh.'

'She has discontinued her course of treatment. Became quite irate, as a matter of fact. She accused him of trying to steer her into incriminating herself, physically assaulted him, and left, but not before virtually admitting to her role in the abuse. She seemed almost proud of it, according to the shrink.'

'He'll write that up?'

'Well, there's the usual confidentiality bunkum, but he says he's certainly prepared to make the recommendation that the kids are not to be entrusted to her in the foreseeable future.'

'That is fucking brilliant.'

'There's more. She's leaving town.'

'I don't know if that's a good thing or a bad thing.'

'Does it matter?'

'S'pose not.'

She wasn't at the townhouse, so I drove to the Gothic edifice in Oldtown. A taxi was idling out front, and the huge, oak door was ajar. I went on in.

I could hear cursing and clattering from the kitchen, and followed the sounds down the long, wooden hallway to the filthy, cobweb-strewn room. The Byrnes' original home was a bizarre, almost surreal collection of knick-knacks and oddments, piled here and there with no forethought. Every item clashed with the one beside it, almost as if that had been the point in the first place. It made the place deeply unsettling to be in.

Vera was packing random pieces of crockery, pictures and ornaments into a huge suitcase. Her hair was awry and her clothes stained with dirt and grease. She looked much more like the Vera I had met months before than the assured, powerful woman who had attended the case review.

'What are you doing, Vera?' I asked her.

She whipped around, and sneered at me. 'I'm taking what's mine and I'm going. You do-gooder bastards won't give me a moment's peace. Everywhere I go there's prying eyes. I'm going away for a while. But I'm not leaving without my stuff.'

'And that doesn't include Larry and Francey?'

She stopped in her frenzied packing. 'And why do you ask that?'

'Because I've called Rivendell to let them know you might be on your way over there, and suggested they take the twins out for the rest of the day. Just in case.'

She laughed — a horrible, mean cackle — and closed the lid of her case. 'Don't think you've beaten me. I'll be back, when none of ye expect it. And when I do, I'll claim everything that's owing to me.'

'You need help, Vera,' I said. 'You're a sick woman. Do you know, if you'd even once said you were sorry for what you did to the twins, if you'd expressed a second's remorse, I'd've tried to help you. But you just don't see it. You have no idea what you did to them. Even poor, simple Malachi understands it, but not you.'

'You're the one that doesn't understand,' she said. 'But don't worry. I'll return, and then I'll make you all see.'

She stomped past me, dragging the heavy case. I followed her to the door, and watched as the taxi driver helped her load her luggage into the boot. It was only when the car disappeared over the brow of a hill that I realised I was soaked in sweat. I heaved a sigh of relief. At last, the twins were safe.

———

Johnny Curran's funeral took place on Christmas Eve. As tends to be the case with traveller funerals, it was a huge affair, with members of the extended families on both sides coming, some for hundreds of miles, to be there. Gerry did not arrive, out of fear that some of the mourners might see the death as being partly his fault. It was not an unreasonable assumption.

The ceremony was beautiful, and afterwards the throng retired to a nearby pub for drink and music that would last long into the night.

I went along for a while, but felt uncomfortable and irritable. I was about to make my excuses when I noticed Tilly slipping out the door. Putting down my pint glass, I followed her. Once outside, she ran across the road, to the riverbank. She smiled when I caught up with her, and, crying softly, took my arm. We walked slowly, neither saying anything, each lost in our own private thoughts. I knew that, somehow, Johnny's brief life, and the small part I had played in his final weeks among us, had altered me completely. I couldn't explain it, but things could never be the same again.

As we walked, a light snow began to fall, soft flakes settling on the black surface of the water before melting, becoming part of the Torc as it raced towards the sea.

'Happy Christmas, Shane,' Tilly said.

'Merry Christmas, Tilly.'

And the first star of the evening came out above us, a single pinpoint of light in the gathering darkness.

AFTERWORD

Hush, Little Baby is a book about parents, and the responsibilities being the mother or father of a child brings. Of all my books, I found it the most difficult to write. The process reminded me of the countless families I have encountered, and the ways in which I affected the dynamic of each one. Some of them had me forced into their lives, and tolerated me with grim resentment. Others welcomed me with open arms. Through revisiting the cases in this volume, I realised that I did not always leave the homes I entered better for my involvement. I always tried, but all too often the damage that had been done, by traumas or abuses that occurred long before I came on the scene, was too great for my meagre skills.

Hush, Little Baby also caused me to think about my own parents, and my relationship with them. I am blessed to have come from a home where my mother and father loved one another completely, and where I knew that I was loved. Yet any examination of the complex emotional interactions between children and their primary caregivers gives one pause, and I spent many long evenings pondering where I have come from, and how it contributed to who I am today.

And, of course, I am a parent now. I have two children who make me proud and who I love and worry about and miss when they're not around. Somehow, when I think of Katie or Patrick or Clive, I see the faces of my own children. Maybe I always did.

The story of Tilly and Johnny Curran is based on a case I was involved in very early in my career. The travelling community has, as I discuss in the text, been a feature of my life for as long as I can remember. I wanted to show them as I see them — a culture of much beauty and with many wonderful aspects, yet a dying one, for all that. There just doesn't seem to be a place in post-modern Ireland for their way of life, which is, I believe, a great tragedy.

Clive Plummer was taken off all medication shortly after his father finally faced the truth, and was allowed to go home shortly after Christmas. Roberta took a career break, to help her brother cope with the reality he had been forced to accept, and she and Clive are, to the best of my knowledge, still in therapy. Jensen Plummer died a year later.

While Clive is based on a specific child I worked with, the events surrounding him and his family are a composite of three cases I was involved in, in various capacities. The Roman Catholic Church has left a legacy that will continue to reverberate through Irish society for many decades to come. It is a shameful thing that they continue to duck and dive, and to harbour individuals they know are a danger to children. The man I based Edward Downey on was, eventually, prosecuted, on a lesser charge. He served ten months, and is at large again, now.

Children and teenagers continue to be put in adult psychiatric facilities. The need for child and adolescent beds has been highlighted countless times to no effect.

Patrick Bassett/Kealy remained in the foster home he was placed in after leaving my care, until he moved out to go to college. He is still in contact with Gertrude and Freda, and he still likes Eric Clapton. Freda remains a challenge for everyone who is involved with her, but, as Patrick told me once, love isn't supposed to be easy. He never found his father.

Katie did not move back in with Alphonso, but they continued to see one another on a weekly basis until his death, at the grand old age of ninety-two. Katie remained in care for the rest of her teens. Shortly after her reunion with her uncle, she returned to mainstream school, and not long after that made the transition into a group home, with other children.

Vera Byrne was never heard of again. Malachi served out the rest of his time in prison, and, on release, moved into the little townhouse he and Vera had been given, where he continues to live. He needs help with the day-to-day stuff of living, and a family support worker sees him for several hours a week.

Larry and Francey, who appear little in this book, but had a major part to play in my previous title, *Last Ditch House,* were, understandably, upset when their mother vanished without so much as a goodbye, but they see their father often, and are slowly rebuilding a relationship with him. The Byrne homestead, in Oldtown, still sits, derelict, radiating a sense of other-worldliness and menace. A friend once told me she felt it was waiting for its mistress to return. I hope she is wrong.

LAST DITCH HOUSE
SHANE DUNPHY

'A genuine page-turner. Heartbreaking true stories, written with a novelist's flair.' *The Sunday Business Post*

When Shane went to work at Dunleavy Trust, an organisation that specialises in dealing with severely traumatised children, he wasn't sure what to expect.

> *'Karena told me about the Byrne twins: "A man had come to their house to sell insurance. He went to the rear of the building, and saw Mr Byrne leading the twins, both naked and covered in cuts and bruises, across the yard to an outhouse. He was screaming at them, although the salesman couldn't make out any of the words. The police were called, and they found the children in that shed. The place stank of shit and piss, the floor was covered in rags and newspaper which the children used as bedding at night. The twins have told us that they were locked up in there with no food at all for days or even weeks at a time. These children behave like wild animals, Shane. We don't know how to help them — we need a miracle."'*

What Shane finds is a series of families in extraordinary circumstances: Bobby and Micky, six and four, controlled from beyond the grave by their evil father; Mina, seventeen, with Down's Syndrome, desperate to be the same as everyone else, and falling into the clutches of abusive men; Sylvie, fourteen, a child from Shane's past, being pimped by her father; twins Larry and Francey, ten, scarcely human after an upbringing of unmitigated cruelty.

Last Ditch House is the true story of these amazing children's battle to survive in a world where cries for help are rarely answered, and where the cost of defeat can be impossibly high.

Wednesday's Child
Shane Dunphy

'**Wednesday's Child** is that rare beast: a serious work of non-fiction that reads like a thriller ... by turns funny, angry, touching and, ultimately, almost unbearably moving, it is a stunning achievement.'
John Connolly, bestselling crime author

Shane Dunphy walked into a nightmare on his first day as a child protection worker, finding himself caught up with a family on the brink of chaos.

> '*With a thunderous roar Mrs Kelly lumbered back into the living room, this time brandishing a bread-knife. She was glaring at me with a savage intensity, her left hand bunched into a fist, her right hand clamped around the handle of the knife.*
>
> *"Now, you big bastard!" she seethed through clenched teeth and a constricted throat. "You will listen to me!"*
>
> *She drew the jagged end of the blade over her arm in a swooping arc, grating the flesh rather than cutting it. She grunted and did it again. The blood came immediately, running in thin sheets down her forearm.*
>
> *"This isn't helping anyone, Mrs Kelly," I said, barely aware of the tremble in my voice.*
>
> *The woman before me was growling, and continued to make red, raw grooves in her arm. I could hear the sound of the drops spattering on the floor.*'

Follow Shane as he reveals the true story of a year spent working with children who are surviving against all the odds: Gillian, fifteen, who is starving herself to death; Connie, fourteen, an A-grade student with a terrible secret; Cordelia, Victor and Ibar, three siblings who love their alcoholic father despite years of terrible neglect.

Wednesday's Child reveals a hidden Ireland, where happy endings are a rare thing, and where the only currency that matters is hope.